THE SUM OF
THE PARTS

MICKLE PRESS

THE SUM OF THE PARTS

THE EVOLUTION OF THE PERFECT TEAM

JON KEEN

First Published in hardback in Great Britain in April 2016 by Mickle Press

ISBN: 978-0-9935175-0-1

MICKLE PRESS
www.micklepress.com

Subscribers

The author would like to thank the below subscribers for their support. Without this, production of "*The Sum of the Parts*" would not have been possible.

Brian Allen, *Reading*

Thomas Allen, *Middlesbrough*

Ben Britter, *The Village*

Andrew Brown, *Orpington*

Peter Bryant, *Berkshire*

Jamie Butler, *West Reading*

Andrew Calladine, *Guildford*

Martin Calladine, *London*

Bob Chandler, *Reading*

Nichola and Chris Cook, *Chichester*

Hannah Cox, *Wallingford*

Stuart Croucher, *Reading*

Stephen M Day, *Reading*

Linda & Martin Dubber, *Wiltshire*

Tina and Gary Ellison, *Reading*

Paul Ellix, *Melksham*

Paul Evans, *Y25*

Ben Fasham, *Reading*

Colin Ford, *Chiswick*

Simon Glass, *Blairgowrie*

Dan Green, *Newbury*

Barry Greenaway, *Waukesha, WI*

Les Hart, *Edinburgh*

Chris Harris, *Stowmarket*

Colin Harris, *Munich*

Dave Hunt, *Great Kingshill*

Antony James, *G7 & Vancouver, BC*

Daniel Kasaska, *Bracknell*

Martin Kent, *GU4*

Keith Machin, *Maidenhead*

Paula Martin, *Riseley*

Gavin Megnauth, *Y22*

Jason Oakes, *The Village*

Steve Peters, *York*

Matt Pitman, *Y21 Didcot*

Neill Rees, *Y24*

Rolf Rumley, *Wokingham*

Judie Self, *Newbury*

Martin Sims, *G10 seat, Y25 mind*

Dave Stevens, *Las Vegas but Reading in spirit*

Michael Tait, *Andover*

Roger and Mark Tillcock, *Y25*

Donald Wilson, *Reading*

Author's Note

This book is not an official product of Reading Football Club and is not associated with them in any way, except that many of their past and current staff have cooperated greatly in its production – freely sharing time, assistance and memories.

Originally conceived on the day in May 2009 day that Steve Coppell left Reading Football Club, this book was written between June 2015 and March 2016, based upon my own personal material and my memories as well as media sources from 2000-2008, and interviews with those who were involved with the team and with supporters from this period.

I discovered early in the process of researching and writing this the most interesting stories and the most valuable insight would come from those behind the team and around the pitch, rather than those on it. So contributions from players are minimal and included only where I feel they add something extra.

Whilst everything in this book has been researched diligently and every fact checked as far as possible, it's inevitable that it will contain some errors, especially as the passage of time blurs memories (in fact, I have been given contradictory accounts of incidents by some people). For any errors I apologise – everything has been written in good faith and as objectively as possible, and I'll happily correct any notified to me in later editions. For simplicity, I've used the term "Premier League" throughout this book, despite this being rebranded from the *"FA Barclays Premiership"* to the *"Barclays Premier League"* in 2007.

This book started out as a celebration and an analysis of the achievements of Reading FC in the two greatest seasons in their history, 2005/06 and 2006/07. But as research and interviews took me forward it became clear that the story wouldn't be complete unless I also looked at what went wrong at the end of this period, in addition to what went right during it. So for some Loyal Royals the final chapters may be painful reading. They were certainly painful to write, as it's hard to recognise that your heroes aren't always perfect. Anyone who doesn't want to relive the low points as well as the high points is might want to put this book down at the end of Chapter Sixteen.

I'd like to offer my sincere thanks to everyone who has contributed time, memories and assistance – those who helped make the 'perfect team' and those who followed it. This includes Wally Downes, Linda Dubber, Alex Everson, Ron Grant, Nick Hammond, Nigel Howe, Rob Langham, Sir John Madejski, Paula Martin, Michele Mead, Mark Reynolds, Roger Titford and many others, especially at Reading Football Club and Supporters' Trust At Reading, who have helped in numerous ways.

Finally, special thanks must go to three people without whom this book would probably not have seen the light of day. These are Dave Harris, a walking football-spreadsheet (with a real spreadsheet as backup) and Neil Maskell, always ready with an astute observation or an acerbic comment. Both have supported me tremendously through the whole time I have been working on "*The Sum of the Parts*", providing boundless encouragement as well as useful memories and invaluable statistics in abundance.

The third person is my lovely wife Fiona, who has shown great support and patience, not least whilst being asked to proofread chapters on football matches and players in which she doesn't have the slightest interest – and for only referring to "*The Sum of the Parts*" as "*that f*cking book*" once.

Jon Keen, March 2016

Table of Contents

Author's Note	vii
Introduction: I Still Haven't Found What I'm Looking For	xi
Chapter 1: Rescue Me	1
Chapter 2: The Changingman	15
Chapter 3: Don't Leave Me This Way	31
Chapter 4: (Just Like) Starting Over	46
Chapter 5: Come As You Are	58
Chapter 6: Downtown Train	74
Chapter 7: We Didn't Start the Fire	86
Chapter 8: Smells Like Team Spirit	97
Chapter 9: You're Unbelievable!	125
Chapter 10: The Winner Takes It All	140
Chapter 11: Take My Breath Away	154
Chapter 12: Do You Remember the First Time?	165
Chapter 13: Once in a Lifetime	179
Chapter 14: Making Plans For Nigel	187
Chapter 15: Even Better Than The Real Thing	200
Chapter 16: The Final Countdown	216
Chapter 17: You Can't Always Get What You Want	227
Chapter 18: I Think We're Alone Now	235
Chapter 19: What's the Story, Nicky Shorey?	248
Chapter 20: Here's Where the Story Ends	265
Postscript	278

INTRODUCTION

I Still Haven't Found What I'm Looking For

BLACKBURN. SUNDAY 13TH MAY 2007. *"We might as well just stop watching now – it's never going to get any better than this."*

Those were my words as I walked away from Ewood Park after watching Reading draw 3-3 with Blackburn Rovers in a dramatic final match of their first ever Premier League season. With qualification for Europe a near certainty should they win, Reading three times fell behind and three times equalised, but in the end the draw meant they missed out on a UEFA Cup place by a single point.

Just a few years earlier, the possibility of Reading playing in Europe would have been risible, and worthy of the time-honoured old gag: "They'll be in Europe next year – if there's a war!" For although Reading is the oldest professional football club south of the River Trent, their long history is one in which they've only rarely made a significant mark on the game's record books.

So to be following the team then was a time of wonder and marvels. The team, its supporters and just about everyone else associated with Reading enjoyed a period of unimagined success and exciting new experiences – experiences that just a few years earlier no-one could reasonably expect would ever come to 'Little Reading'. But all of a sudden Reading weren't so little any more – they were mixing it with the big boys and giving as good as they got, and to be a part of it, even just as a supporter, was a time of almost endless joy and wonder. The football gods smiled on a small corner of Berkshire, and Reading were a quantum leap above anything they'd ever been before.

Looking back on this, ten years older and ten years wiser, this all probably sounds like over-blown hyperbole, but anyone who experienced this incredible period in Reading's history will testify that it was anything but. It really was that wonderful, with everything about the team seeming to have meshed together perfectly, like the teeth of a Smooth-running zip. As a result, Reading supporters were suddenly spoilt – experiencing highs that many supporters don't get to enjoy in a lifetime of following a team, and which most Loyal Royals never realistically expected they'd ever experience.

This time of miracles had started 23 months earlier in August 2005, with an inauspicious start to their Championship season in the form of home defeat to Plymouth. But after that there was no looking back, and Reading didn't lose again in the Championship until the middle of February – 33 matches later. In the meantime they had blossomed into a perfectly balanced and ruthlessly efficient team, playing an attractive style of fast-paced and highly competitive football that swept aside all opposition at this level. A record-breaking total of 106 points; 99 goals scored; 31 league matches won with just two defeats; and that unbeaten run of 33 matches – their list of achievements shows their level of dominance, but the figures alone don't explain what it was like to watch this team in action.

It's interesting to talk to any Reading supporter who was there and who witnessed this time of achievement – even ten years on, the team is almost always spoken about in hushed tones, as a mythical fable or wondrous tale from the past might be. This is a subject that seems to invoke emotions like no other – supporters tend to go slightly misty-eyed as they recall with obvious fondness their own personal high points from among the many. And if you ask them – or indeed anyone associated with the football club at that time – exactly what made that team so special and why they loved it so much, you're likely to be given a wide variety of reasons. The quality and mix of the players will probably be given as a reason, and inevitably the management of Steve Coppell will be cited.

For instance, Reading supporter Linda Dubber thinks the team was so good: "*...thanks to their belief and will to win, they all seemed to get on, on and off the pitch, even though it may not have been the case. They always encouraged each other and there was always that sense that we would go on to win, even if we went behind – the 'never give up' attitude. And for me, most importantly of all, having the master tactician and all round nice guy – Steve Coppell – you really got the feeling back then that all the players WANTED to play for him and do him proud.*"

In the same way, Reading CEO Nigel Howe attributes much of the team's success to Coppell, saying: "*I think it was the unit and I think it was the fact he was able to brief them off the back of his studying of the videos. He was able to basically give them enough confidence when playing an away team that they'd know. He'd say 'this is how they're going to come at you, this is how they're going to play. All you need to do is do this, but just be aware of that.'*"

This unity and team spirit mentioned by Howe is also a

common theme from those both inside and outside the club, while others argue in favour of the role the coaches, Kevin Dillon and Wally Downes, played in the team's success. Many others also suggest that this team was the result of an evolution started six years earlier when Alan Pardew was appointed manager of Reading, while some make a case for the importance of sheer dumb luck in this success story!

Another frequently mentioned aspect of this team is their approach to the game. There's great love for Coppell, frequently described as one of the nicest and most genuine men in football, and many ascribe Reading's approach to the game at this time to his personality, honesty and integrity. This team didn't just win, they won in an old-fashioned, almost Corinthian way, with a minimum of nastiness, fouling or arguing with referees. I don't remember any incident at this time when a Reading player could be accused of diving or cheating in any way to win a decision – but I do remember clearly the sense of outrage when one of them, Kevin Doyle, was actually booked for simulation in a match at Luton. That was utterly outrageous! Steve Coppell's players didn't dive – they didn't need to!

And this approach showed in their disciplinary record, which was quite out of kilter with a team that was so very competitive. The back four gained just 11 yellow cards all season, with the two centre-backs received just three of these, and didn't miss a single match that year. Quite remarkable in such a physical league where referees tend to be quick to reach into their pockets at the slightest contact. This sensible, disciplined attitude that was synonymous with Coppell's whole approach was a feature of the whole team, so that across that wonderful season no Reading player was sent off nor were any suspended.

Off the pitch, too, there was something special about Reading's approach. Epitomised by club captain Graeme Murty, the longest-serving member of this team and its public face, who was always a consummate professional with a mature and sensible voice, dampening down any excesses or the threat of over-hype. As the voice of the team, his manner was completely in tune with the quiet, even-tempered approach of Coppell, and also that of chairman John Madejski, now Sir John, who is well known for his honesty and integrity. That triumvirate of Madejski, Coppell and Murty projected an ethos of decency, honesty and doing things the right way that delighted Reading supporters, and flew in the face of football's perceived wisdom that good guys finish last.

As well as the role of Coppell, the remarkable level of unity and team spirit is often cited as one of the key factors in the team's success. And that unity was extraordinary, extending out to encompass not just the team and others in the dressing room, but also their wives and girlfriends, to the extent that they created a charity fundraising initiative, the 'Royals Families', to harness the team's sudden fame for good causes.

It's clear to anyone who witnessed them that this team certainly was something special, and I have no hesitation of calling them the 'perfect team'. And although supporters each have their own personal theories on what gave this team their 'x-factor' the reality, of course, is never quite that simple. Very few things happen for a single, simple reason, and especially in a team, by definition a highly complex entity consisting of many individuals, each with their own personality, preferences and peculiarities. Add in those who manage, select and motivate them all, and then consider all the other variables that can crop up in a single game of football. Now extrapolate that across two whole seasons.

Considering this, it's astounding how everything did mesh together quite so well – so much so that that virtually every player in that squad seemed to have the peak period of their career at exactly the same time, regardless of whether they were seasoned professionals nearing the end of their careers or relative youngsters just starting theirs. In this little corner of Berkshire, for this brief period of time, all of the various factors that affect a team's performances happened to coalesce at exactly the same time.

But how? And why?

I've always been the sort of intensely irritating person who wants to know the reasons behind things and instinctively wants to analyse every cause of every effect, so this book is the result of my quest to uncover as many of the reasons for Reading's success as possible, and to understand just how they all came about at exactly the same time. This has involved me talking to many of those who around the team, managing and coaching them at this time, as well as others behind the scenes – both in the dressing room and in the boardroom making the big strategic and financial decisions. I set out to understand and to share how such a wonderfully balanced and effective team was created – and just when it happened. Did everything happen all at once or was it the culmination of work performed many years earlier? And who exactly were the key people making the crucial decisions that made it all happen? And was there something extra about this team that none of their competition had – something that gave them an extra edge?

As well as looking at how and why this happened, I also set out to celebrate what it was like to be a Reading fan at this time. I wanted to capture the depths of emotion and the heady mix of elation and disbelief we went through so many times. As supporters tend to have many different views and many different memories, and indeed often see the same game in many different ways, I decided I needed a variety of supporters to give a balanced and objective view. So as well as talking to those at the club who were at the centre of the action, I've recruited what I'm calling the 'Loyal Royals Panel' – a group of Reading supporters who watched the action and remember it well and who love this team as much as I do. Through their words as well as my own, I set out to trace the story of this team from before the magic started, through that record-breaking Championship season, past the feelings of initial trepidation before the first Premier League season started and into the feelings of relief and exhilaration as Reading punched well above their weight at that exalted level.

For instance, Alex Everson from this panel sums up what he loved about Reading: *"The beautiful simplicity of the team is what did it for me. It was a classic 4-4-2 formation, with two pacey wingers, a solid back four, great strikers. It all added together to form such a perfect team. There was never a week watching them in the Champion-ship where you turned up wondering whether or not they would win. It ended up each week being a question of how many they would win by and how entertaining they'd play that week versus the previous week."*

Dave Harris sings their praises in similar tones, saying: *"Quite frankly, it was the perfect team that had everything in the classic English sense of the word. Pace in abundance, defensively superb, midfield guile and fluidity, flanks that worked like clockwork, goals from all over the pitch, clean sheets, mental strength, unknown youngsters – and it had character. To watch that team play at their best, no team could live with them. They had the ability to strike at any given moment, the attitude to look at themselves when they conceded and say to each other 'what the hell are they doing?' and simply go up the other end and score themselves. But most of all they were exciting. The style of play was fast paced, structured around the classic 4-4-2 but with players who had a licence to express themselves. Brilliant to watch at times, a joy to behold."*

Of course, nothing lasts for ever, not even a perfect team, and as well as uncovering the factors that created these highs, I found myself discovering what happens when those factors are taken away. Because, looking back, that glorious day in Blackburn can be seen as a high point in the team's fortunes. Just 12 months later the smile of those football gods had moved elsewhere, that smooth-running zip was sticking and Reading's brief period in the spotlight was over as they were relegated back to the Championship on the last day of the 2007/08 season.

For, as I found out while researching this book and following through the story of that team's incredible rise, it's not just a question of finding those critical success factors that all must be present to make a team function perfectly – you need to keep them there, too. If you lose just one of them, you'll almost inevitably lose others as a result – these factors are often intricately linked, balancing each other out perfectly like a kinetic sculpture. And their absence means that the perfection will quickly evaporate, and the whole structure of the team could come tumbling down, as if you'd removed the bottom few bricks in a wall.

This book is the result of my quest – not just an account of that amazing couple of incredible seasons when 'Little Reading' had a perfect team that took football by storm, but also a discovery and analysis of what were the many factors that made it all happen – and of just how quickly and easily the magic can be lost when those factors aren't properly nurtured and maintained.

CHAPTER ONE

Rescue Me

MY SEARCH FOR THE INGREDIENTS that made up Reading's perfect team has to start with the background to the football club, and a brief overview of their largely uneventful history. This will provide a context that will hopefully help people to understand just how astonishing and just how out of character the three seasons 2005/06 to 2007/08 were, and just why Reading supporters reacted the way they did.

The team's supporters have always been a pretty tolerant and long-suffering bunch, a relatively small hard-core who, over the years, have watched their team reach precious few highs or lows. So when the team delivered a high in 2005/06, the resulting excitement was greater than it might be at other clubs, but maybe only due to the long years of mediocrity that preceded it. And as this high reached ever-greater altitudes, this excitement was joined by sheer astonishment and a real sense of wonder at just how good this team was proving to be, just how perfectly everything seemed to be going and just how far the high might eventually reach.

But this disbelief becomes quite understandable when you consider the history of Reading Football Club up to this point. Although they were formed in 1871 and turned professional in 1895, this switch to professionalism was too late for the club to be involved in the birth of the Football League, a situation exacerbated by their location deep in the south away from major industrial conurbations. Instead, they were a founder member of the Southern League and had a relatively undistinguished record in that competition until it was absorbed into the Football League as Division Three in 1920, morphing into Division Three (South) a year later.

Reading's subsequent years in the Football League were hardly more distinguished. Early promise shown by winning promotion to Division Two (South) in 1926 and reaching the FA Cup semi-final the following year was unfulfilled, and 'The Biscuitmen' – Huntley and Palmers was the middle 'B' in the town's celebrated 'Three Bs' of 'Beer, Biscuit and Bulbs' – were relegated after just five years back to tier three. There followed a 40-year period of stasis until the club's next move, which was again downwards – relegation to Division Four in 1971.

So far, so much like the story of so many other small town clubs who have rattled around the lower leagues without ever significantly troubling the keepers of football's record books. Like so many other clubs of a similar size, their attendances steadily declined as the 1980s were reached, and in order to remain in existence the club needed to either sell a player every season to cover their losses or to receive a cash injection from their owner. This financial environment, together with a virtually non-existent regulatory framework relating to ground safety, meant that the grounds of most clubs, both big and small, deteriorated through neglect and lack of investment, and Reading's Elm Park, their home since 1896, was no exception. With minimal maintenance or improvements apart from an occasional lick of paint from the supporters themselves, with no corporate facilities until 'executive boxes' (in the loosest sense of the word), with crumbling concrete walls (providing ideal missiles for visiting supporters when matches got 'tasty', for instance when Bristol City visited in April 1984) and with toilets in the South Bank as primitive as can be imagined, Elm Park was well past its sell-by date and needed considerable investment. In fact, at the start of the 1985/86 season when safety authorities at last started looking at football ground safety following the Bradford City stadium fire of May 1985, the maximum capacity of Elm Park was reduced to just 6,000.

But although the ground was described by notable football ground observer Simon Inglis as "the least interesting ground in the League" in his book *The Football Grounds of England and Wales (Harper Collins Willow 1983* – a statement that drew predictable anger from Reading's hard-core support, down to an average of under 3,500 that season – who were happy to accept its many shortcomings.

This was a time for football clubs at all levels, and even more so in the lower reaches of the leagues, and it was also a time when the ownership of a club became increasingly significant and moved much more centre-stage. Reading themselves had a very narrow escape in April 1983 when media tycoon Robert Maxwell, already owner of local rivals Oxford United, attempted a takeover of Reading with the aim of creating a wholly new – and wholly artificial – club, 'Thames Valley Royals' to play in a new stadium close to the Oxfordshire/Berkshire border in Didcot. Fans of both clubs took to the streets in protest, but it was legal manoeuvres by Reading director Roy Tranter that finally thwarted the plan, and Reading survived to face the rest of the 1980s, still in existence but with the finances no less secure.

Their immediate future secured, 'The Royals' – as they'd become in 1976 after Huntley and Palmers left the town – rallied on the pitch as well, and in May 1984 gaining promotion back to tier three. Two seasons later they returned to tier two, after an absence of 55 years, by winning Division Three in emphatic fashion on the back of a run of 13 straight wins from the start of the season. This equalled the Football League record, and two seasons later came what was, in the eyes of many Reading fans, the club's greatest achievement of their existence.

This was triumph in the Simod Cup final over Luton Town at Wembley on 27 March 1988. I think the fact that this victory is so revered demonstrates just what slim pickings Reading supporters had had to celebrate over the years, and how low their expectations levels had become, because it's probably fair to say that the Simod Cup is today only remembered by football anoraks and the supporters of the five clubs that won it in its various guises. After all, a competition that was created in 1986 as the 'Full Members' Cup' in order to give English clubs banned from Europe something to play for, but which was shunned by several of the larger First Division clubs, and which only lasted seven seasons in total, is not one of the game's glamour trophies.

However, winning this trophy proved to be the club's pinnacle in the 1980s, and they were denied the chance to defend it the following season through relegation, and as the club reached the 1990s things looked bleak. Owner Roger Smee had had enough of perpetually bailing out the club's ever-increasing losses – running at a reported £11,000 per week now the clubs was back in tier three – and was desperate to find a buyer. Without such a buyer, Reading were looking down the barrel of administration or even receivership.

But in the closing months of 1990 when things seemed to be at their darkest, Reading experienced what was probably the most significant turning point in their whole history – as the first of the pillars on which the perfect team's success was built came to be in place.

In the great lottery of football club ownership, Reading rolled the dice and came up with a winner. While other clubs of a similar size and history found themselves owned by characters liable to either sell the ground from under them or to hire someone to burn down the main stand as an insurance job, Reading found themselves under the ownership of John Madejski. It's hard to think of how the club could have done better at this time, for Madejski turned out to be a perfect fit for the club, and under his stewardship they would change practically out of all recognition, playing at a level – and in a setting – almost beyond the imagination of those who'd followed 'Little Reading' over the years.

The story of Madejski's rise, starting with a typewriter and a rented garage and turning that into a substantial fortune, initially through the *Auto Trader* range of titles, is well documented elsewhere and doesn't need repeating here. But it's significant that although born in Stoke-on-Trent Madejski had lived in the Reading area since his earliest years and his business interests were also centred there, and he explained that his decision to rescue the football club was down to his pride in the town and his own resulting desire to make his own contribution to it. As such, Madejski was somewhat of an 'old-style' owner – by which I mean a local businessman who genuinely recognised a football club as a local asset, of intrinsic value to its community and worth supporting financially for the good of that community. At a time when the money-obsessed Premier League was already less than two years from creation, and when various property developers and asset strippers were increasingly looking at football clubs as a way to make easy money, whatever that meant to the club in question, Madejski was somewhat of a rarity and his modus operandi was just as rare.

The majority of owners of football clubs have typically believed that the only way to achieve success is through the team, and so have lavished their money on managers, players, transfer fees and wages. Madejski, however, did things in a way somewhat different to these accepted practices, investing far greater sums in the bricks and mortar of the club's facilities and its infrastructure than in on-field expenses.

Perhaps this novel approach to football finance was partly down to Madejski's lack of experience in the game – he didn't watch the team before buying it, and he has many times unashamedly admitted to having minimal knowledge of the game or its methods and peculiarities – or maybe it was forced onto him by the general state of dilapidation of Elm Park and the lack of scope for expansion or improvement of the old ground. But whatever the exact reasons behind it, this strategy of investing in infrastructure turned out to be absolutely ideal for both the club and the owner – an almost perfect symbiosis.

For Madejski's investments, relatively small at first but increasing in size and significance as the club's scale and profile increased, directly led to a quantum transformation in the club and its facilities. And as the club's scale and profile increased as a result of these investments not only did its book value as an asset increase with it, but the 'soft benefits' of owning a successful football club, the profile and prestige that came to its owner, also increased.

In hindsight, Madejski's strategy has to be regarded as a stroke of absolute genius, and one that flew in the face of perceived wisdom which said that the only certain ways to profit from owning a football club were to convert a big-name 'brand' club into a PLC and profit from resulting sale of shares or to just dispense with the football side of the club altogether and to realise the profits to be made from any land they owned. Instead, Madejski found a 'third way' – to take a small, relatively insignificant and run-down club and to turn it into a much larger and much more successful club. And although those financial rewards might not have been immediately realisable in strict financial terms, there are also those 'soft benefits' to consider – just how many people would have heard of John Madejski (or 'Sir John' as he has been since 2009) if he'd not taken that decision to rescue his hometown football club in 1990?

But it wasn't just about the finances and the prestige – Madejski has always been clear that his purchase of Reading, just like his financial support for numerous organisations in the worlds of art and education, are genuinely motivated by community spirit and a real desire to help. He is on record as saying: *"People can think what they like about me. I don't care. It's never been a popularity contest. I do it all for the community. In my view, you start life with nothing and you end it with nothing. I'd like to enjoy it all before I kick the bucket."* – and I have no doubts that this is genuine altruism. When I interviewed Sir John for this book in the summer of 2015 it came across clearly to me just how genuine he is about the club and his involvement in it. His pride in how the club has changed and what it has achieved during his ownership was also clear, but equally his pride in the way it has been achieved and his involvement in that is just as striking. For instance, he speaks with great fondness of his pre-match visits to the team before games: "*As I still do today, I'd go into the changing room before each game and say a few words to the players, which I enjoy doing and fortunately every manager wanted me to do that so I'm happy to do that, which I think is quite unique in some ways.*"

What struck me most when talking to Madejski about the team's success, though, was that despite his role at a high level in these events, he speaks with the same wonder and enthusiasm as any other fan – that same fond smile and those same misty-eyes of someone retelling unforgettable, once-in-a-lifetime memories. Although his highlights of Reading's first Premier League season may be more grandiose than those of most fans. He recalls them with the same affection as any other fan would: "*They were all a joy to me, I mean going to all those wonderful games and so on. I always liked going to Manchester United because I knew, as everybody does vaguely, Alex Ferguson. I get on well with him and whenever I go up there, he invites me … well he did, he'd invite me into his little sitting room. It was a nice bit of claret, very nice guy, very normal, very relaxed, so going to Manchester United was great, a sort of joy, but all the clubs were fantastic. I think probably the most impressive club I've been to has been Newcastle, it's such an amazing stadium, without a doubt, but they're all pretty fantastic … of course, when you go to the likes of Liverpool, Manchester United, Arsenal, they were the three really big clubs, and I know Chelsea has emerged, a big club again, but it was such a thrill going to all those big clubs and just seeing how the other half live. Of course we'd never been anywhere like that before, when I took the club over in 1990 there we were in the boondocks, the most wretched place imaginable. It's certainly been different.*"

It is patently clear to me that without Madejski's rescue of Reading in December 1990 there would have been no 'perfect team', and in fact there might not even be a Reading FC now, since many clubs of a similar size and stature to Reading in 1990 have suffered dire crises in the quarter century since. Similar provincial clubs, peers of Reading in 1990 such as Stockport County, Lincoln City and Grimsby Town, have suffered bleak times both financially and in terms of league status, while other clubs, including Oxford United, the would-be predators of Thames Valley Royals just seven years earlier, would eventually find their hopes of advancement forever limited by the size of their ground. Reading's other long-term local rivals, Aldershot FC, had resigned from the football league and gone out of business altogether in 1992.

Reading, however, set their sights high and in August 1998 they moved into the 24,200-seater Madejski Stadium, including hotel and conference centre, built on the site of the old Smallmead refuse tip south of Reading and close to the M4 motorway. Plans for the stadium had been talked about for many years, but they finally started to be seriously discussed almost as soon as Madejski bought the club. The land itself was sold to the football club for just £1 by a local council that was among those few rare local authorities to recognise the value to their community of a local football club – however, decontaminating it and removing decades worth of toxic waste cost over £6 million, and a further condition of sale was a contribution of another £6 million towards construction of the A33 relief road down to the motorway junction. The final construction bill came in at £37 million, and even after the sale of the Elm Park site for housing and of extra land next to the relief road for retail use there was a shortfall of over £10 million, which Madejski himself guaranteed.

Looking back, it's hard to appreciate just how much of a quantum leap this move was, but virtually every aspect of the club and the way it operated was changed in some way. Long-term Reading kit-man Ron Grant, who worked at both locations, shared with me just how run-down the facilities at Elm Park were before the move to use dedicated, professional-standard laundry facilities at the Madejski Stadium: "*In those days the shirts used to be washed by Gordon Neate* [Reading groundsman] *and his wife, Viv. I used to take the kit up to her to get washed – well, she used to come down and take it and collect it in fairness to her – but eventually I was taking it up there and it used to come back from her and we used to then go in the boiler room downstairs, in the cellar, so it was placed there to air and that's where the kit was actually kept and then we had a cupboard outside the dressing room where all the towels were and all the other bits and pieces, but it was very dated. No investment at all.*"

Many would say that the 'no investment at all' mantra also applied to the playing side of the team during this period, with a clear focus on the stadium development and the long-term future of the club. But in the short-term the team didn't flounder, and in fact prospered under manager Mark McGhee, who had joined the club in the twilight of his playing career after successful spells at Newcastle, Aberdeen and Celtic.

Another example of Madejski's relative unorthodoxy compared to accepted practices in the game has been shown several times in brave appointments of almost totally inexperienced managers – and more often than not these have been successful moves. Madejski explained to me one of his rationales in making these appointments: *"As everybody knows I'm not exactly the most savvy football aficionado but I do think I understand people reasonably well and I judge people by their calibre and their integrity and lots of different things that make up a person. Sometimes in the past when I've interviewed for managers, it's all about 'me, me, me, me, me' and then some more me – and 'oh, what club is it again?'"*

Madejski wasn't taking a complete shot in the dark in appointing McGhee as player-manager in May 1991, though – his potential qualities as a manager came with a recommendation from his ex-boss at Aberdeen, Sir Alex Ferguson. And Under McGhee's leadership the team prospered, and in 1994, with a team largely comprising of young unknowns and relative old-timers – for example Jimmy Quinn, another striker who came with a pedigree gained at more illustrious clubs than Reading – were promoted back to the second tier as champions of what was now called Division Two following the creation of the Premiership two years earlier.

With momentum on their side, the team continued in the same vein the following season, and in December 1994 were placed second in the table. However, this was the point when Madejski discovered for the first time two vital lessons that would be learned several times over the next few years. The first lesson is that a young up-and-coming manager is an extremely sought-after property, and the second lesson is that in the cutthroat world of football, which has for many years operated using a set of ethics quite different to those of the business world at large, contracts have considerably less value than a non-football man might appreciate.

The upshot of what was a messy and unpleasant situation was the departure of McGhee to Leicester City before Christmas as he tried – and failed – to save the Foxes from

relegation before delighting those who criticised his lack of
loyalty by leaving Leicester for Wolves after a stay of less than
12 months at Filbert Street.

Madejski's rationale was once again somewhat unortho-
dox, appointing a manager – or rather four 'joint managers' –
from within the playing squad, in the form of senior players
Jimmy Quinn, Mick Gooding, Jeff Hopkins and Ady Williams.
This very soon became just Quinn and Gooding, but the team
continued to compete on the pitch and finished the season in
second place in the table. However, the experience of 1995 is
another formative moment that has shaped the attitudes and
outlook of Reading supporters, who will all show a grim pride
when they recount how their team is the only one in history to
have finished second and to have not been promoted, for this
was a season when the Premiership was reducing in numbers
and so only the top team was promoted to the highest level
automatically. To make the agony and the supporters' sense of
inevitable disappointment even greater, Reading reached the
play-off final at Wembley in great style, but then famously lost
4-3 to Bolton after extra time, despite being 2-0 up after 12
minutes and being awarded a penalty just after the half-hour
mark. That was missed, Reading conceded an equaliser four
minutes from the end of normal time and Reading supporters
trudged back from Wembley with the idea firmly planted that
their best – and possibly only – chance of ever seeing their
team play in the top flight had been most thoroughly blown.

The inevitable fate of small, impoverished teams who have
relative success is asset stripping by bigger, richer clubs, and of
course that was Reading's fate after that gut-wrenching defeat.
Outstanding 'keeper Shaka Hislop left for Newcastle, inspirational winger Simon Osborn left for QPR, local midfielder

Scott Taylor went to join McGhee at Leicester and equally inevitably their replacements were less effective. By the time the team moved to the new stadium in August 1998 they were managed by Tommy Burns. The ex-Celtic manager had replaced Terry Bullivant after a less-than-successful nine-month period in charge, but was unable to turn around an injury-ravaged squad. As a result, relegation back to the third tier meant the final game at Elm Park was a muted affair, with Reading in bottom place in the table after just two wins in 17 matches since the start of February – both home wins over the two relegated with them, Stoke City and Manchester City.

The move to the Madejski started to change everything, as the scale and scope of the club was suddenly a whole magnitude larger – but that largely applied on matchdays only. Reading didn't have a permanent training base, instead training at a variety of local venues, such as Bradfield College or Reading Rugby Club in Sonning. But they were there as guests more than anything else, with no facilities of their own, and typically with use of nothing more than a field to train on and rudimentary changing facilities.

It was clear that off the pitch things needed to change to both match the new surroundings and to keep pace with changes happening elsewhere in the game at this time. But changes were slow to come about. Instead, with the team slowly adapting to the lower level of the game in what was already starting to become known as the 'MadStad', changes off the pitch were relatively minor.

One such minor change, which nicely illustrates the day-to-day working of the club at this time, was a change where players now had their training kits washed for them each day. Ron Grant takes up the story: "*Up to Tommy Burns coming in, the players washed their own training kit, though I used to carry little bits and pieces. I mean I've had occasions when Ady Williams would arrive and he'd forgotten he had his kit in the boot from the day before and so he had to put the dirty kit on and it went from there – but Tommy Burns changed that and I was actually taking the kit to a wash at the Meadway* [shopping centre] *and had it done there."*

But the tenure of Burns was not a successful one, and he was unable to secure the promotion to a level more fitting to the new. His first full season in charge, the first at the Mad-Stad, resulted in an 11th place finish, and countless rumours of dressing room unhappiness – particularly when eight established players, including long-time fans' favourite Phil Parkinson, were placed on the transfer list and told to train with the reserve team – which itself only existed until the end of the 1998/99 season when it was disbanded. The case of the eight players (known as the 'Elm Park Disappeared') was only resolved after intervention from the PFA, and when results failed to improve the following season and with supporters despairing at the mediocre players and the paucity of points gained, it was clear that Burns's days at the helm were numbered. He was duly sacked as manager in September 1999.

Madejski and his board clearly had some crucial decisions to make at this point – decisions that had the potential to determine the club's long-term future.

CHAPTER TWO

The Changingman

IN SEPTEMBER 1999, FACING THE forthcoming millennium in the lower reaches of the third tier with a brand new stadium but no manager, it was decision time for those running Reading FC. It's clear to me from virtually all the research interviews I conducted for this book just how important the appointment of the next manager was for the future of the club.

Again, an unknown manager was appointed, and again the decision turned out to be an inspired one – as Reading appointed Alan Pardew as their new manager. Pardew had arrived at Reading from Barnet in June 1997 to take on the role of Reserve Team Manager, accompanying Terry Bullivant. But when Bullivant was sacked and replaced by Burns just nine months later, Pardew kept his post – and in fact acted as caretaker manager for a period of seven days before Burns was appointed. This meant managing for just one match, a 2-0 home defeat to Huddersfield Town.

Nigel Howe, Reading CEO, told me the story of the departure and later return, as manager, of Pardew. *"Alan, as you know, worked for Tommy Burns and he was very frustrated with his role as reserve team manager, having worked briefly with Terry Bullivant and kept on by Tommy, and he worked with the young lads but he was frustrated with Tommy's approach to what he did. Tommy took no interest in what Alan did."*

"So Alan came to me prior to the end of the season we got relegated and said 'I've decided I'd like to leave' and I said 'have you got a job?' he said 'No, I'm just going to see what's around' and I think he went off and did a few odd jobs around for people as we started the next season. Sir John arrived back from Kuala Lumpur and, as far as I was concerned, Tommy hadn't succeeded and should be dismissed. Sir John gave him the benefit of the doubt and we started off the next season and made a couple of signings but really didn't change a lot and the decision was made in September to ask him to leave. At the time, I'd sort of mentioned to the Board 'look, we'd had this really good guy in Alan Pardew who had been working along while Sir John had been away in Kuala Lumpur', but Ian Wood-Smith had a good feel for Alan and liked him. He was sort of a likeable chap, he had a lot of good ideas. So Sir John said 'Right, we'll take him on trial', as you do."

This was the start of a fruitful relationship for both Pardew and the club. Pardew certainly knew what he wanted from the role and set out to achieve it, and in doing so changed not only the way the team was managed but the whole mentality and attitude as well.

Everyone I spoke to enthused about the positive changes brought by Pardew as well as his many innovations – the like of which were virtually unheard of at a club like Reading. Ron Grant, for instance, spoke of the difference between Burns and Pardew as managers: *"Alan brought a new feel to the place in actual fact, I mean Tommy was a great guy, good coach, but some of the training sessions were very long-winded and Alan came in and brought a more sharper approach to it I think, and also started to bring in players that he had been with and actually played with or actually managed. He had a good knowledge of the footballers in this area in the pro-clubs, for example, he played non-league football for the London clubs, he'd played football for Yeovil and he'd been involved in Crystal Palace, so he had a good knowledge of the players and he actually brought in players. He certainly brought in a different approach to the game."*

Ady Williams, who had left for Wolves in July 1996, was brought back to Reading by Pardew in early 2000, and so is perfectly placed to summarise the changes between the club he left and the one he re-joined: *"Oh yeah, a lot had changed. Alan Pardew for me started the ball rolling here at this football club. Alan Pardew with his methods and his thinking and his techniques and introducing backroom staff that we'd never seen before certainly started that all off and when I come back on loan, I ended up staying four or five years, whatever it was, I clearly wanted to be part of that and it was a privilege to be part of that."*

When I asked Williams what was special about Pardew's management style, he told me: *"Pards did a lot of it himself, if not all of it, he was still a young man and a good footballer. The difference from Alan Pardew to other managers I've worked for, even Steve Coppell, was that Pards would show you exactly what he wanted to do. I think footballers quite like seeing it, like visualising something, whether it's on the telly or whether it's on the training pitch. If he tells me something that's not bad, but if he shows me something I know exactly what he wants me to do and he still had that ability to show the team, whether it was me at centre-half, or whether it was a winger or a striker, he wasn't long out of football and he was still a good quality, still fit so he did his coaching and not just coaching, he showed us how to do what he wanted."*

Pardew also worked hard on new methods of motivating the team. One, considered 'cheesy' by many fans, was players warming up in T-shirts with the words 'Tenacity, Spirit, Flair' – a slogan that seemed to be displayed in an ever-increasing number of places around the ground as time went and it became a theme for the team. And although slogans don't win football matches, Pardew obviously believed they had their place and could help tip the balance the right way. He also arranged for three wall boards to be put up in the home dressing room. Ron Grant told me that as well as the coaches putting motivational or encouraging words, including reminders of incidents from previous matches with those opponents, onto these before each matches, he was, somewhat reluctantly, persuaded to do the same – although he did say he's not convinced that the players ever looked at them.

Whether they were consciously acknowledged, they were just one of many innovations from Pardew that constantly challenged the players and their attitudes. Even if individual factors such as the wall boards had minimal effect, I have no doubts that no player could remain unaffected by the multitude of motivational factors assaulting them from all sides. Pardew's new broom swept away the old, comfortable attitudes of some at the club and introduced modern coaching and motivational techniques that had never been seen by the team. Another of his innovations, this one more inclusive and much harder for any sceptical player to ignore, were his 'goal cards'.

Williams told me more about these: "*The goal cards – we used to sit down, we used to have blocks of six games and what was good about it was that it involved everybody and we all had an input on it and it wasn't the captain or the senior players – everybody had an input. At first it took a lot of getting used to. He made them and designed them like fridge magnets so we used to put them on the fridge, so that every time you opened the fridge you'd look and see the next six games and where you think you should be and what results and what goals you should be scoring and what goals you shouldn't be conceding and things. It took a little bit of time to get used to but it was really good because we had meetings about it and it involved everybody, whether it was a young lad just making his fifth appearance or whether it was somebody like me probably making their 350th. So it was good – and why not? Most people in businesses I think have got goals and visions and ambitions and aspirations and that was the first time I'd seen anything like that, I bought into it, we had a bit of a laugh about it at first but that was one thing that he introduced.*"

Nick Hammond, Reading's Director of Football, explained where the idea of the goal cards came from: "*He and I went to a conference at Mottram Hall in Manchester and we watched a presentation by Steve McLaren who did a goal-setting presentation and it was fantastic and I wouldn't say we plagiarised that – but we saw the benefits of it. Goal setting individually and for teams as well – it worked really well for us. You had to be careful because if you don't meet your goals where do you go? But I think it helped in terms of focus of the mind with a group of players, so it started and it adapted and it worked very well for us.*"

Pardew's willingness to innovate, and to pick up and incorporate new ideas, is testament to his ambition, and it's not overstating things to say that his approach revolutionised the whole way the team trained and the way they played – and this clearly had a profound effect on their attitudes to themselves and their profession. Williams told me more, giving a very revealing insight on how this change of culture within the squad made each player look more closely at themselves and their role in the club: "*The sports science for me was the biggest thing. Pards employed people like Niall Clark, he was a sports scientist, a nutritionist, and it was a major change for us. We started doing different techniques, we started doing core work, we started doing plyometrics, we started using bungees – big elastic bands for sprinting techniques.*"

"*It was a complete change where none of the lads had ever seen anything like it – and training from 10.30 to 11.45 every day. We were training a lot more serious, we were training maybe from 10.30 am until 12.00, maybe having a bit of lunch and then coming back in the afternoon and doing it so the whole mind-set was changed. All of a sudden if you said 'I can't do the afternoon session, I've got to pick the kids up' – well, you know what, you're a professional footballer, you sort that out because you're back in at 2 pm."*

As we've seen with the introduction of Niall Clark, who was brought by Pardew in the summer of 2000, this 'Pardew Revolution' wasn't a one-man operation. Throughout his time as manager, Pardew had assistance, and in fact this was initially forced upon him as a condition of his employment – but it's very interesting and very revealing that as Pardew's needs and his stature at the club changed over his tenure, he was not afraid to change his assistant managers in order to meet his and the team's changing requirements.

Pardew's first assistant was John Gorman, who had spent many years as assistant to Glenn Hoddle, initially at Swindon Town and, later, the English national team. On Hoddle's departure for the FA job, Gorman himself took charge of Swindon for their single season in the Premier League, although that wasn't a happy one for either as Swindon won just five matches and conceded exactly 100 goals. In 1999 Gorman was available following Hoddle's dismissal from the England role, was well known to the club and Madejski, and also lived locally, so he was the obvious candidate to provide the rookie manager with some experienced advice.

Nigel Howe continues the story of Pardew's appointment: *"I suppose the story follows that Alan was very impressive, the way he set out his stall, he knew exactly how he wanted to do things and how he was going to set about the backroom team and everything else and the only thing that we were insistent on as the CEO and Sir John as the Chairman was*

Alan bringing in a bit more experience with him, he knew John Gorman and John Gorman was the obvious choice. As you know that worked, that got us going and Alan, he brought in all of his ideas about coaching and about motivation, team building, team goals and we were up and running."

Initially, Pardew's rein started badly as his team failed to improve its performances, and in December 1999 he was the subject of what was known as 'pants day'. This was a protest organised by a loose alliance of Reading fans, designed to draw attention to how badly the club was doing. But this illustrates how Reading fans differed from those of many other clubs at this time – while at other clubs dissatisfaction might result in marches, derogatory banners or pitch invasions, Reading supporters protested by waving underwear from the stands.

The nature and intention of the protest are best explained by the organisers of it, who posted the below text onto the main Reading FC fansite – although these were very early days for internet fan activism, Reading was located smack-bang in the middle of the UK's 'silicon corridor', a very affluent area with a high percentage of tech-savvy 'early adopters'. At this time, Reading had the highest proportion of internet-connected supporters of any English professional, and so it's no surprise that was one of the first where supporters mobilised via the web.

A statement from the pants day organisers reads: *"'Pants Day' has been spontaneously inspired by events at Reading Football Club as a safe and fun alternative to the inevitable pitch invasion. Enthusiastically promoted by a number of responsible & genuine fans. 'Pants Day' involves the waving of 'Y' fronts to protest at the pants performance of Reading Football Club; 'Pants for Pants' you might say. This is NOT a demonstration organized against any particular individual, but a novel, humorous and harmless expression of concern, designed to draw the club's attention to the depth of feeling and frustration felt by many supporters. The intention is to have a fun day with plenty of noise and express our serious concern at Reading Football Club's current predicament.*

- *We advocate the WAVING of PANTS as an expression of good-natured criticism for the lack of effort, passion and style shown by our team.*
- *We wish to unite the Reading fans with a catalyst, which is safe, fun and newsworthy.*
- *We wish to raise our club's profile and the awareness of the directors of our passion for the club and the need to invest even more in our hopes and aspirations.*
- *We want to re-awaken the interest of stay-away fans, re-creating an atmosphere at the Madejski Stadium to rival and exceed that of Elm Park.*
- *We want to prevent illegal, unsafe or dangerous activities, such as pitch invasions.*
- *We want to be proud of our Football Club, excited by our team and we want to, once again, enjoy being Reading supporters.*
- *We want all supporters to act responsibly and create a carnival atmosphere in all parts of the ground, except the South stand where we hope the gloom-and-doom of disappointment will settle over the away fans for a change."*

Maybe it's partly the lower expectation levels after years of non-achievement or maybe it's partly down to the club having a relatively high proportion of middle-class supporters compared to many others, but this protest perfectly suited Reading supporters and also caught the imagination of journalists across the country, with significant national coverage – a rarity at the time. On the day, both Pardew and Madejski were interviewed at length about the protest by both local and national media, and it was clear the point had been made. Even Madejski entered into the spirit at one point, waving a pair of Y-fronts (as sold in the Reading FC Megastore, of course) from the directors' box!

It's impossible to quantify just how much influence the protest by the majority of the 6,232 crowd that Saturday afternoon in December actually had on the team, and how much was down to Pardew's influence and the effect of two additional January signings, but it's indisputable that within a month Reading were on the up. Before Christmas, they had won just four and lost 11 league matches, but after that point they won 12 and lost just six, finished in tenth place and with a whole new attitude and optimism. There was a definite shape and spine to the team – there was a clear feeling that Pardew was building something at the club, and as a result supporter numbers had virtually doubled.

While it was seen by many as a trivial protest, I do feel that 'Pants day' was an important part of the club's history – not just because of any galvanising effect it had on the team and the manager, but because it was an important step in the process of Reading fans adapting to their new surroundings and in making the Madejski Stadium their own. For many, that day was the first day at the new stadium that it started to be fun being a Reading fan again after a nondescript and depressing year and the loss of the beloved Elm Park, and there was a noticeable improvement in the atmosphere at the ground almost from that day.

Loyal Royal Dave Harris shared his thoughts with me on

just how important that January in 2000 was to the transformation of Reading and the early days of Alan Pardew's spell as
manager: *"The fans, they took a while to warm to him originally. If
memory serves me rightly, his start was inglorious, then there's a specific
match, in early 2000, where the assistant manager had changed, John
Gorman had left and we'd also made the key signing of Matthew
Robinson. We played Colchester, won for the first time in 13 and that for
me is the key point where it started to turn around."*

The new assistant manager Dave speaks of was Reading-
born Martin Allen, who replaced Gorman. He brought a
rumbustious, no-nonsense style of man-management, in line
with the on-the-pitch philosophy he'd showed throughout his
playing career of never showing any fear no matter what the
circumstance was. It's clear that his approach helped toughen-
up a Reading team that was too easily bullied on the pitch,
and helped instil vital self-belief in them. Away at Preston at
the start of February 2000, for instance, he insisted Reading
warm-up before the match in Preston's half of the pitch, and
refused to move despite requests from Preston's first-team
coach, their assistant manager and Deepdale's safety officer.
When he saw the police match commander approaching down
one side of the pitch, he moved the team across to the opposite
touchline, and only took the team off when threatened with
arrest for breach of the peace!

It was an unconventional move, and a blatant piece of
provocation – but it worked. The players stood by him in the
face of dogs' abuse from the home fans and criticism from
their opponents and the match authorities, and came off the
pitch with heads held high. Allen's public display of sticking up
two fingers had worked, and in his words the players 'showed
no fear!' Allen is known throughout football as 'Mad Dog' and

his in-your-face style of man management came along at a vital time in the development of the team and the re-forging of their attitude, and for a while fitted perfectly with Pardew's management style. It's highly unlikely that Pardew wasn't aware of what 'Mad Dog' was planning at Preston that afternoon, and it's impossible to escape the conclusion that Pardew knew he had a squad that was a little too comfortable in itself and which needed to be 'toughened up' and given a good strong dose of self-belief. Martin Allen was exactly the man to do that.

Under Pardew and Allen, the team continued to progress with Pardew gradually getting rid of most of the players he'd inherited from Burns and building his own team with shrewd player acquisitions. He also had a clear ability to convince his chairman that a certain level of money needed to be spent on players – in his first year at the club, Pardew brought in 11 new players, costing more than £1.5 million, including Martin Butler for £750,000. These were big signings in terms of Reading's past financial context and their status as a third-tier club. Pardew also worked had to find new, undiscovered talent, and in the summer of 2000 at least five unknowns turned out for Reading in friendlies, only one of whom, Joe Gamble, actually signed for the club. These included Micky Longfellow, a serving soldier, who impressed against Reading in a pre-season training match – another of Pardew's innovations was to have pre-season training at a local army base, utilising army training methods and army PT instructors.

The team started the 2000/01 season slowly, but blossomed in the autumn with a fine run of form and some resounding wins, including a memorable 5-0 home win in the height of the fuel crisis of September 2000 when Royals fans taunted the few Oldham fans present with jeers of 'what a waste of petrol'. Runs of nine wins from 13 games in September, and ten from 13 from February, put them very much in contention for promotion, but a late-season wobble and a few too many draws meant they finished third in the table, five points behind second placed Rotherham. It was play-off time again!

After drawing the away semi-final at Wigan 0-0, the home leg started badly with Reading 1-0 down after a 26th minute free-kick and struggling to assert themselves in the game. But a late switch to 4-3-3 by Pardew transformed the match. Nicky Forster, who had been out for most of the season with a cruciate injury, was brought on as an 81st minute substitute and just four minutes later his fierce shot was spilled by Wigan 'keeper Andy Carroll and Martin Butler scored an equaliser. Right at the death of normal time, Forster's pace saw him brought down in the Wigan box to earn a dramatic late penalty. This was saved, but Forster was first to the rebound and scored to send Reading off to the play-off final at Cardiff – and create the first truly memorable 'I was there!' Madejski moment.

The despair of the heart-breaking 1995 play-off final defeat was never far from the minds of the 33,000-odd Reading fans who travelled down the M4 to support their team against Walsall – and, true to form, Reading lost in the cruellest of circumstances. They took a 2-1 lead in the first minute of extra time, but with just 13 minutes more to play in the game they conceded a truly bizarre own goal. A Barry Hunter 'safety-first' clearance hit the head of Tony Rougier, back in his own box and in the process of falling over, and rebounded straight into the Reading goal. Still reeling from this, they conceded a soft goal from a speculative long-range shot just two minutes later, and Reading's play-off jinx had struck again and the over-riding pessimism of Reading fans had received another play-off shot in the arm.

The following season followed a similar pattern, with strong runs in autumn (seven from eight games) and early in 2002 (eight out of nine) placing Royals in strong contention for promotion as the season neared its climax, nine points clear at the top of the table in January. But again Reading were cursed by a run of draws towards the end of the season, and they went into the final match, away at Brentford, in second place in the table and in line for automatic promotion. However, their opponents that day were just one point behind in third place, so Royals needed just a draw to confirm automatic promotion and avoid another potentially painful play-off experience.

This match was effectively a sudden death one, and it pitched Pardew against Steve Coppell, his manager from his Crystal Palace days and in many ways his mentor. Demand for the relatively few match tickets in the Brentford away end was fierce, and so a TV screen was provided at the MadStad to enable an extra 6,000 Reading supporters to watch the match. They saw Reading fall behind early in the second half, but due to a communications glitch they missed the 77th minute equaliser by Jamie Cureton, brought on as a substitute by Pardew ten minutes earlier.

Promotion was wildly celebrated, with the feeling that Reading had a developing team with a real passion and a winning mentality – one that would not be out of its depth in the higher levels as so many had in the past. All of this was down to Pardew's changes and the fact that he'd been given

backing – both financial backing and the freedom to innovate
by Madejski and his board. He'd also been given enough time
for his changes to take effect, and backed even through the less
encouraging times – and that's a luxury for managers that
seems rarer in football as each year passes.

Pardew's relationship with the higher levels of management at the club was always very pragmatic and very positive,
although not always without its rough edges. I asked Nigel
Howe to describe the relationship he had with Pardew, and his
views on the Pardew years. He told me: *"Well, he was the first one
to start bringing in what I would describe as the modern approach to
football. Sports science, analytics, a different approach to physiotherapy
and also the psychological thing with the team goals, which was there
basically to create team camaraderie. As you know, history tells you with
Alan, we went on and had the 'Spirit, Tenacity, Flair' T-shirts – Alan
and I had several conversations whether that was his revenue or my
revenue, there were many things, Alan and I… But I always had a really
good feeling about Alan. He was the sort of bloke who, when he came into
my office, we'd have a conversation, whether it went well or not, you
always felt like you'd had a good conversation. You never felt like, 'what
was the point of that?' It was a 'we're going to talk about this whether you
want to talk about it or not'."*

I asked Howe if this was a two-way process. He replied:
*"From both sides, and when we talked about it, actually, whichever person
left the room, whether it was his office or my office, there was always
something came out of it. I think that's why Reading started to go on the
progressive rise it did, because everything that came out of our conversations
was positive in some way. You couldn't say that there was a negativity
about Alan in any possible way. He hated the training ground at the time,
so he wanted a better training ground, he hated this, he hated that but
those weren't hates in the negative way – those were hates to enhance the*

club."

"And the great thing about Alan is, which I find difficult, certainly of late as the club's grown, is that he understood what the club could afford. He was very adaptive. So you can understand why he's gone to other clubs now and, the very big ones like Newcastle and the not so big like Crystal Palace, and been successful. Because he's adaptable. He knows, he sets out his stall and he knows what he wants. So in terms of squad development, Alan knew he didn't have a great deal of money to spend, but he knew what he needed to do, he knew that he needed to score goals, he needed to be able to defend well and he needed to have a creative midfield. I might be saying things that state the obvious, as people would say, but actually, it's easy to say – but you've got to get the right people in the right place."

Promotion came just at the right moment, with the ITV Digital collapse threatening financial oblivion for many lower-league clubs. But the confidence and attitude of Pardew's team carried them ever upwards, and they adapted to the higher level of football with ease. Pardew's shrewd use of a 4-5-1 formation to utilise Nicky Forster's pace brought dividends, and Reading followed the pattern of runs of good form in autumn (eight wins out of nine from October) and spring (12 wins from 17 between February and the end of the season). This time, however, they kept on until the end and finished in fourth place.

That, of course, meant another tilt at the play-offs – and by now we all know what happens to Reading in the play-offs! They took the lead mid-way through their semi-final first-leg match away at Wolves through a Nicky Forster goal, and with the Molineux crowd starting to turn on their own team all seemed set fair. But lady luck despises Reading in the play-offs – Forster went off injured on the hour mark, and with Reading's whole game plan now nullified Wolves scored twice late in the game to turn it around. Four days later at the MadStad, Wolves won the second leg by a single goal, and the play-off jinx had struck again. But Pardew's team had certainly announced their arrival and shown they were ready to seriously compete for promotion to the Premier League.

CHAPTER THREE

Don't Leave Me This Way

As the 2003/04 season started, even football journalists were starting to take notice of Pardew's Reading after their previous season, with one or two tipping them as outside bets for automatic promotion.

And the team seemed to know this too, starting the season in great style. One game that particular sticks in my mind was the first home match of the season against Nottingham Forest. Reading started badly, but mid-way through the first half Pardew made a tactical substitution, bringing Kevin Watson into the midfield. Suddenly the team clicked, and they played some glorious football to beat Forest 3-0. I remember sitting in my MadStad seat and looking over at a virtually full East Stand, a sea of blue and white hooped shirts on this lovely August afternoon, and asking myself if this was really 'Little Reading'. What on Earth had happened to them, playing in this new stadium, in front of so many people and playing in such an expansive, free-flowing way? Even more so, how could they be beating a team with the history of Forest quite so comprehensively? In my teens, when I started watching football, Forest under Brian Clough were winning European Cups, and there was still a certain mystique about them in my eyes.

I wasn't the only one thinking that the team was on the verge of something special at this time, either, as they won three and drew the other two of their first five matches. Fellow Royal Dave Harris remembers that *"we were playing the best football we'd ever played and we had something going"* and a sublime 3-0 win over Wimbledon at an almost-deserted Selhurst Park moved the team into second place in the table – their highest ever league position.

But this is Reading, of course, and Reading fans have long since come to expect that good times won't last. And in late August, the club was hit by a schism that threatened to derail all of Pardew's good work and put their development back several years.

When researching for this book, I was leafing through copies of the *Reading Evening Post*. In a single issue at the end of August, there are two related articles that caught my eye, one in the news section, one on the back pages. The first was headlined 'Blair – Tremendous Evidence of WMD in Iraq', the second 'Pardew Plays Down Hammers Link' in which the Reading manager committed his future to Reading. The link between these two articles, with the benefit of hindsight, is that both are much more about spin than truth and accuracy.

West Ham, relegated from the Premier League the previous May and having just lost to Rotherham in the league, decided to dispense with their manager Glenn Roeder. Inevitably, they cast their eyes around for a replacement and their gaze fell on Pardew after the transformation he had performed at Reading.

This is where what might as well be called 'Madejski's First Law of Football Management' kicks in. This law states that 'the more successful your manager is, the more likely you are to lose him to a bigger club'. In what was very much a carbon-copy of the messy and unpleasant situation endured when Mark McGhee left to join Leicester in 1994, it was clear that West Ham wanted Pardew, and it became increasing clear that Pardew wanted to go to West Ham, despite denials in the local press.

For two weeks there were denials of interest, confusion and newspaper appeals for Pardew to stay, and towards the end of this period things got increasingly acrimonious. John Madejski, who had twice turned down official requests from West Ham to speak to Pardew, was quoted in the local press saying there'd 'be no easy exit' for his manager, but by 10 September Pardew had resigned although his resignation wasn't accepted by the club, who regarded him as still under contract to them. This meant he was unable to take up employment with West Ham, who themselves were publicly castigating Reading for making it public that they wanted Pardew as their new manager – while at the same time also being publicly castigated by the League Managers Association for encouraging Pardew to breach his contract!

Looking back at the situation 12 years later, it looks no less messy and unpleasant than it did at the time. Although the loss of Mark McGhee nine years earlier was a contributory factor, the key issue was the contradiction between Madejski, a fundamentally decent and principled man who has always believed that contracts are sacrosanct, and the world of football, which is often anything but decent and principled, and where contracts are convenient but often ignored. The situation was further complicated by a clause in new Pardew's contract that allowed him the automatic right to speak to any Premier League Club interested in his services. Although at this time West Ham weren't a Premier League Club, they had been for the previous ten seasons and most people expected them to be one again before too long. So in many ways it was a question of 'letter of the contract' versus 'spirit of the contract'.

This new contract, signed the previous summer, also paid Pardew less money – but included improved performance bonuses – and this only served to muddy the waters further. In fact, several of those I spoke to remain convinced that once those new contract terms were the only ones offered to Pardew, it was a virtual inevitability that he'd leave the club when a worthwhile offer came in.

However, Madejski was determined to make his point and applied for a High Court injunction to prevent Pardew being employed by a competing club while under contract to Reading – and was quoted in the local press as saying 'I'll never give in to West Ham'.

Reading supporters uniformly backed Madejski's stand, as shown by Dave Harris, who recalls: "*The feeling was every bit as acrimonious the second time it had happened in ten years, there was anger – no question there was anger – how could someone who was supposedly loyal to the club just up sticks and leave for a club in the same division? There was desperation, there was a feeling of could it really get any better than what we were having at that time.*"

Not everyone within the club saw things the same way, though, and some weren't so sure. Ron Grant told me "*Well, I felt a bit for Alan in actual fact … I thought in many ways, Alan got a bit badly managed. He'd given his service to Reading, actually brought us forward, our playing style and how we were was much better – and here he was looking to move on and he asked if he could speak to West Ham, and I think it was refused to start with and the way I perceived it – and I think most people out there and the media as well would have perceived it exactly the same – in football the contracts are not worth the paper they're written on and if you've got a man that's being touted for another job, you've got to accept that and go along with it. But to send him out on gardening leave and refuse it, and finish up on the steps of the High Court, was a nonsense."*

That perhaps illustrates the difference in approach between 'football people' and those not involved in the game every day. But the best person to explain Madejski's motivation is obviously the Chairman himself. He recalled Pardew's departure: *"He was a very ambitious young man, I wasn't very happy with him when he left …"*

I asked Madejski how his working relationship with Pardew had been. He replied: *"Oh fine, fine. There was mutual respect I think and we got on well and he did a good job for us, and I was very disappointed when he went off to West Ham which was totally wrong and against the spirit of the agreement that we had with him – and as you know we took certain steps with the High Court and that wasn't particularly a good thing."*

I suggested to Madejski that this was a downside of giving new managers their first opportunity and of them being successful. He agreed: *"Yes, indeed, I suppose everybody wants them if they've got a good track record. There's no doubt about it that Alan certainly had a very good track record. And I'm glad he's still doing well in the game today … but he did Reading very proud indeed I'm pleased to say."*

I recounted how it felt to be a supporter at this time, telling Madejski: *"Everything seemed to be clicking with Alan Pardew, and everybody was looking towards the future – and then he left. You've said how disappointed you were with that, presumably in the situation there was nothing that could be done and it was just one of those things?"*

Madejski replied: *"Well, I think one has to appreciate he was going to a much larger club … and I felt that it wasn't right. But then again I made the point – and he made the point – because he was leaving to go to another club that was in the same circumstance, which was totally against what we'd agreed in his contract and we'd just signed an agreement with him – a very good contract for him – and we basically gave him what he wanted and then he does that, so I was a bit disgusted, which is why I went as far as I did. But at the end of the day, how much can you do without shooting yourself in the foot? At the end of the day, by going the full due process, again they did put him on garden leave for a while. But then if you take the thing to its conclusion you know he can't come back – you're just going to waste an awful lot of money in the High Court."*

"It'd be a lawyer-fest and yes, so therefore the pragmatics – I'd made my point, hence going to the High Court and I think enough was enough so we made the moral point and then we just withdrew, and that was the right thing to have done. Having said all that, I've got no bad blood with Alan now, that's water under the bridge, but at the time I was pretty indignant about the whole thing, especially as it happened before with Mark McGhee, it's happened twice."

Time clearly is a great healer, because when asked by the press on those High Court steps whether he had any plans to speak to Alan Pardew, Madejski's curt response was *"Alan who?"*

Under that agreement negotiated on the steps of the High Court, West Ham agreed to pay Reading compensation of £380,000 for the early termination of Pardew's contract, and that Pardew would not be able to commence any role with them for another month, nor would West Ham be able to take on any Reading Football Club employees until at least the end of the season. Madejski had publicly made his point and drawn his line in the sand over the validity of contracts, but Reading no longer had their inspirational manager.

In his four years at the club, Pardew had made a phenomenal difference to Reading, transforming it massively. Not only was there a chasm in league placings between the club he joined – languishing towards the bottom of the third tier – and the one he left – competing for promotion to the Premier League – but the whole attitude and mentality of the team had changed almost beyond recognition. His ideas and innovations had changed the way the players trained, played and regarded themselves and he'd installed a winning mentality that hadn't always been at the club in the past. He'd also fought and won the case for a dedicated training ground, although he wasn't to see this himself. Planning permission for the facility at Hogwood Park, Arborfield – initially leased from the army but later purchased – was granted in July 2003 and the site wasn't operational until the following year.

But the contribution that Pardew made to the development of the club – and the building of the perfect team – was substantial. It's not over-stating things to say that he laid the foundations at the club upon which everything that came later was built on – without his changes there would have been no perfect team. So Alan Pardew is undoubtedly the third pillar on which this perfect team was built – alongside John Madejski and the new stadium. It's sad that for many his legacy has been overshadowed by the manner of his departure – that's the way of football – but without any doubt Pardew's contribution to the development of this club was considerable and of massive importance.

From a player's perspective, Ady Williams agrees: *"When I left and came back a lot had happened, and the club results weren't great and there were a lot of players that didn't really perform so it was only going to go one way as far as I could see under Alan Pardew. Everyone who knew how much he turned the club around was obviously disappointed that he left, some of the Reading fans might think it wasn't a big loss, at the time 'Alan Pardew's gone on, we wish him well' and that sort of thing, but the players realised what he actually did for the football club and I'd definitely become a better player."*

I'll leave the final words on Pardew's legacy to Reading CEO Nigel Howe: *"I think one of the greatest periods of this club was through Alan Pardew and I always say – and I would argue with any fan – that Alan Pardew did more for this club than many managers that I, under my stewardship, have come across, and the way he set about and organised things have been the bedrock of the club going forward."*

But before looking at that search for a manager, it's worth taking a step back and looking at the stories of others who were at the club at this time, and who would all play their part in building the perfect team. The first of these is possibly the most misunderstood man at Reading Football Club, but one who undoubtedly played a large part in helping put together the perfect team – Nick Hammond.

I met Hammond at a warm and sunny Hogwood Park late on an afternoon in July 2015. Generous with his time, he told me the story of how he came to be at the club and how the departure of Pardew changed his role there.

A goalkeeper by trade, he'd initially joined the club on loan from Plymouth in late 1995, signed by Jimmy Quinn and Mick Gooding, and joined permanently the following February. But soon after a back injury forced him out for the best part of two years. Nick takes up the story: *"I had a back injury which led to me being out. I had a hole in my spine, they found a hole in my spine which meant I had a fusion of the spine, which meant I was out for a large number of months, so I came back into the team in 97/98."*

That season was to end in relegation and the demise of Terry Bullivant, whose injury-ravaged team was sliding down the table. Almost inevitably, Hammond joined the casualty list. *"I'd had a good season and then I broke my knuckle in a game against Manchester City, and was out for a period of time which coincided with Terry Bullivant losing his job. Not to say with hindsight, not to say it was the fact that I wasn't in the team but ..."*

That was to be the effective end of Hammond as a Reading player, as Bullivant's replacement, Tommy Burns, thought Hammond too small to be a goalkeeper. But this was to lead to a major change of role and the start of a highly fruitful relationship with Pardew.

Hammond continues: *"So I went from playing regularly, through the injury and broken knuckle, and then they brought in two goalkeepers, Peter van der Kwaak and Scott Howie. I went down the pecking order and it was quite an interesting period really. Actually I was doing a lot of work for Arsenal, doing some scouting – even though I was still contracted to Reading – because those weekends I was third choice goalkeeper and not being used at all."*

"I was still a contracted goalkeeper and then they released me as the goalkeeper. At that stage Tommy Burns came to me and asked me to recommend a first team goalkeeper for them – so I was effectively finding a replacement for myself! We did that, and I took Tommy Burns, God rest his soul, I took Tommy Burns to The Hawthorns to watch Phil Whitehead play. So I suppose I was sort of responsible, really, in terms of the recommendation of Phil Whitehead in coming to the club. So really then things took the turn, so the beginning of where I am now, that was the end of my playing career, really, under Tommy Burns."

"But when Alan Pardew came back as caretaker manager, Alan had

been running that part-time reserve team and I'd had a good relationship with Alan and I'll never forget he phoned me on the day. I think he met with Sir John – who wasn't Sir John at the time – and the board in the afternoon, and I met him at the Hilton in Bracknell that evening. He said 'I need some help, would you like to come … because I need to know where the team's at, Nick'. And that was the start really."

Initially working as a goalkeeping coach for Pardew, Hammond's working relationship with him flourished. He also found his role growing as time went on, taking charge of the Reading academy 12 months after its inception. *"My relationship with Alan Pardew was a strong one, we built that very, very quickly. And although I was sort of coaching … I was sort of close with Alan and we had that relationship where he'd trust my judgement in terms of certain things. So we built a strong relationship and then John Stevenson left and I took over the academy. But in those days I was feeling almost a dual purpose because I was academy manager but I was with the first team all the time as well. Those were the days before our academy had become quite as big as it is now."*

Looking around Hogwood Park that summer afternoon, I could see just how much the setup had grown in the few years since I'd last been there, and it was a quantum leap larger than it had been in those early days. However, its days are numbered, as Reading have outgrown it since gaining EPPP Category One status – the highest level of certification in the Premier League's new youth development programme – and plans are currently well advanced for a move to a new, larger facility in Bearwood Park, Wokingham. This growth in the training and academy facilities, from a point of virtually nothing just 12 years earlier, is a testament to just how much the club has developed in this time – and is another demonstration of how large the snowball that Pardew started rolling has grown.

But Hammond's role was to change again in the fullness of time, prompted by Pardew's abrupt departure. He continues: *"So I was doing that dual role, but Alan and I worked together, whenever they had a board meeting, whenever they had a meeting upstairs with the directors, Alan and I would attend and I would quite often put a report together in terms of what the plan was, what the strategy was, what we were going to do. So I was academy manager, doing that I built a relationship with the board as well and then of course we had Alan ... a good start to that season and all of a sudden he's gone to West Ham!"*

"And that was when the Chairman and Nigel [Howe] came to me and said 'Director of Football' and I said 'Lovely, what's that?' – didn't really know, but they said 'We'll have a look at that, we'll have a discussion about how we think it'll work'."

"Actually they basically said to me 'You come back and tell us what it is and how you want it to work' because I think what they were concerned about – the board – at the time was losing myself and Alan because the assumption was ... that I would have gone with him to West Ham – although the legal situation in the end meant that he couldn't take any staff for 12 months. So it was sort of 'we need some stability here' and I was seen as the stability and the continuity."

This Director of Football role has evolved over time, but it was quite unlike the concept of Director of Football as understood by many supporters, and as usually found across continental Europe. In Europe, a Director of Football is usually superior to the manager and oversees all footballing activity. But Hammond's role is somewhat different – effectively acting as 'Chairman's Proxy'. As Hammond said the day he was appointed: *"I'll bring football knowledge to the board – although I won't actually be on the board, I'll be working alongside them."*

This role is a recognition that Madejski, as he freely admits, is not a football expert, and he felt that he needed someone within the game who did know football and could advise him and act as his representative – for instance advising him on whether money requested by a manager for a new player was likely to represent worthwhile value. Clearly as academy manager, working closely with Pardew and regularly presenting plans to the board, Hammond had established his credibility and suitability for this role – and it was a role in which Hammond and the club thrived.

But one of his first tasks was to help find a new first team manager, and it was to be a difficult time for him because of his close relationship with Pardew. He told me: *"It was a very interesting time for me because he* [Pardew] *spent two days holed up in my house. Obviously there were some difficulties with him leaving from a contractual point of view. And the club obviously had strong views on that and Sir John had strong views on that – which I completely understand – and it does not surprise me because Sir John is so very proper in the way he acts. So he had a strong opinion at that time and he had a young, ambitious manager who also had a strong opinion – so there was quite a lot of media that went around that at the time, considering it was a Championship club, it wasn't Premier League."*

"So my feeling was obviously to try and be supportive of Alan but also understand the perspective of the club, so it wasn't an easy time – I remember that very clearly! In some ways I think it was the catalyst for my role developing because I think the club felt that they needed someone to act as that conduit, because the board didn't necessarily have that football background and football experience and I think because I'd dealt with them at board level and given presentations – and maybe was the slightly calming influence alongside Alan – probably that thought germinated in their mind and everything else. But it was difficult and it got to the steps of

the court."

But before we examine the search for Pardew's replacement, it would be worthwhile to take a step back and look at the others already at the club who would be available to assist the incoming manager.

In addition to Hammond there was Kevin Dillon, who had been appointed caretaker manager once it was clear that Pardew had left the club. A player at the club for three years from 1991, Dillon had returned in 1995 to become a coach in the academy. After Pardew's promotion to manager, Dillon had stepped up to become reserve team manager, and when Martin Allen left the club, Dillon took his place as assistant manager.

The thought process that led to Allen's departure is interesting, and reveals much about the way the club worked at the time and Pardew's willingness to change things when he felt they were no longer working for him.

We've already seen an example of 'Mad Dog's' unconventional management style in his insistence that the team train in the wrong half at Preston, and he also regularly indulged in other shenanigans, such as astounding the West Stand crowd by leading the players on a pre-match run through the stadium concourse!

But, as Sir John Madejski explains, those original methods only work for so long: "*Indeed, he was sort of a one-trick pony I suppose, he got the players running round the stands, but again he had an infectious enthusiasm, but the trouble with an infectious enthusiasm is you can't keep pulling the same rabbit out of the same hat, can you? So that's the problem with that – but a charming guy.*"

Nick Hammond takes up the story of Allen's departure: "*Yeah, Martin was Martin, and he did a very good job in the role that he filled for that period of time, but there obviously came a point when Alan felt that he probably needed a different approach from the number two and so that's when that change was made. And Martin's such a good fall man – and he's gone on and he's had a good career – and I think Martin always wanted to be his own man anyway because that's his character. I think he's a natural number one, you know he can fulfil that number two but he wants to lead, he's a leader. So things evolve and things change in football and one of the skills is understanding that and seeing it – I think that was one of the great, great strengths of Ferguson in that he would reinvent things. Ferguson was the consistency at United over many, many years, but the people around him would change at times and he would change them and freshen things up and I think that's a great skill to be able to see that …"*

Clearly, Pardew had the strength and determination to see that change was needed and to make it happen. Hammond, who as we've seen was by now working closely with Pardew on a day-to-day basis, explains how Dillon came to be promoted to assistant manager: *"Kevin Dillon was because when Martin left, Alan and I spoke at length and he was talking about who he was going to bring in to do the assistant's role. And of course various names were talked about at the time, but my view was that – and this is what I said to Alan – he was such a hands-on coach, sometimes you get managers and you get coaches, but Pardew's great strength was that he was both. But he was such a hands-on coach, he just needed the right fit, the right character to support him and the deal was internal, he [Dillon] knew the club so I thought he was a good fit at the time and that's how that sort of originated really."*

As caretaker manger, Dillon's first match, just three days after Pardew's departure, was against West Ham – who else? This ended in a 1-0 defeat and although Dillon at the time said he felt it was a 'natural progression' for him to take the top job, this wasn't considered an option at the time.

Another key individual at the club at this time, and who was to play a crucial part in the building of the perfect team, was chief scout Brian McDermott. Ron Grant told me about McDermott's arrival, another masterstroke from Pardew: "*One of the things that Alan Pardew had done was bring Maurice Evans back to the club. He brought Maurice in as the chief scout and that was brilliant, to me personally that was brilliant.*"

"*His office was right next to the kit room at the stadium and I could have a chat to Maurice when I was doing the kit about old times and things. The greatest sadness was when he died of a heart attack, but that was when Alan brought Brian McDermott into the fold. He brought Brian McDermott who had been out of work I believe.*"

In Hammond, Dillon and McDermott, three of the crucial components for building our perfect team were in place. Now they needed a manager.

CHAPTER FOUR

(Just Like) Starting Over

To Reading supporters, the search for a new Reading manager seemed to go on for ever, although in reality it was only five weeks. As always, there was endless debate and speculation, with new names appearing in the local press almost on a day-by-day basis – for instance in a single week Lawrie Sanchez, Peter Taylor and Tony Adams were all linked with the role.

Much of this delay was due to the need to find the right candidate, but it was also down to a determination to do everything exactly by the book, and to do so publicly. As well as being Madejski's natural instinct, I don't doubt that it was important to show the rest of football – and West Ham in particular – the right and proper way to handle finding a new manager.

Nick Hammond told me about how the search for a new manager was carried out, and explains some of the trepidation he felt in his new role: *"Yeah, I managed the whole process. I interviewed a number of candidates, because obviously I was now Director of Football and of course I'm new to the role – it's a brand new role, what does it really mean? When I look back now I wasn't really sure, but I was going to make a good fist of it."*

So I interviewed a large number of candidates of whom I took five, I think, to final interview, which happened at the Chairman's house in Pangbourne. But I'd spoken to a number of people before because my role was new and I wanted to be clear that whoever was coming understood 'This is the role that I've been asked to do, these are the responsibilities I have – are you comfortable with that?' So for me it was a really important process at the time because it was a new model. The club had said that was the way they wanted to go and so it was important for me to do that and I think it's important for any sporting director to appoint a manager. It's very important because it's a line of communication and support, and at the very beginning it builds a relationship between those two individuals, which is crucial if you want to be successful.

Of course, the final selection wasn't Hammond's – once he'd produced a shortlist of suitable candidates, the final decision was made by Madejski, his fellow-director Ian Wood-Smith and CEO Nigel Howe. Hammond continues: *"So I'd narrowed the market down and it was a very intimidating process for me at the time – young retired goalkeeper now interviewing some significant people! … then we took a group for final interview at the house and for me that interview was then the Board's interview. I'd made some points to them on each candidate in terms of 'these are the things you might want to ask, these are the things it might be interesting for you to understand' or 'these are some of the concerns that I would have'. Then that really was Sir John, it was Nigel and it was Ian. It was the three of them, really, and I was in the room but that was their meeting, their interview. It was the second interview and it was where the decision would be made. Looking back, it actually worked well."*

The chosen candidate, of course, was Steve Coppell. Coppell had had a successful playing career for Manchester United, having signed from Tranmere Rovers at the age of 19 in 1975. A condition Coppell made at the time of this signing was that he was able to continue his degree studies, and while this often entailed studying at the back of the team coach after away matches as his teammates slept or played cards, he was successful and gained a degree in economics at Liverpool University.

Coppell played for the Red Devils for nine years, gaining 42 caps for England, but a severe knee injury sustained in a 1982 World Cup qualifier against Hungary effectively ended his playing days the following year.

At the age of just 28 and ten months, Coppell started his management career at Crystal Palace, and was to have four spells as manager at Selhurst Park over the next 16 years. Among his many achievements in this time, he signed Ian Wright as a 21-year-old from Greenwich Borough, and he took Palace to the 1990 FA Cup Final, where they lost to Manchester United after a replay. One of Coppell's key players, who scored the winning goal in his team's 4-3 extra-time win over Liverpool in the semi-final to reach Wembley, was Alan Pardew, with whom Coppell had since maintained a close relationship.

The only major question mark hanging over Coppell's managerial history was a spell as Manchester City in 1996, a post he resigned from after just 33 days as a result of severe stress. Following his latest spell at Palace, Coppell had followed his old chairman Ron Noades to Brentford, where his team was pipped to the automatic promotion place by that 1-1 draw with Pardew's Reading in 2002. Now he was managing at Brighton, despite their lack of a permanent ground and the consequent lack of resources.

Sir John Madejski remembers Coppell's appointment: *"As always with my managers, he was the best man for the job and he showed a tremendous level of commitment and indeed energy – commitment, energy and ability to lead."*

"I knew Steve vaguely – very vaguely – from his Crystal Palace days and I always liked the man. Very astute, very saleable guy, one of the few managers like that was Steve – but a very quiet man and I still can't claim to know Steve. He's very much into himself but very professional and spends a lot of his time watching endless videos and so on at home. A very straightforward guy, he has his agent who looks after his pecuniary side of things."

Considering the animosity and legal acrimony at the time, you'd think it strange that Pardew himself would recommend the job to Coppell, but that's exactly what happened. Ron Grant explains: *"Yes, Alan Pardew and Steve Coppell were good friends – they go back as a Player and Manager at Crystal Palace, and I understand there was a conversation between Alan and Steve, and Alan actually said to Steve 'It's the club for you, it's made for you, you'll enjoy it there'. That's as I understand it – he certainly made sure that Steve was aware it was a good club to come into."*

The fans were not quite so certain, though, with many favouring Peter Taylor, by now at Hull City, and who'd taken Brighton up ahead of Reading and done well in a brief but well-publicised spell managing England Under-21s. Loyal Royal Neil Maskell, who expected Taylor to be appointed, shared his memories of hearing the news that it was to be Coppell: *"I think at the time I thought 'second choice, but not a bad second choice, an experienced second choice'. He was a guy who'd done different bits and pieces, taken teams up, doesn't seem to stay around very often."*

Fellow supporter Dave Harris said: *"Coppell was manager of Brighton at the time, he was obviously a highly, highly regarded man in the game. Brighton at the time didn't have much in the way of resources, they had a temporary ground, they were struggling to get the stadium at*

Falmer approved, they were at the Withdean – totally inadequate ground, 6,000 capacity – didn't really have the resources. It didn't come as a surprise that we went for somebody in the same mould as Pardew with the whole similar style, similar ethos, somebody to continue building. At the time the over-riding feeling was, well, we're going to be in fairly safe hands."

Personally, I was just glad to see a manager appointed after so long – Coppell was appointed four and a half weeks after Pardew had left, although it had been more or less open knowledge that the job was Coppell's for at least a week before he was finally announced. Thirteen years ago it seemed a very long time to find a manager – these days, through the echo chamber of endless social media, supporters would no doubt be in a frenzy of rage and frustration long before the fourth managerless week was reached.

This delay was almost certainly down to Madejski's determination to be seen to do everything strictly according to the appropriate league regulations – by diligently dotting every 'i' and crossing every 't' there was no way he was going to leave himself open to accusations of 'poaching' another club's manager in response to having had his own 'poached'. As such, he was careful to go through the proper procedures, requesting permission from Brighton Chairman Dick Knight to speak to Coppell, agreeing a compensation package of £100,000. In the event, Madejski went even further than required by the league regulations, delaying the appointment of Coppell to allow Knight time to start the search for a replacement and lining up a caretaker manager, so as to not leave Brighton suddenly without a manager.

One of the definite attractions of Coppell to the club was that he would not make too many changes, and would build upon what Pardew had started. In the words of John Madejski: *"The good thing about Steve was he had the mentality – if it ain't broke, why fix it?"*

As just one example of this laissez-faire attitude, Coppell was quite happy to carry on with the goal cards instituted by Pardew – although the consensus among those I spoke to was that Coppell didn't have anywhere as much faith in them as a motivational technique as his predecessor did, but could see no reason to discontinue them.

On the field, results for Coppell were mixed. He won his first two matches, then five out of the following nine, so that the Royals climbed to fifth in the table at the start of December. But the rest of that month was disastrous, as Reading lost their next three matches 3-0, including a humiliating Boxing Day home defeat to Wimbledon, recently relocated to Milton Keynes and who were well adrift at the bottom of the table and destined for relegation. Two draws and an FA Cup exit followed in January before the next win came, and an inconsistent second half of the season, in which they won nine and lost six out of 19 games, meant that Reading finished the season in ninth place, three points and three places short of a play-off position.

It was a frustrating season, as Reading spent much of the closing months of the campaign flirting with the play-offs but never quite doing enough to fully embrace them. Just one point from three crucial matches in April effectively sealed their fate, and although they went into the final match with a mathematical chance of making the play-offs that wasn't to be.

As the season drew to an end, though, there was one change of personnel that was to prove absolutely crucial, with the addition of someone who was to play a vital part in putting together the perfect time – and, in an indirect way, to bring to the club the vital element that made all the difference to the team.

That key person was Wally Downes.

Downes was a product of the Wimbledon FC 'crazy gang' era – and many people attribute a high proportion of their antics of that period to him! He holds the distinction of being Wimbledon's first ever apprentice after they joined the Football League, and made his debut in 1979. After a playing career lasting 12 years, a fourth broken leg ended his calling in 1991 and he made his way into coaching, finding himself working under Steve Coppell at Crystal Palace.

In 2000 when Coppell was sacked at Palace by incoming Chairman Simon Jordan as chairman, Downes followed Coppell to Brentford as his number two, and when Coppell left for Brighton in July 2002 the close relationship was temporarily severed as Downes stayed at Griffin Park to take over the manager's role himself. Despite winning the Division Two Manager of the Month in his first full month in charge, his time in charge was not wholly successful and he was sacked in March 2004. This, of course, was towards the of Coppell's first season in charge at the MadStad, and with Downes now available Coppell was quick to seize the opportunity to bring his former colleague into his coaching team.

I met Wally in a pub in West London, where he was happy to share many interesting details of his time at the club and how he came to join: *"When I got the sack at Brentford, Steve was at Reading and he asked me to come along at the end of the season – just to come down, watch training, have a look, keeping involved. I went down, watched them – and he said 'I want you to come in next season'."*

The role Coppell had in mind for Downes was reprising

the one he had previously performed at Palace and Brentford, although at the time of joining Coppell didn't specify this. "*He didn't say specifically. The only time he specifically got me was when I got the first job at Crystal Palace, he said Ron Noades* [Palace Chairman] *wanted me there. He said 'Wally, I want you to come, I'm creating a role for you because Ron's seen the potential in you as a coach'. He said 'I know you and you're a great one for developing and coaching people, I don't like doing the defence much, I'll work with the forwards, you work with the defenders' – so I had to go home and give myself a crash course in what would make up some defending practices. So I took it at Crystal Palace, at Brentford I did all the coaching there and at Reading I worked a lot with the back four.*"

Undoubtedly the arrival of Downes added a new dimension to the coaching at the club. When I met Central defender Ady Williams he was full of praise for the type of methods Downes brought to the club, for instance his use of DVD analysis of games. Ady tells how this came about: "*When he was brought to the club Wally Downes was the defensive coach – and talk about bringing new ideas to the club, Wally did that. Steve Coppell and Wally Downes were very much chalk and cheese – good cop, bad cop in many ways, and a lot of successful backroom staff are like that.*"

"*Whether it was Wally's idea or the gaffer's idea, basically the biggest transformation was that he started filming, analysing the defensive displays – and we then, in those days, were given DVDs of our defending. We were told to go away and watch the DVD and the next time we had a meeting, whenever it was, we had to bring up three points, each of us … we all came back, and it might have been at a hotel on a Friday night if we were playing up north, and Wally would put the DVD on and say 'we're playing it – just shout out 'stop' when you've got a point'. And we would go through it and I would have a point – I'd say 'stop' and I might say something along the lines of 'Graeme Murty's taken two throws and he's given it back to them every time'."*

Being made to criticise the play of teammates was a change of style, and something that took a while for some players to adapt to. But Ady explained that it wasn't long before everyone realised that any criticism was constructive, and that the aim was to be objective and not nit-picking: *"At first, it's a bit embarrassing because you sometimes think you're singling people out – but we were all pretty senior professionals and we all wanted to improve and we all took it well. Two minutes later, Nicky Shorey might say 'hang on a minute, Ady, I think you were a little bit deeper than everybody else' – and you look at it and think 'you've got a point there, Shorey'."*

It was certainly effective: *"So you've then started thinking about that when you started training the next day or the day after and then in matches. And I guarantee you the next time I was looking along the line and I was slightly deeper than everyone else I'd squeeze up a little bit and it worked a dream."*

This is just one of a number of ways to invigorate training sessions that Downes introduced. He explained the problems of training defensive units day after day: *"I thought it can be repetitive and dull – but that's the thing about defending, you have to be, it's all about repetition and organisation and the dreary stuff that you have to do. So I used to come up with things that I thought might inspire the lads and give them something to think about, instead of it being 'fuck me, a defending drill again today ...' So I used to come up with things like that just to spark them up."*

That is typical of the whole approach of Coppell and his coaching team – always on the lookout for something different to perk things up and make a difference, no matter how small. They realised that in such a competitive league as Champion-ship, where the margins between success and failure could be tiny, small improvements could make all the difference – and the cumulative effect of many small improvements could easily add up to a large improvement.

Going into the 2004/05 season with high hopes, the Reading coaching team was largely complete, with Coppell as manager and Dillon and Downes as coaches. Working with them, on a day to day-to-day basis, were two others we've already come across, kit-man Ron Grant and Niall Clark, who had been brought in by Alan Pardew as Sports Scientist. The squad's medical team was led by Head Physiotherapist Jon Fearn, and there were three others in the background who were to play a crucial part in putting together our perfect team. The role of one of them, Nick Hammond, has already been explained – and this role involved working closely with the other two key figures, Chief Scout Brian McDermott and Academy Manager Eamonn Dolan. The latter, previously manager of Exeter City, joined the club in September 2004 to replace Reading's long-term Academy Manager Brendan Rodgers who had just departed to join José Mourinho at Chelsea.

That 2004/05 was the epitome of the inconsistency Reading had shown over recent years – a highly promising start, with seven wins from their first ten matches putting them top of the league in late September, but after Christmas things started to slip. Seven draws and no wins up until the middle of March meant that they slipped from the play-off positions, although – typically for Reading – they were never quite out of contention. They achieved 16 points out of 21, including victory at runaway league leaders Sunderland that revived hopes, but two more defeats dampened these down again. Reading went into the last match of the season, away at

Wigan, who were themselves pushing for automatic promotion, on the same number of points as sixth-placed West Ham, but with an inferior number of goals scored.

Reading therefore needed to achieve a better result than West Ham to sneak into the play-offs – but this was something they conspicuously failed to do. As West Ham beat Watford 4-0, Reading were comprehensively outplayed and beaten 3-1 by Wigan.

This dispiriting performance, and finishing just three points outside the play-off places for the second season running, was another blow for Reading fans, whose hopes had been so high in the first half of the season where Reading were so impressive and had stormed to the top of the table. But second half inconsistency was their downfall again, and the talk among many supporters was of the team 'bottling it', with theories that the players didn't want to go up or weren't mentally ready for promotion, or even the conspiracy theory that they'd failed because they were scared that promotion would mean they'd be replaced in the squad by players more suited to the Premier League! Much ire was also directed at Coppell, with some fans citing his resignation from Manchester City as evidence that 'whenever the going gets tough he runs away'.

Internet opinion was just as severe, with postings such as: *"In my opinion Steve Coppell is a spent force and will not lead the Royals to future success in this Division or at a higher level"*; *"I really hope that I am wrong but I am not optimistic and certainly do not feel inspired by Mr Coppell"*; and *"This was probably one of the best opportunities the club has had to secure promotion to the Premiership but a combination of bad signings, poor management, poor direction at Board level and general player incompetence has led to another 'so near and yet so far' season."*

But so much for the fans at the time. I'm convinced that something special, and a crucial development of our story, came out of that disappointing defeat at the JJB Stadium, as it was then known. A single image remains etched in my mind from the aftermath of that day – and that is of a very quiet, very pensive John Madejski in the directors' box watching the celebrations on the pitch and the elation of the home directors and their guests.

For beating Reading had ensured automatic promotion for Wigan – a historically small, provincial team with no significant history, a team that had only joined the Football League in 1978, and – thanks to a supportive local businessman who'd invested in a new stadium as well as in the team – they'd reached the ultimate pinnacle of promotion to the very top of the football pyramid.

The National Lottery's famous slogan, at this time, was '*It Could Be You*' – I've always wondered if, as he was watching the sheer ecstasy of those on the pitch and around him, John Madejski was thinking to himself: 'It could be us, too, you know ...'

CHAPTER FIVE

Come As You Are

WE'VE SEEN HOW THE READING'S backroom team was put together, but this is a book about football – and so far we've hardly mentioned the players who made up our perfect team.

But that summer of 2005 saw substantial changes in the Reading squad as eight players left and eight players came in – substantial change by Reading's past standards. This very much seems to be a reaction to the scenes witnessed on the last day of the season at Wigan, and in fact several of those I spoke to confirmed that there was a conscious 'loosening of the purse strings'.

To understand how this came about, it's useful to take a look at the feelings of those who'd seen their team just miss out on play-off qualification at the time. Nick Hammond told me about Coppell's reaction after that game: *"Steve was really flat after that, I mean very, very flat, to the extent where you wondered what his thought process was in terms of going forward to the summer. I sort of said to him 'get yourself away, recharge and rest'. I was concerned whether he felt he could take the team on at that stage."*

There were similar feelings of flatness among many of the fans, too. Neil Maskell recalls: *"For a big chunk of that season we were top six and it felt like another opportunity tossed away. Coppell had had the best part of two full seasons and I remember on the online forums there was a very famous thread about the odds on Coppell to leave Reading. His stock wasn't particularly high amongst the people who like to analyse and write about these things behind online aliases."*

But Coppell, of course, didn't leave, and that summer the changes of personnel started. Among the players leaving were three who'd each made more than 30 appearances the previous season – Paul Brooker, Nicky Forster and Andy Hughes. Forster left for Ipswich as Reading were only prepared to offer him a one-year contract, a deeply unpopular and heavily criticised move for many supporters, while Hughes also moved to East Anglia, joining Norwich.

Coppell told a fans' forum the following August – a meeting where supporters were able to ask questions of club staff – that he'd not wanted to lose Hughes because of the commitment and spirit he brought, but that he couldn't see a settled role for Hughes in his team. There was also a clear feeling that many other departures, especially of fringe players or players with a long career behind them, was overdue. Among these older players were some big-name veterans who'd not been wholly successful at Reading, players such as Les Ferdinand, Martin Keown and, to a lesser extent, Shaun Goater.

Loyal Royal Dave Harris describes some of the fringe players as 'stop-gaps': *"They were journeymen players that Coppell had signed, they seemed at the time just to tide us over, players he knew that could do a job – players who were adequate but who weren't fantastic"* and it's hard to disagree with that analysis. Dave continues with an interesting insight on that Wigan game: *"With players like that, we over-achieved, I think, particularly based on the number of goals we scored and it was clear that something needed to happen. That Wigan game set us the benchmark. Wigan showed us what we needed to do, Jason Roberts and Nathan Ellington up front, Lee*

McCulloch at the side, Arjan de Zeeuw, players like that. They had a good, good side, they had backing – serious backing – from their chairman, Dave Whelan, and when they got promoted to Division One it was literally a matter of time before they got promoted up to the Premier League. They set the benchmark and Reading's shortcomings were shown up that day – big time, soundly!"

It seems clear that this view was agreed by all who'd seen their hopes of the play-offs thoroughly dashed by Wigan in a first-hand demonstration of the type of players and the standard of performance needed to compete effectively for promotion. As Downes told me: *"If we'd have made it into the play-offs, great – but that would have been a major feat with what we were trying to do. There were players who had been at Reading a long time – good players, good lads – but they had failed to do what was looking to be achieved so sometimes you have to make decisions and move players on."*

The player departures were just the first part of the changes needed though, and they left behind a core squad who would all be a crucial part of the perfect team.

First-choice goalkeeper was 33-year-old American Marcus Hahnemann, who'd been signed by Pardew from Fulham in December 2001 – initially on-loan but joining permanently in August 2002. A native of Seattle, Washington, and known as 'USA' to the fans, he moved to the UK in 1999 from Colorado Rapids, but had few first-team chances at Craven Cottage. When he came to Reading he quickly became first choice 'keeper, filling a role that hadn't been adequately filled for several years.

In front of Hahnemann were the two first choice full-backs – on the right Graeme Murty and on the left Nicky Shorey. Of the members of our perfect team, these two were the longest-serving at the club, but their fortunes had taken very different paths. Murty, 29, was the only remaining player signed by Tommy Burns, and the only player in the squad who'd experienced Elm Park. Brought from York as a right-winger, his early days at the club had been unhappy, and in his first three seasons he was plagued by injury and made just 59 league appearances – prompting numerous supporter's jokes along the lines of how rarely they saw the 'lesser-spotted Murty'. With injury problems resolved, and by now converted from right-wing to right-back by Pardew, Murty was rejuvenated in the second half of the 2000/01 season, rarely missing matches from January 2001 and being voted player of the season by fans in 2001/02 and 2003/04. Murty had been promoted to captain in November 2004 following the departure of Ady Williams to Coventry City.

On the other side of the pitch, left-back Nicky Shorey had joined in February 2001 at the age of 19, brought in from Orient by Pardew. He had to wait the best part of nine months before he made his league debut, but since then he'd become an integral part of the team, under both Pardew (who told a fans' forum in 2003 that one of his biggest regrets was waiting too long to give Shorey his chance in the first team) and Coppell. Predominantly left-footed – 'my right leg is for standing on', he frequently joked – he was deadly at set-pieces with that left foot, and also provided a frequent outlet for Hahnemann to throw the ball to in order to build attacks.

In front of the full-backs, the centre-back pairing of Ívar Ingimarsson and Ibrahima Sonko was also a settled part of the team. Ingimarsson had been Coppell's first signing, purchased from Wolves for a relatively modest £100,000 just two weeks after his arrival at Reading, and had previously been with Coppell at Brentford and on loan at Brighton. Now aged 28,

Ingimarsson was one of several players in this team who'd previously had a steady but relatively undistinguished career – although he was an established Icelandic international, the Championship was the highest level in England he'd played at.

Alongside him was Sonko, a 6ft 3in man-mountain. Senegalese by birth, he'd grown up in France and was signed by Wally Downes at Brentford shortly after he'd taken over at Griffin Park, and once Downes joined Reading in the summer of 2004 Sonko following him to the MadStad on a 'Bosman' transfer. Signed at the age of 23 and having only played 79 first team games in England, Sonko's first season with Reading had seen him blossom as Ingimarsson's defensive partner – so much so that at a fans' forum in April 2005 Coppell was asked to nominate his most improved player of the season and immediately plumped for Sonko, who he said had come to the club 'very raw' but was so committed – as well and being a "lovely, warm, human being". Coppell also told the forum he thought Sonko could get better and better.

In front of Ingimarsson and Sonko, the youthful central midfield pairing was just as settled and worked as a pair just as effectively. Both James Harper, aged 24, and Steve Sidwell, two years younger, were products of the Arsenal Academy, and had been brought in by Pardew – Harper in February 2001 and Sidwell in January 2003. Speaking at the time of signing Harper, Pardew remarked that two of Harper's best qualities were *"his athleticism and his arrogance on the pitch"*, and these quickly endeared him to Royals supporters, who voted him player of the season in 2002/03. Always a bundle of energy, and described by one teammate as 'madder than a sackful of monkeys', Harper was the team's engine room, covering more ground in a game than any of his teammates, endlessly harrying in midfield, winning tackles and denying the opposition space and time on the ball – the sort of unglamorous activities that are vital to any team but which so often go unnoticed by so many.

Sidwell also arrived from Arsenal without ever playing for their first team, although he had captained the Arsenal squad that won the FA Youth Cup in 2000. A highly rated youngster who had loan spells under Coppell at both Brentford (playing in the team pipped to promotion by Reading in 2002!) and at Brighton, Sidwell was wanted by both Reading and Brighton when he became available in January 2003. Pardew won the race for Sidwell's signature, beating Coppell – presumably Sidwell's decision was helped by comparing the Madejski Stadium with the Withdean, Brighton's temporary home at the time. Almost immediately upon his arrival, Sidwell formed a superlative complementary partnership with Harper, whose selfless energy and dynamism provided Sidwell with the perfect situation in which to thrive, and to show his own talents. He was also the best-known Reading player at the time – and almost certainly the only known Reading player to many football journalists, who tend to be almost wholly focussed on the Premier League – and in 2004/04 he was voted the 'Best player outside the Premier League' by *FourFourTwo* magazine and was voted into the PFA Team of the Year.

As an ex-winger himself, wide players were an essential part of Coppell's footballing ethos. Again, there were two first-choice players retained in this position, both brought to the club by Coppell but their success at Reading was quite different. The first to arrive was right-winger, Glen Little. Another player who'd had a long but largely trophy-free

career, Little had been brought in by Coppell at the start of
the 2004/05 season, although he had previously spent six
weeks on loan at the end of the 2002/03 season before
Coppell took over. Little had spent the best part of eight years
at Burnley and was regarded as something of an icon by
Claret's fans but had largely underwhelmed Reading fans
during that loan spell under Pardew. Now aged, 29, 6ft 2in tall
and with a personality even bigger, Little came straight into
the team and played 39 times in his first season, although this
was slightly interrupted by a five-week lay-off with a hamstring
injury and Little was reported to have carried a number of
niggling injuries all season. In this first season, his trickery and
unpredictability – Coppell once said of him that Little didn't
know what he was going to do with the ball next, so there was
no way a defender ever could! – as well as his pinpoint
crossing from the right flank proved to be Reading's major
source of assists, and by the end of the season he was well-
established as first choice right-winger and a fans' favourite,
although he was criticised by some for not actually scoring in
his first full season at Reading.

The left wing position was much more problematic. Just
four weeks after bringing in Little in the summer of 2004,
Coppell had also purchased USA international left-winger
Bobby Convey from DC United in the MLS – signed at the
age of 21, he had five years earlier been the youngest ever
player signed by an MLS team. Convey came close to signing
for Tottenham in 2003, but that move broke down as he
hadn't at that stage made sufficient international appearances
to qualify for a work permit, and Reading secured his
signature the following summer. However, his first season was
less than successful, and he only made seven starts and 14

substitute appearances, only playing a full 90 minutes four times and not playing any games after mid-January. At the time, many fans considered him a poor purchase (although being fans they tended to express their opinion using much more strident vocabulary), amid concerns that he couldn't cope with the pace and physicality of the English game – the word 'lightweight' was much used.

There was also considerable speculation about whether Coppell had actually seen him play 'in the flesh' before purchasing him, something he answered at a fans' forum in April 2005. Coppell confirmed that he hadn't, but said that he'd watched numerous videos of Convey, and further rationalised the decision by explaining that Convey was keeping Eddie Lewis, a player he greatly admired, out of the USA team so felt he was worth taking the risk on – he was looking for what he called 'that elusive left-sided player' and didn't think he'd be able to find it at a price the club could afford in this country.

When asked about Convey's disappointing first season, Coppell confirmed that he was just as disappointed, and that he'd certainly not intended to purchase a 'reserve team left-winger'. But this first season was a trying one for Convey, who was relatively young and had not gone to college so had never previously been away from home, and so had initially not coped that well. But Coppell still has high hopes for the player, who was working well to make himself stronger physically and who he believed would still come good.

At the end of the summer, Coppell was even more optimistic, reporting that Convey had benefitted from a settled pre-season with the club when he could have stayed with the US national team all summer – maybe the better decision from a career point of view with World Cup finals in 2006. Instead, he'd made a 'bold decision' to stay in England and he was now one of the three fittest players at Reading. However, Coppell was still aware that the jury was still out on Convey, who still had *"much to prove to him* [Coppell] *and to Reading supporters"*.

After the clear-out of strikers that summer, there was only one front-line striker left at the club, Dave Kitson – possibly one of the most interesting and most enigmatic players ever to play for Reading – as well as one of the greatest bargains in the history of the club. Unlike so many players at Reading and throughout the whole game, Kitson didn't come up through the ranks of football club youth development schemes – instead, at the age of 20, he was discovered playing non-league football for Arlesley while working full-time stacking shelves in his local Sainsbury's. Signed by Cambridge United, his game immediately blossomed and he scored 47 goals in 123 games at the Abbey Stadium, despite playing his first season there as part of a relegated team.

Kitson had a minor injury when purchased from Cambridge in December 2003 at the age of 23, Coppell's second significant purchase. At the time, a number of clubs had been, in Nigel Howe's words, 'sniffing around' Kitson, but most were waiting to see if he'd develop further – after all, he'd only been a professional for little more than two years, and had played only in the bottom two leagues. But only Reading considered the purchase a risk worth taking and so made an offer, and Kitson arrived for an initial fee of £150,000.

A favourite chant from Reading fans was 'David Kitson, what a bargain, what a bargain' and that's completely accurate – looking back it's unbelievable the club was able to sign such a prolific goal-scorer for such a small sum, one who

Nick Hammond calls *"one of the best players that's ever played for Reading Football Club"*, saying *"obviously I've been here 20 years now, I know there's been some great players that have gone before that so I am speaking for myself when I say that certainly in my time I think he was outstanding."* For although he was first and foremost a goal-scorer, he brought many more skills than just being a big target man – often likened to Teddy Sheringham, he had a vision and the ability to drop back and make himself space when necessary that made him an invaluable asset to the team. Almost from the start he was a fans' favourite at the MadStad, and his two goals in April to defeat Alan Pardew's West Ham at the MadStad further cemented this.

A common factor among this squad was the intelligence of the players – you'd not see any of the Reading squad fulfilling the stereotype of the 'thick footballer' grunting their way in monosyllables through interviews. And Kitson especially was highly intelligent and highly erudite – a *Times* reader, happy to share his love of Shakespeare since his schooldays, for instance calling Macbeth 'absolute perfection', he was perhaps as far removed from the stereotype of a footballer as it's possible to get.

You'll notice that although the defence and central mid-field is pretty settled, the other positions clearly needed to be supplemented. An indication of how this was tackled was given by Steve Coppell to that fans' forum at the start of the next season. He spoke of what he called a 'post-mortem board meeting' held after the end of the season, a meeting that he described as 'long and harsh', and in which he and Hammond identified 'three or four positions' in which they felt the club needed to strengthen. Nigel Howe remembers this too, and particularly Coppell coming to him and making it very plain that 'we haven't quite got enough!'

What those three or four positions were is fairly clear from the players brought in – and is reiterated by Coppell telling the fans' forum that he felt the previous season's back five wasn't a problem, but that the team would need to be much more prolific in terms of goal scoring that coming season.

Looking at that previous season, that's easy to see. In finishing seventh, Reading scored only 51 goals, with 19 of those coming from Kitson. Nick Hammond told me more about the need to score more and the conversations held that summer: "*If you look at the season before [2004/05] we hadn't scored enough goals, it was as simple as that. You know that you've got to score 80+ goals generally for automatic promotion, you've got to score high 60s for play-offs, there are exceptions to the rule, if you looked at our goals scored the previous year it was low 50s.*"

If the team had scored more goals that season would have almost certainly ended much more profitably – because there appeared to be few problems with the defence coached by Downes. The previous season Reading had conceded the joint fewest goals at home of any team in the division, and fewer overall than the four teams who finished above Reading in the play-off positions.

The priority, then, was to create more chances and to score more goals from them – and that meant concentrating player recruitment around strikers and wingers. The search for players was on!

The first to arrive were both completely unknown to Reading fans, who as a result were largely nonplussed by the signing of Kevin Doyle and Shane Long from Cork City for a combined fee of approximately £100,000. They arrived due to fortuitous family connection – Cork City's manager at the time, Pat Dolan, reported the players' potential to his brother Eamonn, Reading's academy manager, and the deal was set up. Although there is massive demand for football in the Republic of Ireland, this is almost entirely focussed on English and overseas leagues and so League of Ireland clubs survive on gates of just one or two thousand, and for many years have tended to stumble from one financial crisis to another. As Cork at the time were in the midst of such a crisis, this deal was a win-win for them and Reading – the sum was large by the standards of Irish football, but relatively small by English standards.

However, the fans who were less than impressed by the signing of players who were not 'proven' weren't the only ones, according to Nick Hammond when he was recalling the purchase of Doyle and Long: *"One of the funniest deals I've ever done, but they were a little bit more under the radar. And to be honest, that summer there was quite a bit of negativity around those trades – externally as well as internally – because it was 'we've just missed out, we need to have a go ...' and taking a couple of boys from the Irish League – there was a little bit of negativity around that."*

Doyle, aged 22, had played two full seasons for Cork, scoring 25 goals, whereas Long, who was just 18, had played only a handful of games for Cork. Raw as he was, though, he was an obvious athlete, accomplished at hurling (he played in two Under-18 All-Ireland Hurling Championship semi-finals for Tipperary) and also regularly playing Gaelic football. Despite Long's lack of experience and looking somewhat out of his depth at his earliest training sessions, Ron Grant told me that as he and his colleagues looked out at the training ground they felt that Long would one day be a better player than Doyle.

The next player to arrive, at the end of July 2004, was also an Irishman – but one much better known to both Coppell and Downes. Energetic left-winger Stephen Hunt, aged 23, had been a trainee at Crystal Palace when Coppell was manager, and Coppell signed him for Brentford shortly after taking over there. He had been virtually ever-present for the Bees under first Coppell and then Downes, but had now rejected a new contract and was a free agent and about to sign for Bradford City – literally on the way to put pen to paper on a contract! But a last minute offer from Reading caused him to reject the Bradford offer and sign for Coppell once again. Downes explains the rationale: *"We had Stephen in from Crystal Palace, we signed him at 18 when he was at Brentford, he did great for us, we knew what he was like and it was a no-brainer taking him, really, he was on the train to go somewhere else when we signed him."*

The next acquisition was a back-up goalkeeper, Graham Stack, another signing from Arsenal. Stack, 24, had played in the same FA Youth Cup-winning team as Sidwell, and had made five League Cup appearances for Arsenal as well as 30 starts for Millwall while on loan the previous season. He initially joined on loan as there was a pending charge of rape hanging over him, but when he was cleared of all such charges the following September the way was clear for him to sign permanently, and this happened three months later.

The most eagerly anticipated signing – and what seemed the most drawn-out one – finally happened in the middle of July, and involved Reading breaking their existing transfer record. This was 20-year-old Leroy Lita, signed from Bristol City for £1 million despite competition from numerous other clubs.

Throughout this period, Reading were unlike many other clubs in that they didn't have a formally set 'transfer budget' –

instead, budget for each new player was requested on a case-by-case basis, and if the justification was made at a price the club felt was the right one, the purchase was made. This was the case with Lita – following that 'post-mortem board meeting' the potential for spending was agreed, but the player and price still needed to be identified and the justification to purchase them proved.

Downes told me about his recommendation of Lita to Coppell: *"Leroy had scored two goals for Bristol City against me the year before when I was in charge at Brentford, and I can't remember if Steve had said it to me or I said it to him, 'if we've got money to spend we need a centre-forward, this kid Lita is a goal scorer, he can score goals'. I did a bit of reading up on him and he'd been at Chelsea and they'd let him go because he was a 'bad boy', not a really bad boy but a bit feisty, and he was what Reading needed really."*

With the player identified, it was over to Hammond in his role as Director of Football to make the justification and make the deal happen. Hammond told me the process: *"That was purely me getting to a point where I had to go to the Chairman and say: 'Chairman, here's a player that we want and this is what it's going to take'. And the Chairman was brilliant and he backed us, he absolutely backed us, because at that time we wouldn't have got the player."*

This willingness to break the transfer record underlines the desire throughout the club, right up to the Chairman, to 'go for it'. As Nigel Howe relates: *"At that point, we'd got the Chairman to the point where he knew that he had to get the club to the golden place at some stage and he kept thinking 'I'm running out of opportunities here, I've been in the new stadium for seven or eight years and I've got to get moving'. So we persuaded him to do what we do – which was to underwrite a loss and that was it, that's how we did it."*

But even then, Reading's budget was much smaller than

that of many competing clubs. Coppell told the fans' forum shortly after signing Lita that negotiation for him and enquiries into his background took longer than anticipated but despite that Lita hadn't been watched as much as he liked, considering the outlay, as there had been few opportunities since their interested in him started in May. Coppell reported that a dozen other clubs had been watching Lita, and if he'd stayed at Bristol City and started the season in good form, then his price would have gone up, which meant Reading would have had no chance of signing him. He felt, though, that the forthcoming season 'would be determined by finding a goal scorer'. But Coppell did get his man, and one of the deciding factors, according to Lita at the time, was Coppell's reputation as a manager, and particularly in his role in discovering and developing Ian Wright, who Lita, a keen student of the game, saw as his hero and role-model.

Before the season started, there was still time for three additional signings to be made. An experienced right-back, Chris Makin, 32, joined from Leicester City to provide cover in that position, and right-winger John Oster signed from Burnley. Oster had started his career at Grimsby, but was sold to Everton as an 18-year-old but had few chances to shine, and he soon moved on to Sunderland. However, two incidents blighted his career – the first, in 2002, involved the accidental shooting of a reserve-team player with an air pistol, and two years later a loan spell with Leeds was terminated after a 'breach of discipline at the club's Christmas party'. Coppell, who has always said he is happy to sign players who have had problems elsewhere and so 'have something to prove' offered him the change to resurrect his faltering career at Reading.

The third player signed was hard working and versatile 29-

year-old midfielder Brynjar Gunnarsson. This signing, in particular, delighted Hammond, who told me: *"The other really good signing for me was Bryn because there'd been a change at Watford in the manager and they didn't quite understand what they'd got, and we nicked him. We sort of nicked him out really cheaply and I thought he was a big player for us, not always a starter, but just very, very reliable."*

The core squad was now complete – a total of 18 players, assembled over a period of seven years and costing a total of just £3.875 million. Of them, 13 had signed within the previous 22 months, eight of whom were completely new and had never played a match for Reading. Age wise, half of this squad was under 25 while five of them were 28 or older. Coppell and his coaches clearly had a lot of work to do as the team left for pre-season in Sweden.

Steve Coppell came back from that training camp at the start of the season feeling that more transfer dealings had happened in the summer than he had anticipated, but that there were indications of a real tightness and unity in the squad in the pre-season just gone. With real goal-scoring capability now in the team, he said there was a groundswell of opinion that the team had a real chance this year, even though he felt the division was likely to be harder than the previous season's.

Nigel Howe, however, was not so sure, saying: *"We thought – we being me, Sir John and Ian – this is either going to go tremendously well or it's going to be a nightmare!"*

CHAPTER SIX

Downtown Train

ASK MOST READING SUPPORTERS WHO should take the credit for building the prefect team, the vast majority would immediately name Steve Coppell – in the period since he left a strange mythology has developed about Coppell and his time as manager. And while it's obvious that his management was just one of a number of complementary factors that all came together at the same time to create such a period of success, its undoubtedly true that Coppell's role in many of these was absolutely critical.

But was he as inspirational and as important as so many people believe? To try to answer this question, I looked closer at what happened at the training ground, Hogwood Park, during Coppell's reign – trying to discover for myself the characters of the main protagonists, who among them did what, how were the coaching sessions structured – and just how did Coppell and his coaching team turn this disparate group of 18 players into an all-conquering team?

There were distinct roles among all of those at Hogwood. Coppell, of course, was manager and so had the ultimate say about the first team, but his working relationship with Director of Football was absolutely crucial to developing and managing the team, although this relationship worked in a very interesting and quite possibly unique way. In many clubs where there is a Director of Football, the holder of that role will tend to be the manager's superior, hiring and firing as necessary. At Reading, there were no such hierarchical reporting lines. While Hammond was, as we've seen, the board's representative on the football side of the business, advising them on all football-related matters and playing a major part in recruiting a manager, in many ways he was also a peer and a partner of the manager – there to assist and advise, rather than to manage or supervise. This structure functioned perfectly for Reading, and was perhaps the best possible way of working to allow Coppell to be at his best. Naturally quiet and pensive, studious and almost completely focussed on football management, Coppell disliked many of the trappings that traditionally came with the manager's role – such as negotiating player contracts and dealing with their agents, etc. To have Hammond take these responsibilities off his shoulders was a godsend, and this method of organisation – with Coppell managing, Hammond dealing with player recruitment and contracts and specialised coaches doing the day-to-day coaching – was, I'm convinced, something that greatly contributed to the effectiveness of our perfect team.

Of course, a high degree of mutual trust and respect between those involved is critical to make such a structure work, and these appear to have been in place from the very start, almost from the point during the interview process when Hammond outlined the club's stipulations to incoming managers.

Hammond explained to me what these initial conversations with Coppell were: *"The important things for me were to say to the manager, or potential manager, 'here's the structure of the club, here's how it runs and here's the financial situation you're coming into' – because those are the two important things for me. Does he accept the model and does he accept how it works and does he come in here expecting £20 million to spend when he's only going to get five because that's not right? Those are the two pertinent things, so Steve understood that we were building something that we believed in and that people could believe in and he was happy to come and work in that framework so that was very much part of the interview process."*

Another stipulation for an incoming manager was that he retain the existing coaching team, and Hammond's comment about this gives an interesting insight into Coppell's character. *"And the great thing about Coppell is that he's that comfortable in his own skin and what he does, he doesn't need – I won't call it a comfort blanket because that would sound disrespectful to other managers – because I also understand, absolutely understand, managers needing to have certain people around that they trust. But for Steve it wasn't a massive issue."*

Of course, this structure wouldn't have worked at many other clubs or for many other managers – can you imagine Harry Redknapp not dealing with player contracts or financial negotiations? And as many observers frequently express surprise or scepticism at a manager not directly controlling the player recruitment process, that's worth looking at in more detail, so I asked Hammond to explain how this worked at the club.

He told me: *"It's always a joint effort, the way we've always worked, so as the Director of Football I run the recruitment process. People still don't see this but I run the recruitment process and drive that and I have a chief scout who works for me, or now Head of Recruitment, so it was me and Brian McDermott at the time. That process was driven by us."*

"Steve's focus is the team, working with the team and preparing the

team and we would drive the other part of the process – understanding what he requires and making recommendations and the manager would then, off the back of those recommendations, look at video footage or if we can get him to a game."

Hammond then shared stories of Coppell's level of involvement in some of the players who were signed at this time: "*Steve famously has told about the time – was it once or was it twice? – he went to see Kevin [Doyle] – with his beer goggles … because he liked the Irish because he could always go and have a Guinness. But by the same token he hadn't seen Shane Long play, so that was where we got to at that stage – you build relationships and there's a degree of trust there."*

"*But the key for us, and I'll reiterate again I'm talking Madejski regime, as Director of Football I would run that process – but the manager always has the final say, that's always been my way of working."*

"*The manager has the power of veto but the truth was Steve never used that and that's where you build relationships over a period of time. So Stephen Hunt, for example, would be complete because Steve knew him, he'd played with him and I would support that because he knows the player, he knows exactly what he's going to get and the player fits within the confines of the budget. Another player may come, so Bobby Convey he didn't really know – but I had a belief in Convey and he went with that, and Convey for 12 months was not great and then instrumental in the promotion season."*

On the training ground itself, roles were just as split. Ady Williams told me about typical training sessions. "*Sal did the goalkeepers, Wally took most of the defenders and did the defending. Dill [Kevin Dillon] would put on the sessions for the midfields and strikers, being a midfielder he knew how to pass a ball. And the gaffer occasionally would put on a session but he was much more – I can see him now – standing on the side with his shorts on and his rugby shirt with the collar up and his baseball cap on and just overseeing everybody."*

This image of Coppell quietly standing on the sidelines, thoughtfully supervising training, is one that comes up again and again among the people I spoke to. But he was by no means idle or uninvolved, although he was sometimes accused of being so. Downes told me how training worked under Coppell: *"Steve would be first in in the morning and he'd say to me 'what do you want to do today?' and I'd set out what I'd planned for the day and he'd go 'okay, that's fine with that'. And if he'd been looking up – which is what he did, he studied the opposition a great deal and he knew exactly what was coming at the weekend – he might say to me on Monday afternoon 'tomorrow or Thursday have something in your mind'. And when we'd do the 11 v 11, I'd put on the 11 with the opposition, something that they did and we would counter that so he might give me a couple of points to watch, 'their winger cuts back on his left foot and puts it in'. He'd find a couple of specific things for me to work on with the group towards Saturday's game but other than that it was fine and he never stepped in on a session, he would never step in."*

Hammond gave more information on Coppell's approach: *"He had his coaching staff who he trusted so he allowed them to deliver the bulk of the coaching. He always dictated what was going to go on, how long it was going to last, what was required, but he very rarely delivered. 'This is what I want, you go and deliver' and then he would observe and talk to individuals. That was his style – and then at the end of the session, after lunch, whether it was here or at home, he would be analysing the opposition to come and setting his team up to play against that opposition. He was methodical, very methodical."*

Hammond also recalled how Coppell brought this laid-back approach, always observing but only rarely intervening, right from the start. *"I remember sitting with him the night before, talking to him the night before in terms of the arrangements when he'd come in, his first day. 'Steve, what do you want, do you want them in a* meeting room, do you want them at the stadium?' 'No, just let 'em train Nick, and I'll have a chat'. That was his way, that was what he did, there was no massive introduction, he turned up at training, he spoke to a few individuals, he gathered the group together at the end and it was just – it was sort of fluid really. I think he was very, very conscious because the team had been promoted, there was some good stuff going on and again that's not his way. He's not a revolutionary is he?"

This was a change of approach from Pardew's time as manager, but it was nonetheless extremely effective as a management technique. I asked Ady Williams to tell me about Coppell's management style, and what made him such a good manager. He gave a brilliant insight into the way Coppell worked, which is worth quoting in full: "I think Steve's unbelievable to try and work out because since finishing I've tried to work out what made him so good. He didn't do all the coaching himself, he did very little of it but he was there, he was overseeing it. Whereas Pardew would get out there with his boots on and show you everything and do everything, Steve wasn't like that. Dill took sessions, Wally took sessions, but Coppell was watching everything."

"But what I realised he was so good at, he was good at the things you thought he wasn't good at. As captain I used to collect the fines, and we had a certain group of players that were always late because of the M25 – whatever it was, it's just the way it is – and it used to annoy me and it used to annoy other players, and I used to have to try and get the fine money off them for being late. Steve Coppell would hold the training back, he wouldn't train until they were all there and we felt like we were being punished because we were all ready to go – but others thought 'I'm not going to get here till 11.00 so we'll start 11.30'."

"I'd say 'they've not paid their money' and he'd say 'well you look after that'. He didn't want anything to do with any of the nonsense outside of training and picking the side. But the way he dealt with it was in six *weeks' time those players weren't playing football. He didn't puff, he didn't get hot about it, he didn't show any emotion at all – but slowly but surely the players that were regularly late or regularly under-achieving or whatever, slowly you could see that they weren't at the football club anymore."*

"But he did it in such a nice way it was unbelievable, because he did have every player's interests at heart so he would tell them that 'at the end of the day I can't see a future here for you, why don't you go here – it's much better for your playing?' Whatever it may be, I don't honestly think he was lying through his teeth – he was actually being one of the gentlest with it and footballers like honesty. You know they're wrapped up and pampered sometimes, but he was really good at seeing. He didn't want anything to do outside of football – if that makes sense. He's not interested in fining people, he's not interested in curfews, he's not interested in any of that palaver – he couldn't care less if you've got a suit or a tracksuit or whatever, flip-flops or jeans – he doesn't care. All he really focused on was the football side of things."

Of course, Coppell and his coaches all had their own personalities, and again this mix was a complementary one. Kevin Dillon, according to Nigel Howe, was a talker and always had a lot to say and a lot to offer in terms of what he gave to the coaching, especially with strategic play and set pieces. But Wally Downes, also brought a contrasting approach: *"Wally was very important to the overall thing – how his humour and how he was. He went in and he looked after the defence and he was the loud voice to counterbalance the softer voices in there ... Wally was a much louder voice and different personality, he was a louder personality than say Kevin or Sal Bibbo ... Wally had his sense of humour."*

This 'crazy gang' sense of humour was counter-balanced by the most-noticeable quality that Coppell brought to the role – his unflappable calmness. Coppell's quietness was often criticised by people who didn't quite 'get' him or understand his methods, but those who worked with him fully appreciated it and it was one of the reasons that he was able to motivate his players quite so well.

And there's no doubt he was an exceptional motivator, and that he managed to instil in his players an intense desire to please him. Downes provided astute observations on why the players had so much respect for Coppell: *"I think it was still close enough they may have remembered him as a player, they may have just about remembered him as a player; they knew he'd had Wright at Palace which was a good team that he'd managed there; we'd run them close at Brentford the year before when Pardew took them up ... so he's a respected manager. And I think Steve is not a great one for wasting words so when he talks, you listen – and they were out to impress him every day. I'd be taking the training, they were probably sick to death of the sound of my voice – but if he spoke, they listened!"*

Ady Williams echoed the theme that Coppell didn't say very much, but what he said was always worthwhile, saying: *"Someone once said to me 'don't talk unless it's relevant' and in the dressing room I've always had a lot to say, that's just my nature, the way I played. Steve Coppell taught me that the fellow that's sat next to me in the dressing room who said nothing after the defeat, he's still hurting as bad as I am if I'm throwing teacups about – and it took me a while to work that one out. And Steve Coppell taught me that, really. When he says something, we stop and listen. If it's relevant, say it!"*

"I'll always remember that because footballers, particularly after a defeat, we've all got so much to say and it's all nonsense most of it, in the heat of the moment – 'he's crap and he's shit and why didn't he do this, he missed out on a chance!' – It's all rubbish and what you've got to do is look at it constructively and talk sense and improve so it doesn't happen again. And that's what the gaffer was good at, he was calm."

This calmness had a grounding effect on all those around him, including his players, and helped damp out excessive and possibly harmful emotions – win or lose. When the perfect team really took off, it was Coppell's calmness that helped keep their feet on the ground. As Nigel Howe says, thanks to Coppell's lack of emotion: *"We used to sit there at the top of the table and we'd think 'oh, it's just another win'."*

Coppell, of course, was challenged and criticised many times about this 'lack of passion'. His response, as given to a fans' forum in April 2005, was to say: *"Look around football, take Arsenal. They play good football and you cannot imagine Wenger throwing cups. In this division it seems you are expected to be the jump-up-and-down monkey on the line. 'Passion' is going to watch the reserves and missing the Champions league semi-final last night! 'Motivation' comes from setting standards pre-season and making the most of ability."*

We've already seen that the level of intelligence of the 18 players that made the core of our perfect team was considerably higher than usually found in the average professional football squad. This is no coincidence – Coppell said many times that he always favoured intelligent players, because once they crossed the white line they were effectively on their own and had to make their own decisions, adapting as necessary. As such, the level of responsibility he handed over to his players was noteworthy – as Ady Williams says of the pre-match briefing session: *"He used to come in, he used to name the team, he used to say who's marking who and then it's like 'that's it, I've done my work Monday to Friday, you all know what you're doing, you all know what you're in the team for. If you do what I want you to do you'll be in it next week'. It's quite simple really."*

Coppell underlined this point in another forum four months later, telling fans that he felt that his players needed a 'pre-match speech' to motivate them before a match then there is something wrong with them as a group. Similarly his handing over of responsibility to the players frequently influenced his substitutions, where his attitude in many situations when things weren't going well on the pitch was that his players had the ability and the intelligence to get themselves out of the problems, so he was happy to leave them unchanged, with the responsibility to turn things around themselves.

Coppell's delegation of responsibilities also applied off the pitch. Ady Williams told me how this applied to curfews: *"We'd been away on pre-season tours and there was never a curfew. He was the only manager where there was never a curfew and he was like 'well you're grown men, you know what you should and shouldn't be doing, you know what time is a reasonable time to come in when you've got to get up at 8.00 in the morning for training. Now do it'."*

"Do you know what? I can remember nobody took the mick, nobody came in at two, three, four o'clock in the morning drunk or anything like that. He said 'no curfew', the lads respected it and 11.30, 12.00 or whatever it was: 'I'll tell you what boys, we'll finish these and that'll do us'. It's amazing psychologically how it works when someone gives you a bit of responsibility. I'm sure we pushed the limit even with Steve, but when someone gives you that responsibility – 'you're a grown man, you know what you should and shouldn't be doing' – I think players, men respect that."

Hammond agrees that this was a vital part of Coppell's way of motivating his players: *"It was unheard of.* [He'd say] *'Listen, stay at home with the family and we'll meet at seven, get on the coach and go ...' but again, that was discipline. The discipline of the team came from the discipline of the manager, 100 percent. That was where he was so good really ... his players were like kids with a father.*

They all looked up to him and they all wanted to please him, and he just had this way. He never gave them much, but they were always striving for approval really, it was just his style."

Clearly, the relationship that Coppell had forged with his players, and the respect they had for him as a manager and a mentor, was exceptional. But more and more these days, the relationship that managers have with those above them in a club's hierarchy is critical. I asked Nigel Howe about Coppell's relationship with the Chairman: *"I don't think you could describe Sir John and Alan Pardew's relationship as fantastic, certainly in the latter months. You could describe Sir John and Steve Coppell's as a bit of a love-in. Steve absolutely got where Sir John was coming from and he would play to Sir John's tune in terms of he would talk to him, he would be very sympathetic to Sir John's not-detailed understanding of football, so he would go along with a lot of what Sir John wanted to do."*

I asked Nigel if this made it easier for Coppell to get approval for player purchases and other funding requests.

"I have to say, as needy as Alan Pardew was, as un-needy Steve Coppell was, he had a grasp of the realities. He'd been through the rock and roll of football, he'd been to the very highs with Man United and the manager at Crystal Palace and places like that, so he'd seen the lows and he was very grounded. There was no doubt that his approach to everything was borne out by him having a very bright intellect, so his needs were only when necessary and ones he felt important."

"If Steve wanted something it was a very indirect approach about how he'd get it, it was more 'this would make us better' and 'let's do this' and in that way Sir John would try more to help then he would if he had the 'you must …'"

As Howe said, Coppell had a good understanding of the financial realities the club operated within, and he elaborated more on this when speaking to the fans' forums in April 2005.

He explained that the Championship roughly divides into three sections – the group of six teams receiving parachute payments, a group in the middle and a group at the bottom. The bottom group will cut wage bills and will be spending enough to avoid relegation, while the group of eight-ten teams in the middle will aspire to promotion but will not commit sufficient spending to be sure of that – and that he felt Reading were at the top of that group.

Coppell added that while he didn't have a set budget as such, if required the Chairman would finance a new player. But Coppell fully understood why the Chairman wanted the club to 'wipe its own face' (i.e. to be self-funding, without needing cash injections) and he had no complaints with that – and that he treats the club's money like his own and strives for a 100 percent hit rate from it.

With the summer signings, those tight purse strings had been slightly loosened, although not to the point where Reading were competing on equal financial terms to those clubs receiving parachute payments. But heading to Sweden for pre-season training there were ground for optimism, and Coppell now had the chance to take his squad of players and turn them into a team.

CHAPTER SEVEN

We Didn't Start the Fire

So FAR IN THIS STORY we've seen how Reading managed to put together the potential elements to be successful – an environment where they could thrive, a talented set of coaches and a group of players with real potential.

But lots of clubs have those elements – and, it could be argued, bigger clubs with more spending power potentially have them in greater abundance or with greater potential. So what was the extra ingredient that created the extra magic of this team? What made them so much better than the competition?

The answer to that question starts with a presentation delivered to those attending a UEFA pro-licence refresher coaching course very shortly after the end of the 2004/05 season. That presentation was delivered by Mark Reynolds, someone completely outside the football industry – and among the attendees at that presentation was Wally Downes.

I'm absolutely convinced that Downes's appreciation that day of what Reynold's company, Catalyst, might bring to Reading – and of the potential difference they might make to the team – is one of the most crucial steps of all those that lead to the creation of the perfect team. For Downes shared his thoughts with Coppell, who was always on the lookout for anything that would add a little extra to his team.

Downes takes up the story: *"I came back and Steve and I met in Chiswick. And he said 'we need to do something different, we need to shake it up because looking at it, if we're not in the top two after six or eight games, I think the chairman will go whack and get someone in – we've got a very short time'. He thought we'd have a very short time to get it right. I said I'd seen Mark and he was a smart guy and I thought he'd be good to come in and talk to us and he did and he came in."*

Clearly it wasn't just fans on an internet message board who were aware of Coppell's potential future at Reading. But Coppell shared Downes's enthusiasm for Catalyst, as did Hammond when he met with Reynolds shortly afterwards, so it was time to make a deal. Downes gives his perspective on how this happened: *"It wasn't a great deal of money and I think it was incentive-based but Steve went to the board and said 'I want to get this guy on board, do the deal'. So it was like signing a player – there was a bit of to-ing and fro-ing – the club wasn't open to things like that, I had to battle them to get the ProZone in for £30,000, I said to Nigel Howe, 'if we don't get this in now, you'll be falling behind' and they were 'do we need it?'"*

"So I would imagine Steve said to Mark Reynolds 'I want you' and he's gone to Nigel Howe and said 'I want him' – and then he's put them both together, they're both businessmen, they got together to do the deal."

In fact, it was Hammond who was just as instrumental in setting up the deal, and he quickly became a major force in championing Catalyst within the club. He told me about this deal: *"Wally had … really liked them, he fed it back to Steve, Steve met them, fed it back to me, I met them and then I talked to the board and we did a deal to get them in and that was it really."*

I asked Hammond if he had any difficulty in getting this additional expenditure agreed. His response was: *"No, not especially, because the Chairman was always okay about the things that might give something different – and although we'd spent £1 million on Lita, we weren't spending three, four or five million pounds on him which was a lot in those days. So no, the answer is no, it was always about the money – how much is it going to cost?"*

In some ways the ease with which this expenditure was agreed seems surprising, especially for something completely new to the club, but Nigel Howe explained that one of the deciding factors was Coppell's determination to engage Catalyst – as he says, Steve was so 'un-needy' – he asked for so little that when he did he usually got it.

So what did Catalyst actually do, and how did they make all the difference? I asked several people this, and they came up with subtly different answers. Hammond, for instance, described their role: *"Mark had no input on the football side, didn't profess to have any input on the football side but he taught the staff to work smarter. He brought in those charts. I mean they'd been around in football forever – Mark didn't invent them – they'd been around forever, the six-match plan. But clubs that had been up before you kept them amongst yourselves, amongst the staff, short-term goals and long-term objectives."*

"So Mark took the players from us and gave them an open forum amongst themselves about what they wanted and how they saw it was going – because no matter how much of an open group you've got, players aren't forthcoming with staff and managers because they want to look after their own arses basically. They don't want to say anything because they're worried about their own futures, but after a while Mark got them to talk openly and that's when he encouraged them to put their own goals and objectives up – I think he did it on a six-week cycle."

We'll look in more detail at those changes later in our story, but for Downes one major difference was the level of communication from the players. He told me: *"It didn't change how we coached but we got better feedback from the players via Catalyst and the regular staff meetings that we had made us work smarter as a group."*

As we spoke more about the role of Catalyst, Hammond told me more about their role with the players: *"They were a sounding board for the players and we would talk about a thing called hygiene factors – it's all the issues that go around performance. So if we got Marcus Hahnemann sleeping in a single bed on an away trip, he's got the hump and when Marcus has got the hump, we know about it – so we used them to take away as many of the peripheral issues as possible so they were very useful in that respect."*

"They would run meetings with the players, and the players would get all their gripes out and then that would come back to me and I would deal with the issues I could. It was 'no names, no pack drill, this is the issue, what can we do Nick?' And of course we don't deal with everything – 'sorry guys, that's not possible ...' But if we could make things better, if we could facilitate things, if we could help, then we did. You create this non-excuse environment, the players have got no excuses – 'the bed's big enough Marcus; the food's great, go and perform, because if you don't, we'll go and find someone else who can. It's a bit like that really'."

Hahnemann himself echoed this 'sounding board' role, speaking to a fans' forum in January 2006: *"We have a firm called Catalyst come in to look at the club with different eyes. This has given the players a chance to express their ideas more easily – it does means players are listened to rather than being dismissed as moaning!"*

But after a little investigation it became clear that there was much more to Catalyst's role and their influence than helping the players communicate with the coaching team. Ron Grant, who positively enthused about Catalyst, gave me some more information about their impact: *"Catalyst – they actually used psychology and also part of good management techniques. Everybody had one-to-one interviews, very similar to this, with questions being asked. There was a report for Ron Grant – I mean the whole book is for me! The comparison report and in that, what did they have? 'Action people in system', 'blocking' – every person was actually identified whether they were blockers or whether they were sustaining – and all the psychology of it was worked on. A really modern approach to it."*

Speaking to others about Catalyst, it seems there are many different views on what they did and what their role was. As far as most fans were concerned, if they'd heard of Catalyst at all they were some 'bunch of sports scientists' working away in the background and responsible for organising a couple of events before matches to boost the crowd noise.

But whoever I spoke to inside the club, one thing was coming across loud and clear – that Catalyst had made a difference that season. It was time to find out more about them.

I met Mark Reynolds, Managing Director of Catalyst, twice in London and I was tremendously impressed by him. He immediately struck me as one of those rare people who seem to exude wisdom and experience – someone who I felt could give me an astute and well-thought through answer to literally any question on any subject I might ask him.

Reynolds, who had been Saatchi & Saatchi's youngest Managing Director, had founded Catalyst several years earlier. As 'performance consultants' they had already worked with a number of global, high-profile businesses such as Apple, Virgin, Mercedes-Benz, Nike and Microsoft. I asked Reynolds what 'performance consultants' actually do. He told me: *"Getting the best performance possible out of a team, advising them how to improve that team in order to enhance the performance. So if we had to sum it up in one line it's the art of winning. It is an art – it is not a* science."

"*All we did with any client was realign and manipulate the resources that we had already. You can't have more resource when you want to – life is not like that. You've got to get the best out of what you've got. And we were very good at getting the best out of what we had.*"

That sounded like a perfect match to Reading's situation in the summer of 2005 – although Coppell did have slightly more resources than he was used to, those resources were still relatively small in comparison to those of many of the clubs he was competing with to gain promotion. Reynolds told me that he was asked by the FA to present to the coaching course, and that's where Downes saw him and was impressed and intrigued enough to ask him to meet Coppell. It appears there was an almost instant rapport between Coppell and Reynolds – both highly intelligent, they seemed to perfectly understand the other's situation and what they could offer each other.

Reynolds speaks very highly of Coppell, as he told me about the state of the club he found when he first came to Reading: "*Where I admire Steve and still believe he is one of the best managers this country has ever had, is that what he was looking for was something different. Bobby Convey gave us something different; Leroy Lita gave us something different; Glen Little at his best gave us something different. He was always looking for an edge. For a way to out-think, out-perform, out-tactic an opponent. And I would say he was worried that they didn't have an edge going into that Championship season. He wanted an edge. There wasn't the money available from the Chairman. The Lita transfer was a way off at that point. Steve wanted an edge, he was looking for one and he had nothing to lose. So the difficulty in the first few weeks/months was – 'so, what are you going to tell us?'*"

I asked Reynolds how the relationship with Reading started from his perspective. He told me: *"This is where I have to give enormous respect to Nick Hammond, because Wally made the original introduction. Wally said 'come and meet Steve'. So I met Steve at West London Sports Club or Birmingham or somewhere in his shorts, just come off the golf course. Steve said 'yes, but you will have to meet Nick'. Nick said 'the Chairman is not going to like it and I have a real problem with Nigel' – and Steve said 'I don't give a fuck. Nick, fix it'."*

"So Nick went away and fixed it. And the trick with any proposal is you have to win before you get there. So we had the manager and the coaching, elements of the coaching team and the director of football saying 'we want to do this'."

And so Reading became Catalyst's first sports customer. I asked Reynolds if Catalyst made a conscious effort to get into football at this time. He agreed that they had, not just because of the money but because: *"there was nobody doing what we were doing at that point in time in football."* With this in mind, pricing was set in order to help make that first sports deal happen. Reynolds told me: *"We had made it extremely affordable and then were surprised when the club thought that was expensive."*

And so the relationship started. One of the first tasks was to visit the Hogwood training ground and Reynolds was brutally honest about what he saw there: *"So faced with a paucity of resources the club had allowed itself to descend into 'get by' tactics. So the drinks cabinet was locked when the academy players were around. When I say locked, it was a motorbike padlock and chain."*

"So Hogwood was a heap of shit. A flood plain by the Thames, very muddy. A mini – I wouldn't say city, a village – of Portacabins."

This locked drinks cabinet is something we discussed at length, and is almost a perfect image of the state of the club at the time and the way, perhaps, some in management felt. You have highly-trained, highly-paid sports professionals, but you don't actually trust them to help themselves to a drink from the fridge at the end of training – they have to go and ask the chef who has the key to the padlock! An unbelievable situation to many, and unheard of in the real world of business that Reynolds was used to working in.

Reynolds told me more about the training ground at the time: *"It was dirty, grimy, ill-kept. Pretty much reflecting where the team and the club was at that time. Meanwhile up the road is this brand new stadium built by property developers from the old Elm Park days … to move to Madejski was fantastic. Unfortunately as with any club getting a new stadium, you have to put a good team in it – and we didn't have a good team to put in it. We didn't have a new team to suddenly pull out of the hat and say 'wow, we've just hired 11 players and we are going to dominate this league'. So we had to get the best out of what we've got."*

But, as with any new organisation coming in from outside, things don't always go smoothly, especially in an industry such as football where for many change is difficult and lots things are done in the same way they've always been done. Reynolds explained to me that with any change or new initiative, those it will affect typically spilt into three groups: *"A third who think it is brilliant. A third who think it is shit. And the floating vote in the middle, not sure which way to go. So the job of a consultant is to win a majority in that parliament."*

And this split applied at Reading just as much as it did in any of Catalyst's previous customers. Reynolds explained to me in wonderfully descriptive terms: *"The second you mention 'consultant' you might as well walk into a dinner party and say 'let's talk about gonorrhoea'. Nobody wants to talk about gonorrhoea – nobody wants a consultant!"*

"So if your question was unpopular, absolutely [there'll be re-sistance]. *But if you go to somebody and say 'how do I become a better*

lover?', the advice you receive is not going to be popular. It is going to make you angry, it is going to make you frustrated, it's going to make you spiky, difficult. And we encountered all of it."

"We had the usual third, third and a third, and that was no different. Where Reading I think underestimated us was that we had met much worse than Reading – in some of the biggest corporate names in world industry."

As our story progresses, we'll see how and where Catalyst made an impact across all aspects of the club. But one underlying theme that was repeated again and again is worth exploring here, because I think it sums up very simply and succinctly one of the absolutely fundamental changes made to the team and the way they were motivated. And this is summarised neatly by Reynolds when he explains that the various objections encountered were overcome: *"Slowly through logic, through emotion, through common sense – but mostly through turning skilfully the environment from push to pull."*

This concept of changing from push to pull is absolutely critical to our story. Catalyst knew from their experience in many other organisations that any team has a much better chance of succeeding in its objectives if those it needs for this task are pulled there and made to want to succeed and share the success – rather than being pushed (or shouted at, cajoled, threatened, bullied – call it what you like!). And Catalyst implemented a number of small changes, all of which worked to this 'pull not push' aim.

For instance, we've heard how Hogwood was dirty and ill-kept. On one occasion when most of the players were away for a few days, the changing rooms were quickly decorated – no vast amount of effort needed, no massive budget, but just a simple change that improves the environment for the players.

Ady Williams previously told us how good it felt as a player to be given responsibility – now they were being given respect too. As part of the same process, the chains were taken off that locked drinks fridge!

As time went on, this drive for 'pull not push' carried on – not with big expensive changes but in small, incremental ones – as rewards for the players for achieving objectives. Many might call this bribery or incentivising but it was much more sophisticated than that, involving rewards the players themselves were involved in choosing. For instance, one reward was a 'float' behind the bar when the players went on a racing day to Cheltenham – relatively inexpensive, and a sum that the players themselves could have easily put up between them and hardly noticed the loss. But the effect of something shared between them, benefitting the whole squad – and earned by the players themselves – has significant positive impact.

As Reynolds explains: *"You had a bunch of players who were massively overpaid for the performance that they were delivering. So we were more interested in intrinsic awards then making well-paid players better paid. The money behind the bar at Cheltenham Festival made no player better off."*

"So, we were more interested in getting a professional dart board, exactly like the one on the telly, into the training room. We were more interested in getting PlayStations into the training room. We were more interested in getting stainless steel ice baths into the training room."

"Ice baths were a new technique in those days – and Reading's version of an ice bath, it was a wheelie bin. So watching Dave Kitson being lowered manually into a green wheelie bin behind a Portacabin in a muddy car park gives you a rough idea of where the club was."

"Six months later we had a Cleveland Brown, because one of our

consultants had worked in the NFL and we knew the Cleveland Brown had the best stainless steel ice bath system. And that was installed in Reading – to Nigel Howe's credit, to Nick Hammond's credit, to the Chairman's credit – because by that stage we had a high performing team."

In this way, and in other ways we'll see across the whole of the team, Catalyst slowly changed the culture and the motivation within the club.

Meeting Reynolds was an eye-opening experience for me – not only did I learn some very interesting facts about psychology, motivation techniques and human interactions, I had previously had no more than a vague idea of what Catalyst did and how much they helped shape our perfect team. But that's fine as far as Reynolds is concerned. He told me: *"All the credit we can take is behind the curtain. So our job is to wear a black T-shirt, black trousers, black gloves – the credit must go to Steve Coppell and Nick Hammond and that coaching team. And then in front of them the players. And alongside the players, the Chairman and Nick Hammond – despite his best effort to position himself in different places – because they did it. Nigel contorted and twisted himself, as a Chief Executive must to make it add up."*

"So, I think we need to define what we did. What we did was we lit a fire – in fact we didn't light the fire. We provided the petrol and the matches!

CHAPTER EIGHT

Smells Like Team Spirit

WE'VE ALREADY SEEN HOW CATALYST helped change the way the players were managed and motivated from 'push to pull', and how they were given more of a voice, helping resolve what they called 'hygiene factors' – issues that might have been affecting their performance. But their work wasn't just about the playing squad. As Ron Grant outlined to us, they also worked closely with the coaching team in order to increase their effectiveness as a team.

This process started immediately Catalyst were engaged, prior to the squad's pre-season tour of Sweden and involved one-to-one sessions with all of the coaching team, including Grant, undergoing an exercise, two or three hours long, to identify their typical behaviour profiles in a number of scenarios. I won't even try to detail this in full – or even try to pretend I understand it in full – but the outcome from this exercise was a graph of each individual's typical behaviour profiles in a number of categories: 'accelerating performance' (behaviour that changes the way things are done, that creates and drives a vision forward, that engages the skills, ideas and energy of others and which improves overall effectiveness); 'sustaining performance' (behaviour centred on consistency and attention to detail that makes things run smoothly, achieves plans and hits targets); and 'blocking performance' (behaviour that, while not always wilful or intentional, inhibits the previous two behaviours). This performance-blocking behaviour typically comes from people who feel frustrated, anxious, uncertain, insecure or threatened, and often shows itself as avoidance of responsibility or conflict, anger or aggression.

It goes without saying that while the first two are positives that drive a team forward and help it carry on moving forward, the third is wholly negative, and generates destructive forces that create resentment, destroy commitment, generate tensions, undermine loyalty, decrease creativity and drain people's energy – and not just the energy of those it immediately affects! In fact, research has shown that such blocking behaviour often destroys upwards of 25-30 percent of a team's performance.

For each of the behaviour attributes in these categories, each individual's results were graded as a percentage – for the positive behaviours, a score around 70 percent was seen as the most effective value, while a score below 30 percent was seen as ineffective. A low score meant that behaviour made no contribution to the desired outcome – or even hindered it – while too high a score over 70 percent meant that energy was being wasted in over-achieving, with over-performing individuals often seen as single-minded zealots and therefore easy to ignore. For blocking behaviours these were reversed, with the optimum a value around 30 percent.

As you'd expect in any group of diverse individuals, there was a wide range of scores, with some scoring almost exactly 70 percent in some attributes but low scores in others, while others had almost opposite profiles. The key point from this exercise wasn't to criticise anyone for low scores or to castigate them for not contributing to the team, it was to identify areas where improvements could be made and then to work with individuals to help them improve in these areas. As Reynolds succinctly put it: *"So I can change behaviour. I can't change personality. I am not interested in measuring personality. I couldn't care less if you are a left-handed Aquarian dolphin – but I can give you techniques today in our conversation that tomorrow in the training ground you can use so that people can see you doing a different or better job."*

Such techniques might be minor or major, but were all targeted to the specific attributes and individuals concerned in an effort to raise the effectiveness of the whole group. One such example Reynolds outlined to me was in helping an individual improve their visibility – there was no question that they worked hard, but this was often on background tasks and so they felt over-looked and unappreciated. Another case I particularly enjoyed was someone who frequently felt they weren't listened to, and felt that when they raised an issue it was frequently ignored or not taken seriously. By the simple expedient of teaching them that when raising an issue they should touch whoever they were talking to, they were much less likely to get a resolution to their issue from the other person. As Reynolds said: *"The very fact that you touched them means they have got to do something about it. If you don't touch them then their engagement is optional."* This is just one of the many thought-provoking things I learnt myself from talking to Reynolds about Catalyst's techniques – so the individually-tailored sessions that each member of the coaching team received must have been incredibly useful and instructive.

Again, with a diverse group of individuals the response and the acceptance of these new techniques varied across individuals. Reynolds told me about one of the coaching team: *"We were able to make a difference and he would listen to it. It was like watching a sunflower come out within a week."* Others, however, were not so accepting. Reynolds continues: *"With others they would say 'fine'. And the definition in consultancy terms, if you hear the word 'fine' – start worrying. Because it means fucked-up, insecure, neurotic and emotional. And there were so many 'fines' on that training ground."*

I asked Reynolds if this was a better or a worse profile than other teams he'd worked with. Saying that the overall profile was 'average', he explained: *"What this tool does is it takes a Polaroid picture at a point in time. So this is preseason, this is the opportunity as opposed to the solution. I would say the answer to your question is probably worse but I think if you took that same Polaroid of highly effective teams, the teams who are over-performing their capabilities, you would see the reverse of those graphs."*

The aim, therefore, was to reverse those graphs as much as possible – to change the behaviours in the group as far as possible. But Reynolds emphasised that although they'd measured individual behaviours the aim was to improve those of the whole aim collectively, rather than single out individuals, and that one resistant to change would not impede the whole group's progress: *"The technique from a consultant's point of view is not to enhance the performance of an individual unnecessarily. If we can get an achievable performance out of the lot by manipulating an individual to overcompensate to make up for his slow-to-change compatriot, that will do."*

And with this coaching, the profiles of the coaching team – for some individuals and for the group as a whole – did change to become a closer match to the optimum values on the graphs. As Reynolds said: *"Suddenly, some of the people had shot up.*

Not with our opinion – but with logic and data – we showed them what they looked like and then we offered them a better way to do this. And that applies to the players as much as it did the coaches."

As we've seen, Coppell himself was a firm believer in these techniques and embraced them enthusiastically. I asked Reynolds for his views on Coppell's managerial techniques and the manager's way of communicating with his players, together with how he felt Catalyst had changed these. His answers were very revealing and worth quoting in full. *"Steve made some of the bravest decisions I have seen any manager make. He backed players who I think would have been dropped or abandoned by other coaches. But he believed in them* [the players] *and they believed in him."*

"They found him difficult to deal with because he was singularly one of the most silent communicators. Pre-game he was great. Post-games he was pretty good too. The bits in between, namely Sunday, Monday, Tuesday, Wednesday, Thursday, he was silent."

"The respect the players had for him was enormous. And I agree they were desperate to please him. He was the gaffer in everybody's eyes. He was head and shoulders the boss in terms of every single person on that training ground."

"So as far as those players were concerned they would run a mile naked for him. Their problem was that they didn't know in which direction to run sometimes – because he hadn't told them. He had thought it, and so in terms of match tactics he would be explicit. In terms of his satisfaction/dissatisfaction he sometimes wouldn't."

"So I guess we were the ideal foil – the complete balance to that approach. I would say that we got the best out of Steve … I don't know if we could necessarily make that commitment to a promise, but if I look back to those seasons now that was Steve at his absolute best."

"And by graphically showing him a graph of what he looked like we

probably accelerated his development at whatever ripe old age he was at that stage into weeks rather than the years it would have taken for him to grasp a different way of doing things. As we get older you know our learning slows down, as our choices to refuse increase."

"In Steve's case he was desperate to learn, desperate to do things better but didn't know how to. We either reaffirmed, challenged or in some situations said 'no, that is a bad idea, don't do that'."

"And I think he welcomed that. We made him rethink so many aspects. I am pretty sure that having rethought them, 70/80 percent of what he was doing anyway, he was happy with. But if we had made a 10/15/20 percent difference that was sufficient. The team had to produce a 25 percent improvement over the full season."

"And that improvement had to come from the coaches – and it had to come from them first. And some of them found it extraordinarily difficult to deliver and some of them couldn't. That's okay, it doesn't make them bad people, it just means they struggled. And it didn't matter providing we achieved the objective – if the goalkeeper's backside put the ball in the net – it didn't matter. We wanted an edge and Steve found that edge in ourselves and we stood cheerfully behind the curtain to deliver it."

I'm convinced that the work Catalyst did with the players and coaches – improving their communication, their techniques and their overall effectiveness – was absolutely critical and one of those factors that elevated this team from being merely good into being great. Steve Coppell, as virtually everyone in football will testify to, is a superbly intelligent tactician and a highly skilled manager. With Catalyst helping him fine-tune his communication techniques this raised his effectiveness as a manager even higher – and made a real difference.

With work in progress to improve the effectiveness of the coaches, and the transition from push to pull underway,

Catalyst met with the whole group of players and coaches in Sweden to set targets for the season. As consultants, Reynolds told me, they specialise in collecting and using data, but not the sort of data that football is awash with, the sort of data beloved by fans and the media, such as "how many years it is since Reading have lost to Oxford United". Instead, he focussed on the data that counted, performance statistics, and presented the group with targets needed to secure promotion – the 25 percent improvement on the previous season's performance just mentioned. Reynolds challenged the team to create history – to be the first Reading team to reach the top division, and showed them how much of an improvement they needed to make – and that challenge was accepted by the team. Reynolds recalled: *"What we wanted, we wanted them to say right at the beginning of the season: they wanted to create this dream, they wanted the best championship team ever and that sort of thing, which is very easy for a group of players to say."*

Planning for this involved the season being divided into cycles, and the players collectively setting their own targets for these – on the surface quite similar to the old 'goal cards' introduced by Alan Pardew, but under that surface much more sophisticated in the way they were set – in sessions facilitated by Reynolds, and the way they were backed up by real data and targets brought in by Reynolds – who started each objective-setting session with a presentation of progress so far and what was achievable and necessary to stay on target. For the games in each cycle, each player would predict what they felt the result would be, and put their name to that to take ownership of their predictions. Once the papers were collected in, Reynolds would facilitate the session to help the groups reach agreement. He gave an example: *"So let's go around the*

room, and say 'Right Sonks, tell us why you've got three points there ...'
And so if we had common denominators we group them – 'so you guys sit
over there because you are all a group. You guys go sit over there, you
disagree. Now between you and you, let's fight it out in the next few
minutes. Can we get you to come over here or do you lot have to come over
here?'"

This process was allowed to run on as long as needed even if it delayed training for several hours. By the end of it the players have an objective that they had put together themselves, and they owned. As Reynolds says: *"So they owned it. They had the choice. They put their objective on the wall. Their handwriting. Monday they get back in for training – guess who would write in the points achieved in the box on the wall? Even if they lost."*

This further helped turn the squad into one with common purpose and a common objective. As Reynolds said: *"What united that dressing room is simple declared shared objectives. 'We can do this. We can't do it on our own. We have got to all pull together'".*

However, it would be unfair to try and suggest that there was disunity in the squad that Catalyst resolved – in fact, the squad was already very close and had been for several years. The club had recognised that financially they were often unable to compete for players against bigger clubs, and that geographically they were at a disadvantage against some other clubs (young players typically are drawn more to living and playing in cities, especially London, than to a relatively quiet, provincial town like Reading) and so worked hard to keep players happy and to create an environment where they would want to stay and prosper. This ethos clearly helped make Catalyst's 'pull not push' easier to implement but the padlocked drinks fridge shows us that this wasn't applied universally.

I'm sure the closeness of the squad was also partly down to

Coppell's quiet, even-handed and undemonstrative management style, and Ron Grant confirmed that since Coppell's
arrival in late 2003 the spirit and togetherness in the squad
had been getting stronger all the time. He shared with me an
example of the spirit within the whole club: *"There was a real
collective feel about the place and I know from a personal point of view. I
had my 70th birthday in that season and they surprised me with a party
in the canteen at the training ground. I'll have been 70 in 2005, the
September of 2005."*

*"That was all part of that as well, they'd all collected up for me. In
fact they sent me to the Savoy Hotel in London for the weekend with my
wife and a visit to the theatre next door – the Savoy to see 'The Rat Pack'.
And John Madejski sent me up in his Rolls or Bentley with the wife. The
wife thought she was the Queen going there and then it came round and
picked us up on the Sunday as well. They were very important, because my
wife was part of my being there and so she was part of the family as
well."*

As Ron says, this togetherness extended across the whole
club including the wives and girlfriends of those involved, so
much so that, as we'll see, they were later to combine to form
the 'Royals Families' charity. I asked Nick Hammond whether
this was a deliberate policy or just a happy accident. *"It just
evolved, it just evolved – and, of course, winning does that – but it's
people, it's 100 percent people. If you put – and I said this to the
Chairman of the Board – if you put the right people in the right environment you've got a chance of being successful, but we'd certainly bought
good players that summer and the goals were key – but it was a whole
coming together of things really."*

As well as the large-scale initiatives we've seen, there were
also smaller ones – for instance players' lockers were personalised with their pictures, and Reynolds also instigated a policy
that every letter, fax or email sent in by fans, even negative

ones, was shared with the players. Even though this idea was initially laughed at, the players came to appreciate this – as Reynolds says: *"There is nothing nicer as a player than to see that some bloke in Turkey thinks they're great. And this was all hidden stuff – we just pulled them together. They were there, they were collated – but the stadium knew about them, the training ground didn't."*

I remarked earlier upon the level of intelligence of the players in this squad. As well as helping them to take responsibility on the pitch, this also enabled them to participate fully in Catalyst's initiatives, and to understand them sufficiently for them to be effective. I'm sure this was another important advantage that meant that Catalyst's methods might not have worked so well at other clubs, and I don't believe that the remarkable level of dressing-room harmony could have been possible at many other clubs either. Reading's financial state meant that it was not a place where overly-ambitious players, who often had egos to match, would ever be likely to sign for, and so Reading's squad was made up of players who certainly weren't star names – even the record signing, Leroy Lita, was attracted to sign primarily by the managerial reputation of Coppell. This lack of egos and absence of the kind of greed that afflicts some footballers all helped in the creation of an environment conducive to team spirit and harmony – another of the vital factors required for the success of our perfect team.

The transformation of the club didn't just involve the coaches and the playing squad, though. In one way or another, everyone at the club was involved – with, as we'll see in forthcoming chapters, initiatives that emphasised the part that they would play in getting the club promoted.

At the end of my interview with Reynolds, I asked him if he would sum up what he felt he had achieved at the club. *"It is amazing what a small group of people can do if they put their minds to it. So what we did was take a highly paid group of people – and I include the coaches in that – and reorganised, realigned and – no excuses – manipulated the scenario to equip them with best thinking, best approach, best practice and to encourage them to make the best decisions – and then we kicked their arses hard!"*

"I think everybody out of that period of time delivered the best they could possibly be. And that was all that was ever the request."

"But the environment we built, and I say 'we' in the collective of us and club, club and us, was extraordinary. The excitement around that agenda. The atmosphere at the training ground. The people in the canteen were desperate to improve. The people in the media room were desperate to improve. The stewards were desperate to improve. The groundsmen – I had loads of conversation with the groundsmen, when we put in the new pitch, when we redid the pitch at the training ground to make sure that the pitch and the training ground were exactly the same as the pitch at the stadium, despite the efforts of rugby – that became passion."

"So all we did was added new metrics to the same people. We didn't recruit/transfer players. We didn't have to bring in new chief executives, new managers, new coaches. We got the best out of what we had on the table. You can only play what you've got. And we played what we'd got superbly. They were phenomenal, and I doubt if any of them collectively or individually can probably replicate that period of their careers again."

By the start of the 2005/06 season, after a highly successful tour of Sweden where the team played three games and won them all, with an aggregate score of 14-1 – admittedly to inferior opposition – and with the new players integrated into the squad, it was time to see whether all the analysing of behaviours, all the crunching of data, all the planning of objectives and the improvements in communication styles would make a difference where it mattered – on the football pitch.

John Madejski (now Sir John) on his purchase of Reading Football Club, 1st December 1990.

Elm Park, June 1992.

A new era starts for Reading FC as The Madejski Stadium opens to the world, 22nd August 1998.

Alan Pardew is appointed manager of Reading, 13th October 1999. L to R: John Gorman, Alan Pardew, John Madejski and Nigel Howe.

*Alan Pardew (R) directs assistant manager Martin 'Mad Dog' Allen in training,
16th August 2001.*

*John Madejski tries to avoid the flying Champagne, sprayed by Andy Hughes,
following promotion at Brentford, 20th April 2002.*

Reading's rudimentary (and borrowed) training facilities as Alan Pardew (L) speaks to scholar Darren Campbell, 23rd December 2002

©*Reading FC*

Nick Hammond (L) and Kevin Dillon take temporary charge of Reading with Alan Pardew subject to a high court injunction, 16th Sept 2003.

©*Mirrorpix*

Steve Coppell is finally officially appointed Reading's manager, 9th October 2003. (L to R) Nigel Howe, Steve Coppell, John Madejski, Nick Hammond.

©*Reading FC*

Nick Hammond and Steve Coppell face the press in July 2004.

©*Reading FC*

The new training ground at Hogwood Park – but still a relatively basic facility at this stage, 23rd August 2004.

©*Reading FC*

A squad game! In one of his six substitute appearances, Eric Chukwunyelu Obinna creates a dramatic image as he competes for the ball against Southampton, 28th September 2005. ©*Mirrorpix*

Reading coaches Wally Downes and Kevin Dillon discuss tactics.

"Bring it on" – 31st January 2006

Reading FC v Norwich City FC - 31st January 2006

Dear Loyal Royal

It's time to be the best we've ever been.

Over the last 16 years, I have worked very, very hard to create an environment for success at Reading Football Club.

Our stadium, training facilities, conference centre and our hotel are among the very best in the country.

Only a handful of clubs in the UK, or even Europe, can boast the platform that we have created here at Reading. All these superb facilities are brought to life week in and week out with the passion, energy and commitment of a fantastic team of people – both on and off the pitch.

This has been a great season – so far. Now we have to finish the job.

And that's where you come in. No 13 on every team sheet – the Reading Fans.

We need to ask for your help. We need to ask for you to power our club and our players to higher levels of performance over the next few weeks.

We need your help to create an atmosphere, an electricity that you can feel in our stadium at every remaining home game. I want us to unite with a passion and fervor and get behind the players and the club.

Let our players see the fire in your hearts. Let's show our courage to roar our team on like never before. Let's unite as one voice and dare the opposition in each game to match our intensity. Let's make it personal.

When I took up the role of chairman – 16 long and expensive years ago – I declared that our objective must be to reach the Premiership. Thanks to the performance on and off the pitch this year, we have created a platform from which we can now reach our goal. We can smell success. We can almost touch it.

Now, more than ever before, I'm asking the people of Reading to be the best that we can be. I want our stadium to glow with passion. I want to terrify the opposition with our confidence and enthusiasm. We can do this. But we need your help.

Now is exactly the right time to be **Proud** and very, very **Loud**.

Getting Reading into the Premiership? There can only be one answer.

Bring it on!!

Best Wishes

John Madejski

Inspired by Catalyst. John Madejski's letter to Reading fans before the home match with Norwich.

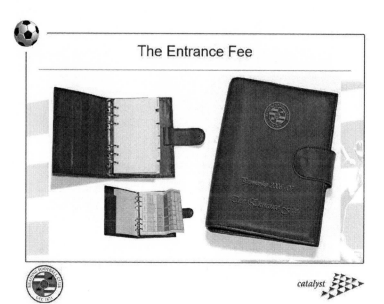

Catalyst's "The Entrance Fee" – a challenge presented to the playing squad to return from summer Premier League-ready, March 2006.

Steve Coppell and his coaches celebrate Reading's promotion to the Premier League after the draw at Leicester, 25th March 2006.

©Mirrorpix

Reading fans celebrate promotion outside The Walker' Stadium, Leicester.

Winning the Championship at home – Reading captain Graeme Murty celebrates with the crowd, 1st April 2006.

John Madejski and Steve Sidwell celebrate winning the Championship, alongside Kevin Doyle.

©*Reading FC*

Volunteers from Supporters' Trust at Reading prepare the MadStad for 'Raise the Hoops' before the visit of QPR, 30th April 2006.

John Madejski gives Stephen Hunt a 'piggy-back' as they celebrate the presentation of the Championship Trophy.

Dave Kitson takes his turn with the Championship trophy, watched by Glen Little (R) and Bobby Convey (L).

Leroy Lita scores Reading's third as they come back from 2-0 against Middlesbrough to win their first ever Premier League match in style, 19th August 2006.

©Reading FC

Michael Essien's face is a picture as his late own goal gives Reading a 2-2 draw at Stamford Bridge on Boxing Day 2006. Leroy Lita celebrates behind him.

Possibly the highest point – and for many fans the most satisfying point – of Reading's first Premier League season. 1st January 2007.

Steve Coppell's body language speaks volumes after his team's 2-0 home defeat to Fulham, 12th April 2008.

The pain of relegation. Pride Park, Derby, 11th May 2008.

A few signs and a "Save Our Steve" t-shirt which would grow into a clamour for Coppell to stay at Reading, 13th May 2008.

The day in May 2009 when The Messiah finally left Reading – bearing gifts from the fans, organised via Supporters' Trust At Reading.

CHAPTER NINE

You're Unbelievable!

THE FIRST TIME THIS TEAM was tested in action was Saturday 6th August 2005, with a home match against Plymouth. In front of a crowd of 16,836, of whom the best part of 4,000 were away fans, Reading started with the core of the same team that ended the previous season with such disappointment. Of the eight new players, only Lita and Doyle started the match – with Kitson, a substitute after recovering from an injury although he was joined on the bench by four of the new signings: Stack, Makin, Hunt and Oster. Convey, looking fitter and stronger after a full pre-season, started wide on the left.

Reading began well, passing the ball around neatly and with confidence, but conceded a goal midway through the first half – very much against the run of play, and a prompt for Plymouth to close things down at the back. Although clearly the better team and playing with some style, Reading struggled to break down the Plymouth defence, and it took until nine minutes into the second half before they equalised. Convey thought quickly in taking a short free kick to Murty, whose cross was headed in emphatically by Lita for his first goal for the club. Thereafter Reading continued in positive style, looking for a winner, and had a number of good chances – notably a header from close range put well over the bar by Sonko late on, but were unable to score against a Plymouth side happy to defend and looking to attack on the break.

With 15 minutes to go, Coppell had even switched to 4-3-3, a relatively unusual move for him, although later that month he did tell a fans' forum that the team had played it in the pre-season tour In Sweden and that he felt it worked provided the team was stronger than the opposition. Reading clearly were, but unfortunately in making this switch Coppell had taken off the two wingers who'd created much of their attacking threat, Convey and Little, and brought on just one, Hunt, for his Reading debut. Although there were now three up front there was much less ammunition, and this looked destined to end up as a disappointing draw. Right at the death, though, a major injustice was done as a poorly-hit Plymouth free kick was scooped into the Reading goal and the visitors claimed all three points.

That late goal was a real sickener for fans and team alike – Reading had played some very nice football, and had looked bright, if a little bit disjointed at times. They'd created enough chances to win the game but had failed to put them away, and the previous season's habit of silly defensive lapses clearly hadn't left them, and ultimately cost them the game.

Fans' reactions to this defeat were surprisingly muted. Certainly, Reading fans had much lower expectation levels ten years ago than they do now (when even a single defeat can lead to the words 'relegation candidates' trending on Twitter and calls to the local radio phone-in calling for the manager's head) and most focussed on the performance and the potential shown by the team, rather than the result.

Loyal Royal Dave Harris summarises the match and his

feelings at the end of it: *"'How the hell did we lose that?' is the first thing I'd say. We dominated the game. To all intents and purposes we were an injury-hit side as well at the time – we'd gone into the season without Kitson and a number of other first-teamers, but still absolutely battered them. Did everything we could but possibly score – I still think Sonko's header with ten minutes to go, that's still in orbit. Six yards out, free header and it's still rising now!"*

"Looking back it was massively disappointing, it looked like it was going to be another season of similarity to the one before, with inconsistent performances and inconsistent results attributed to that. I still look back on that game, though, and think 'how the hell did we lose it?' – the way we played set the tone for the rest of the season, if not the result, because we battered them."

Ron Grant told me that the feeling in the dressing room after the game was very similar: *"All pretty down actually. 'Don't tell me this is going to be another season like many other seasons ...' I can remember Glen Little was very upset about it at the time. We got beat 2-1 that day but we played so well. Shouldn't have got beaten but we did."*

Wally Downes was more realistic and philosophical, though, saying: *"We played okay – it was unlucky, the goal. I knew we didn't expect to lose that game but there's not a lot of bearing on the first game of the season. Certainly there is probably a little bit more now because they heap the pressures on more ... but first games don't necessarily reflect how the season goes. After six games, the bottom six and the top six rarely change, but not after one game. We were disappointed to have lost it but we played well enough, we had all the chances. If that had happened later on in the season in a regular season you'd have just said 'okay, don't worry about it'"*.

The team had the chance to atone for that defeat just three days later with a tough away trip to Brighton, now managed by Mark McGhee.

The coaches knew just how important this match was to
get the season back on track, and Downes told me about the
preparation for the game: "*Well, we got to Brighton on the Tuesday
night, and Steve did his meeting. [*It was]* 4.15 before he put the board
up, and then he'd tell the players the team for the night and then a couple
of little reminders. I'd said to Steve beforehand, 'when you've done your
meeting, you go and I want to have a word with them'. So Dill and I
stayed behind and I didn't read them the riot act, but I said to them 'look,
this is now – we've got to win this fucking thing. We've put a lot of
fucking work into it, if we're going to go up you don't lose two games on
the trot! Forget Saturday – it was unlucky – but tonight is where it fucking
turns round. We've got to make sure, whatever you've got to do to win this
game, you don't come to Brighton and lose. If this was February and we're
in the top two in the league you come here and you win, you don't lose –
you make sure you get that mentality tonight! Don't think it's Tuesday
night, there's no time for that – tonight is a fucking big night for all of you
and for the staff. We've got to show that Saturday was a one-off and if
you lose tonight those two games on the trot and everyone's shitting
themselves for Saturday!*'"

This 'old-school' coaching seemed to serve its purpose in
lifting the team. As Grant said: "*Withdean Stadium – I can
remember going over the far side and we were really up for it, really were –
the whole squad, the bench, the back room, we really wanted that after
what had happened the previous game, we were really looking to do it.*"

Nick Hammond was also significantly aware of the importance of this match to change his normal arrangements. I
asked him how he felt before it: "*Worried, because the manager was
really flat – very, very flat, to the extent that I went to Brighton on the
Tuesday night, I went to an away game. With Steve, nearly always I'd be
at the home game because you want to understand where the team's at, but
the away games, when the team was away, I'd generally go away scouting*

and watching players – that's how I normally worked. I actually went. There was a full programme on that Tuesday night, but the 2-1 loss to Plymouth and a home game as well. Based on, obviously, the last game of the previous season, again I was concerned enough to go to the Brighton game and watch that. Not concerned, just to see where it was at and the vibe. Again, that for me was a massive, massive game."

However, the side won 2-0 with relatively little trouble, and according to Grant: *"Yeah, that was the first signs that we did have a decent side out there in a game."* Hammond agrees, saying: *"I actually thought that night we were okay and I wouldn't say we won comfortably but it wasn't too hairy-scary."*

The first goal, early in the game, was scored by Little, a floated free kick that went into the net without a touch from anyone, and Kitson – now restored to the starting 11 – scored the second goal after an hour. Little's goal was his first in 41 games since joining Reading permanently, a goalless run that included the whole of the previous season. Since a frequent criticism of that season's team was its paucity of goals from midfield, the Little goal was widely seen as a significant mark of progress.

I don't intend to chronicle the details of every single match in that incredible season, but rather to pick out some key matches in it, matches that hopefully demonstrate the progression and transformation of the team. The next match was, for me, one of the most significant of the season, because it marked the first time I thought that the team might just be on the verge of something quite unexpected.

This match was just four days later, as Reading travelled north to Preston for their third match in a week. Deepdale had always been a nightmare ground for Reading – they'd not won in their last seven visits, and the draw earned on the back of

Martin Allen's 'warming-up in the wrong half' shenanigans represented their only point at the ground since April 1992. Preston was also regarded as one of the favourites for promotion, having been beaten play-off finalists the previous May and not having lost a home league match since November 2004.

And Reading smashed them! Almost from the start Reading played with a fluidity and a confidence that knocked Preston off their stride, and two almost identical Leroy Lita goals – both created superbly by Bobby Convey – killed the game off. The icing on the cake just before the hour mark was another Glen Little goal – his second in two games – and with a header, too. A real collector's item! Coppell later told a fans' forum that Little had boasted about scoring 'two goals in three games' after this match, until Coppell reminded him that including the previous season it was actually 'two goals in 50 games!'

This was the first match since the last days of the Alan Pardew era that I came away from thinking *"wow, that's not what I'm used to from Reading – there really seems to be something about this team."*

Dave Harris also remembers this match as a significant one in the team's development. He told me: *"Nine months previous to that we'd gone up to Preston over the Christmas break and we'd been absolutely annihilated 3-0 and we reversed everything that day – we deserved to win 3-0, if not more. And this was against a team that ultimately finished fourth, they had a better defensive record than us, they conceded two fewer goals than us throughout the whole season and they only conceded 12 goals at home all season so they went another 21 games conceding just nine goals at home. We beat them 3-0 and the manner of the victory suggested there was something going on. We'd gone to*

Brighton mid-week after the Plymouth game and it was a routine team victory, but going back to Preston, they'd been in the play-offs the season before, they had a gnarly, wily manager, Billy Davies, and a good side – a very, very physical side. And we rocked up, we had a classic away performance in many ways, we withstood early pressure but then got a goal just before halftime and that net is still shaking, Lita hit that shot so hard! Of course the cream on top of that little pudding is Glen Little's towering header at the back post – I'm still cheering, I'm still going absolutely nuts at that one. If we go in chronological order I suppose that's a big one, Preston away is a big, big one."

That performance and the emphatic victory, at a venue where Reading traditionally failed to compete, clearly bred confidence – a confidence that was visible in the team for the next home match, against Millwall on 20th August.

And that confidence showed straight from the start, as Bobby Convey scored what was one of my favourite goals of that season just six minutes into the game. A Millwall corner was cleared to Convey just outside the Reading area – and he just ran with the ball, virtually the whole length of the pitch, and beating two Millwall players, before calmly sliding the ball in just inside the far post. A brilliant goal, and a further sign that the Convey of this season was a world apart from the disappointing and largely ineffectual Convey of the previous campaign.

Everyone in the stadium knew from that point that there would only be one winner to this match, and this was confirmed when Millwall's 'keeper was sent off for handball outside the box after 23 minutes. Two minutes later Convey scored a second goal, Reading were 4-0 up at halftime and playing with a clear swagger, and the match ended with a 5-0 victory that took Reading to the top of the table on goal difference – although as Coppell said at the time *"I'm not too excited about being top of the league at this stage of the season."*

More significantly, though, with Harper and Sidwell also grabbing goals, in just four matches the Reading midfield had contributed six goals – a sharp contrast from the previous season when they scored a total of just ten from 46 matches.

For the next match, a home League Cup tie against Swansea, Coppell made five changes to give some of the fringe players a chance, and they made hard work of the task, needing two extra-time goals to win 3-1 – a suggestion at this early stage in the season of perhaps a lack of depth in the squad. Many considered this a cop-out or 'not taking the competition seriously', but Ron Grant explained Coppell's philosophy in doing this: *"It was about giving all your players a game, wasn't it? It wasn't actually that we were putting out a weaker squad, you were putting out part of your squad – those players could come in at any time to the first team anyway. But that's what he was doing, so it was an opportunity he gave to the younger players – he was a real team player. I think it was part of his makeup."*

For the next league match though – a dour and largely uneventful 0-0 draw at Watford – Coppell reverted to his preferred starting line-up.

The contention that the squad lacked depth was put to the test for the next match on August Bank Holiday against Burnley. Although they took an early lead through a deft flick from Lita, the final six minutes of the first half looked to be calamitous for Reading. In this time they suffered injuries to three key players with Shorey and Sidwell suffering almost simultaneous knee-injuries, and Kitson taking a knock to the ankle. Shorey and Kitson were substituted and Sidwell played on, but clearly suffering impaired mobility – and to add insult to injury Burnley equalised in the midst of this mini-injury crisis just before halftime. The Reading of previous seasons might have crumbled at this point, but as well as flair and confidence this team also had an abundance of resilience and character, as they showed to grind out a fairly ugly 2-1 win, achieved through a 70th minute header from Kevin Doyle, who'd come off the bench to replace Kitson. In fact, Doyle was inspirational, a bundle of energy and mobility, often having to win the ball for himself as Convey and Little were forced to help out in defence.

For Loyal Royal Paula Martin, the significance of this match was that it was the first where the team was shown to be more than just a starting line-up of 11 players. She told me: *"We played Burnley and Kitson, Shorey and Sidwell all got injured and I thought 'oh shit, this is it – we've lost three players, that's the end of the good run, we're not going to be able to cope without them!' – but we did. We didn't win every game without them, but we carried on playing well, the people that slotted into their places were seamless and I just thought 'we've got a good squad here. We haven't just got a good team, we've got a good squad'."*

This was confirmed by Coppell when looking back at the season to a fans' forum the following April: *"We suffered three injuries and three people stepped in and the transition was seamless. We have the best fringe players in the division."*

All three injured players missed the next match, a 1-1 draw away at Coventry, but their replacements had good games as part of a visibly confident Royals team – but one that not only missed a penalty but conceded a late goal from a corner to lose two points, which they probably deserved.

The next match was one which I can truthfully say is absolutely the best game of football I've ever seen in 40 years of matches – a match that had everything you could want, and a match that I literally dare not take my eyes off even for a second for fear of what I might miss.

Crystal Palace, just relegated from the Premier League and still with most of their big-name players, gave Reading their sternest test so far. Both sides were confident and completely up for this match, a match that pulsated with action from start to finish. Doyle, still deputising for the injured Kitson, scored his third in three matches after 26 minutes, but Palace equalised through Andrew Johnson, who was always a threat, just three minutes later. Although Palace fans at the time said that Johnson's loss through injury just before halftime was the deciding factor in this match, once he'd gone off Palace looked a much better side, offering more variety, and very early in the second half they took the lead. More like a basketball game than a football match, both teams took it in turns to attack, and both goalkeepers were under almost continual pressure, with Hahnemann in particular producing some excellent saves.

Still the game pulsed, and Lita, who'd been largely ineffectual, produced a stunning moment of brilliance to level the scores – an overhead scissor kick, from a very tight angle and with his back to goal! But still this game had more to offer – as Doyle won a penalty, missed by Lita but ordered to be retaken, with the second attempt from Little spectacularly saved! But three minutes from the end, this breathless match was settled by a bullet-header from Sonko at the far post. Superb entertainment, and a match that no one who was there will ever forget. As Michele Mead commented: *"The only time I've ever said this – even if we lose this game it's been a privilege to watch."*

You'd think that with all these wins, Reading would easily be top of the division, but in fact they were only second, as Sheffield United had started even more emphatically and were four points ahead. In a real 'hare and tortoise' race, Reading strove to overtake them – although of course Coppell emphasised all the while that he didn't look at league tables – and won their next three matches by 1-0 scorelines before going to an away match at Southampton.

This was possibly Reading's toughest match of the season so far, and a real test of their character, as they defended resolutely for 90 minutes and came away with a 0-0 draw to stretch their unbeaten league run to ten games. At the end of the season, Coppell cited this match as his hardest of the season, saying: *"We were fortunate on the night, it was a testing evening and terrible weather that was great for attacking football but we predominantly had to defend."* He added that he felt that passing that test with a goalless draw was a key indicator that the team could do well. The defence, and particularly Ingimarsson and Sonko as well as 'keeper Hahnemann, performed heroics in the pouring rain on the South Coast, and that match produced one of the most iconic pictures of the season, as Sonko rises head and shoulders above six Southampton players to head the ball clear.

But while Reading were drawing, Sheffield United had won again and were now six points clear at the top as they came to the MadStad. This was another frenetic game, with bags of controversy – particularly when United 'keeper Paddy Kenny clearly handled the ball outside the area but was only booked. Reading crowds are typically fairly subdued, but nothing gets them enraged quite like a clear injustice such as this, and the sheer fury at this error created a magnificently hostile atmosphere. The league positions of the two teams, and the presence of Neil Warnock, Sheffield United manager and purveyor of a well-publicised and long-standing feud with Downes, only added to the needle. Reading scored through Brynjar Gunnarsson – deputising for the injured Sidwell for the sixth consecutive game – after just three minutes, but 12 minutes later United were level. Later injuries to Little and Convey meant that Reading played the second half with just five of Coppell's likely first-choice line up, and United had the bulk of possession but were unable to create any meaningful changes as Reading performed another resolute defensive display worthy of Rourke's Drift.

As the final whistle drew closer, United had what looked like a clear-cut penalty claim turned down – prompting predictable apoplexy from Warnock, or 'Colin' as anagram-inspired Reading fans were wont to call him, but there was still time for the home team to launch their first real attack of the second half – from which Gunnarsson scored his second, winning, goal. Ten years later, it's still easy to remember the sheer elation and the total release of emotion at winning such a tight and crucial match in such circumstances. The free-kick for that decisive goal was sent in by Sékou Baradji, signed on loan from West Ham at the start of September and making his single substitute appearance for Reading – truly this was a squad in which even those who had bit-parts were critical to the squad's overall success.

Despite clawing a crucial three points off Sheffield United's lead at the top, it stayed neck and neck between the clubs until late November, when a 3-0 win over Ipswich at Portman Road finally took Reading into top place in the championship. Dave Harris remembers that match well: *"We played Ipswich twice quite quickly, within three weeks of each other. We beat them 2-0 at home on the TV and it was embarrassing, embarrassing, just how many it should have been – remarkable it was only two. And three weeks later we went to Portman Road and did exactly the same again, scored three this time – went top of the league that night. Again it was embarrassing, they barely had a chance and of course not forgetting they also had one of Reading fans' favourite strikers of all time playing for them, Nicky Forster. So actually going top of the league that night in front of about 300 Reading fans, there weren't many Reading fans there that night, Portman Road is a notoriously – sorry, excuse the cliché – tough place to go ..."*

As Harris says, Reading had now settled into a groove of playing with flair, pace and above all confidence – and going out onto the pitch knowing that if they performed to their usual standard then victory was virtually assured – and with the self-assurance that if an opponent had the temerity to actually score against them, they'd almost certainly be able to get straight up to the other end and take a goal back themselves. This feeling of invincibility had spread to the crowd, too, and was reflected in the noise they made – the noise of a crowd who were loving every minute of such on-field style and confidence, even bordering on arrogance, from what had previously been 'Little Reading'. Glen Little told fans about one of his favourite memories from the period, a home game against Hull, three days before the match at Ipswich. He recalled that Reading were leading 1-0 and playing well, but hadn't got a second goal when Hull equalised. His vivid memory was of Reading scoring twice in a minute – he scored the second – and the place going 'absolutely potty'. He wasn't sure if it was disbelief at scoring twice in a minute, but he said that the crowd are *"really getting this now – the timid Reading crowd are really getting this."*

One match in particular stands out for a number of Loyal Royals – away at Plymouth in late November. As well as gaining revenge for that opening day defeat, for Alex Everson this was the first game when he, in his own words: *"Realised we had a special team. Although we were top and had been for two months by that point, I don't think I'd realised what we were watching until then. It was after that game when I realised I was going to games and not hoping for a Reading win – but expecting it. After that, it was not a case of 'would we win?', but a case of 'how many by?' in nearly every game for the rest of the season."* Michele Mead also remembers this game with affection, particularly Little's goal – following a fine save from Marcus Hahnemann the ball came to Little inside the Plymouth half. He beat three players and put in a beautifully weighted chip to beat the Plymouth 'keeper. For Mead this was her 'goal of the season': *"The save from Hahnemann and his distribution which then led to Glen Little's goal. It has to include the save as it epitomised the season in one move – very much about the team with occasional pieces of individual brilliance."*

Of the nine league matches played since beating their rivals, Reading had won seven and drawn two in the league, and they were also going well in the League Cup, having beaten Swansea, Luton and – gratifyingly – Sheffield United. This had been achieved with a team consisting mainly of fringe players – and Coppell followed this policy in their fourth-round match away at Arsenal. With Reading playing so well, and Arsenal – a team Reading hadn't met since 1987 – in their last season at Highbury, this was bound to lead to a scramble for tickets, and as a sideshow to the league there were the inevitable controversy and arguments about ticket allocations before this match. Reading lost 3-0 to the Gunners, their first defeat in any competition for 23 games and 90 days – but they were by no means outplayed in any aspect except the quality of their finishing. Arsene Wenger summed them up by saying: *"I think Reading are a good team. They have good team play, a very mobile team, they are tuned in together – there is a good understanding. And they have a way to play that looks fluent and dangerous – for me it's a good side."*

The Cup exit didn't affect the team in the league, and with the likes of Sidwell and Kitson returned from injury they steamrollered on, with 3-0, 5-1 and 2-0 wins over Luton, Brighton and Millwall, until at Christmas they were six points clear at the top of the table, on the back of eight consecutive league wins. As Ady Williams described it: *"That winning snowball effect happens – winning is a habit and they didn't get out of that habit."*

All thoughts, though, were on the Boxing Day match against Wolves at Molineux. Considering the form the team was in it's surprising there were such worries, but there was a very real feeling that this would be the match that ended it all. For many months there had been discussions about when, precisely, the 'wheels were going to come off' – and the universal consensus was that this Wolves match would be the one.

Fans knew that over recent seasons, no matter how well they had started the season, Reading's form inevitably plummeted after Christmas, and Wolves were among the pre-season favourites for promotion. Additionally their manager, Glenn Hoddle, had also been piling the pressure on Reading in the media, saying: *"The pressure's all on Reading, they're top of the league, they always fade after Christmas."* So there was a definite level of trepidation among those Loyal Royals who made the journey up the M40 to Wolverhampton.

CHAPTER TEN

The Winner Takes It All

DESPITE THE FEARS THAT IT was all about to come crashing
down at Christmas 2005, this phenomenal first half of the
season was no fluke – on the pitch it was a combination of a
superbly balanced and motivated team, combined with the
effectiveness of Steve Coppell's tactics. Even Coppell's critics –
of whom there are noticeably very few – would not deny just
how astute an observer of the game he is, with a knowledge of
tactics and formations second to none. Combined with his
intelligence and guile he was able to put together tactical
solutions to suit most eventualities. But on the surface level, the
tactics of the 2005/06 Reading team didn't appear to be
particularly sophisticated.

Instead, their main game plan consisted of doing relatively
simple things – but doing them supremely well. This would
have been clear to a visitor at the club's open day in August
2005, who would have seen a training routine that epitomised
Reading's approach to attacking, and consisting of the
goalkeeper playing the ball to one of the full-backs, out wide,
that full-back playing the ball forward along the line to a
winger, that winger taking the ball forward and crossing it into
the area, where an advancing forward would put the ball into
the net.

Of course, it's a massive over-simplification to suggest that's all the tactics consisted of, because with opponents on the pitch there would often be a need to use the midfield or for the wingers to beat one or more men, but in essence that was Reading's style – fast, counter-attacking football, particularly down the wings. Or, to reduce it to just ten words: "Get it out, get it wide, cross it in – goal!"

To achieve this, Coppell deployed a fairly standard 4-4-2 formation, but with orthodox wingers on both flanks, a superbly solid back four and a highly mobile and energetic central midfield pairing. Although he'd experimented with 4-3-3 on the pre-season tour to Sweden as well as towards the end of the home defeat to Plymouth, Coppell seems to have abandoned the idea and spent the rest of the season resolutely playing 4-4-2. He'd also told a fans' forum in August 2005 that he felt 4-4-2 would always be most effective against closely matched opposition. But another hallmark of this team was the intensity at which they played – Nick Hammond called this 'relentless' and that's a perfect description of the high-energy, fast-paced game they invariably played, always in the opponents' faces, never giving them a chance to settle.

To watch this in full-flow was quite breath-taking, and a real revelation for Reading fans after decades of relatively meagre fare, and as the team's confidence increased their play seemed to get better. But one facet of this team's make-up is quite unique, and worth looking at in more depth. As Dave Harris points out, most teams that gain promotion to the Premier League tend to do it through one or two outstanding 'Premier League-ready' players: *"You take a look at QPR, they had Adel Taarabt; you take a look at someone like Portsmouth who ended up with Paul Merson and Svetoslav Todorov – they spent heavily. Wigan spent heavily — Jason Roberts was superb."*

But this Reading side was known to many as the 'team without stars' — as we saw earlier, at the start of the season the only member of the team that most national football journalists would be able to name was Steve Sidwell. Instead of being built around a few stars the whole squad was perfectly balanced, with a mix of players who complemented each other wonderfully, and with fringe players able to step seamlessly into the team when required.

Wally Downes went further, saying of the team: *"I think it was a very symbiotic team — all the time we were there it was, you couldn't really pick out any one person, every unit worked well together. It was a perfect storm of people coming together at the right time. Steve was at the right time with his career, I was 44, I was with the lads coaching them. It was everything coming together, the boys were rarely injured and played every game; the three forwards you had up front, you weren't bothered if one was suspended or one was injured because you knew the other two were capable of doing something, never a problem up front."*

When I asked Downes to name the standout player of the season for him, his reply was telling: *"I couldn't — it's like trying to murder your darlings, isn't it? You could look back and every one of them contributed right through the team; Graham Stack, the reserve team goalkeeper; Johnny Oster, played in all the cup games. John Oster — it was a tragedy we couldn't get John in the team, he was a terrific player, he raised the standard of training every day, his technique and ability, top quality. Hunty as sub — Stephen Hunt as sub, Irish international — can't get in the team! Leroy Lita, £1 million — can't get in the team! Shane Long on the bench — can't get in the team!"*

Coppell also paid testament to the whole squad when talking to a fans' forum at the end of the season, when he said that he felt that eight or nine players had had the 'season of their careers'. He also cited the contribution of Chris Makin, who came in for Shorey in six games early in the season before himself being injured at Southampton, and who otherwise might have played 40 games but *"didn't get a look in through no fault of his own."*

Nick Hammond expanded upon the balance of the team, talking about 'teams within the team': *"You have the balance of the two centre defenders – you've got Sonko who was a man mountain, aggressive, and alongside him you had Ivar, and that's the calming, Slavic influence and the balance of the two. The goalkeeper was very, very solid, the balance of the full-backs, so you had a runner in Murts and you had a cultured left-foot in Shorey. Central midfielders balanced. You had a sort of winger in the old fashioned sense of the word* [Convey] *and then you had Glen Little who was a bit of a maverick – and then you have strikers who score."*

Ady Williams, who returned to play against this Reading team with his new club Coventry, agrees that the balance of the team was perfect: *"For me a brilliant side. The best Reading side ever ... people go back to the 70s and say a great side, they go back to our Wembley side, 94-95, which was a very good side but the 106 side was the best Reading side for me. Full of flair, energy, pace, power, goals. For me a great side – they just gelled as a team. The balance of the team was spot on, the energy was spot on. You had Ingimarsson alongside Sonko so you'd got experience and calmness with sheer determination, power and pace – that worked well. It worked quite like that when I was playing with Matty Upson – he had the pace and I had maybe a bit of organising skills and everything. You had Murty and Little – they combined so well down the line, like Convey and Shorey. In midfield? Sidwell and Harper – they're just great players and gelled well ... and the manager managed them so well, because when they won he played them again, and he played them again and again. And training must've been a joy – it's Butlin's when you're winning games, training."*

These teams within teams were a key to Reading's play – of course, the whole defensive unit was a team in themselves, coached intensively by Downes. One remarkable statistic of the Championship winning season is the disciplinary record of the back four – between them, Murty, Shorey, Sonko and Ingimarsson received only seven yellow cards all season, and the whole team suffered no red cards all season. In today's game where referees are frequently 'card-happy' and where defenders – often finding themselves the last line of defence – can easily be sent off for simply mistiming a tackle in a key area, this is a quite astounding statistic. It's also a real testament to the discipline installed in the defence by Downes, and another example of the character of the team.

I asked Downes how this discipline came about: *"That was something I drummed into them. In the meetings we used to say that over and over again – we used to work constantly on staying on your feet, not giving free kicks away because so many goals are scored from set pieces. We prided ourselves on that, not going to ground, staying up. We used to do it all the time, every match. 'It's hard enough to win a match with 11 players, don't make it ten!'"*

It was also noticeable just how well the back four moved, another example of the level of discipline within the defence. I asked Downes if any specific player had responsibility for marshalling this: *"No, that worked as a group, that was drilled in – and all four moved as one, and if one was a bit slow then he called a stop and they stayed with him. There was no signal, we worked every day – the ball moved, we moved, and they worked in relation to where the ball went and there was no signal or anything like that."*

Dave Harris believes that there was more to the paucity of yellow cards than just excellent discipline in the defence, saying: "*I think a lot of that is down to team set up. The back four under Coppell weren't got at by the opposition. Coppell's team was always based around a solid back four, back six players, and it wasn't easy to get at the back four which is why that season the disciplinary record was superb. Sonko and Ingimarsson had, in the league, two bookings between them. Suspensions-wise, that's not luck – that's design, its good defending, its good team set up. That's having good defenders who do the right thing. No question that they would have been happy to take one for the team had they needed to, but the team set-up meant they didn't need to do that.*"

When discussing the strength of the defence, Ady Williams emphasised the role that both Marcus Hahnemann and Graeme Murty played, telling me: "*Marcus always marshalled from behind. I've always loved goalkeepers that talk and Marcus was very, very vocal. None better than Neville Southall, playing for Wales, but Marcus was like a sweeper and his distribution and kicking were phenomenal. You had Ingimarsson who was such an underrated player – I've played with him and honestly he was quicker than people thought, he was better in the air than people thought, he was stronger than people thought, he was better on the ball than people thought – he was underrated so much and he was a great player, he had experience. So although Murts was marshalling, Murts was never as vocal as someone like myself but he'd been in the game a few years as well and he was an organiser – and with the help of Hahnemann and Ingimarsson and Shorey, it just worked well. They didn't concede many goals and they certainly didn't concede soft goals.*"

Williams is right – the role of Murty cannot be underestimated. At the club since 1998, as captain and elder statesman of the team he was the public face of Reading as their success mushroomed and as the world of football media took an interest in what was happening in this small corner of Berkshire. Erudite and intelligent, he was a superb ambassador for

both the club and the players, always calm and level-headed –
in many ways perfectly in tune with Coppell's tranquil
approach to management.

His early days at the club had been challenging, though.
Nigel Howe gave me his views on Murty's career at Reading:
*"Graeme was majorly important to the club. He'd started off with a bit of
a chequered career as you know, he came in as one of our most expensive
players and played at Elm Park, then got injured and then got injured
again – and everybody called him 'sicknote'. But he stuck at it and he
became part of the fabric. Graeme never moaned – he got through his
injuries, he'd work like a Trojan, he'd change shape and became this really
developed guy from a stick insect. He stopped being a winger, turned into a
full-back and just got himself sorted – and then started becoming a leader.
I heard conversations, but as people get older they change, and he changed.
People would say 'Graeme Murty, he's a bit of a wimp isn't he?' No, he
wasn't a wimp at all."*

*"He was the one who would get all the players and it was borne out
when the team all wanted him to score. It wasn't actually the crowd, it
was the team, so you got to see how important Graeme was in terms of the
fabric, and he was a great one as a player who'd talk to me and say 'come
on, you've got to get behind this, you've got to get behind that'. He's the
sort of player who I wish was still here."*

Nick Hammond told me more about Murty's role as cap-
tain: *"He was a good captain, he got things done for the group, he is a
very good player, far and away Tommy Burns best signing, and he proved
to be good value because I remember he was expensive at the time, I
remember he was a good player then. Generally the best full-backs tend to
be converted wingers, but a strong, strong runner, and again the thing
about Murts was he'd played the games, he'd got through that ... he got
another knock, another injury, he played the games."*

There is a popular feeling among fans that Murty acted as

'Coppell's conscience' on the field, making sure the game was played honestly and fairly as Coppell would want. I asked Hammond if there was any truth in this: *"I think every player recognised what was required with Steve. There were certain things that were expected and not tolerated so I think it was more of a group thing really ... Steve Bruce was maybe Alex Ferguson's man on the pitch or something like that, but I wouldn't have said that about Murty, he was just good for the group in terms of he was a focal point for them off the pitch, to get things done with the manager or with me."*

By all accounts, Murty wasn't a traditional blood and thunder captain, reading the riot act to his team in the dressing room and on the pitch. But that would tie up perfectly because we've already seen that Coppell wasn't a traditional teacup-throwing manager, so this consistency of approach between manager and captain makes sense – and the levels of intelligence in this team clearly meant that they could be talked to, rather than shouted at – although as we've seen before the Brighton match, Downes and Dillon were always available if a good old-fashioned bollocking was required!

Mark Reynolds also shared some interesting perspective views on Murty's role as both player and captain, and how Catalyst were able to assist: *"Graeme is not the most gifted of players but the crowd loved him ... Graeme was a very good leader. He didn't have the full support of all the dressing room – some players just didn't like the captain, and that is not unusual in a football team."*

"But we were honest enough to square up to that. We asked people if we needed a different approach and we asked people what they wanted the captain to be. And Graeme stepped up and did that in difficult circumstances. He was approaching the end of his career as opposed to the start of his career. He was the brunt of many a joke and many a piss-take. And he absorbed all of that and more besides."

"I think in that season and the subsequent Premier League season I would say that player Graeme went from playing at 80 percent of his capability to about 150 percent of his capability. And I think he enjoyed his football more in that season and the Premier League season than at any stage in his career."

"What did he do differently? We encouraged him to be more honest. To be more open. Not so much in what he said but in the way he handled some of the backchat, some of the background chatter."

Ron Grant agreed that Murty's voice as Captain was not the loudest in the dressing room – but also that it didn't need to be. He told me: *"He'd have his say in the dressing room. He wasn't that vociferous, that's the truth of it, but Graeme would have his say. If there was a younger player coming up, he'd go and have his chat with him and have his say ... but you had Sonko there, Kevin Doyle, Glen Little, Nicky Shorey, Ivar Ingimarsson – I mean you had some leaders. Forget Murts, you had some leaders in there anyway – and the old saying was 'you could do with a team of captains on the field, a team of leaders' and we did have quite a number in that squad that were leaders. Bags of banter!"*

On the opposite side of the pitch to Murty, fellow full-back Nicky Shorey was the principal outlet for Hahnemann. Both full-backs clearly knew what the job of defending was all about, acting as orthodox full-backs who occasionally went forward rather than as wing-backs constantly joining the attack. But as well as being crucial components of Downes' defensive team, Shorey and Murty were each also part of a team of two with the winger in front of them, invariably Convey on the left with Shorey and Little in front of Murty. The understanding along each wing was critical, and both of these pairings seemed to quickly gain an understanding close to the telepathic.

The performances of Both Convey and Little were vastly improved from the previous year, not only creating numerous chances from the flanks but also contributing with goals themselves. Part of this was down to resolution of the various minor injuries that plagued them the previous season, and much of Convey's improvement was undoubtedly down to the hard work he applied to building up his strength and presence during the pre-season – although he denied this when asked at a fans' forum in January 2006, saying that he wasn't actually any different this season, but that Coppell had now decided to play him. He said that despite how badly the previous season had gone, as he'd signed a three-year contract he was determined not to leave and give up, and also that Coppell had been very happy when Convey decide to turn down playing with the USA national team in order to spend the pre-season with Reading.

Another factor that may well have been significant was that there was now competition for places on the flanks. While Convey and Little were Coppell's first-choice wingers, the presence of Stephen Hunt and John Oster in the squad meant Coppell had four capable wingers now available and plenty of options.

These options made a real difference to Reading's effectiveness in attack. The previous season when the team often had only one effective or in-form winger on the pitch, opponents were able to easily nullify this by concentrating defence down that one side of the pitch. Two in-form wingers took away this defensive option, leaving opposing defences continually stretched and their full-backs occupied and unable to join any attacks. As a former winger himself, Coppell obviously rejoiced in good wing-play and he regularly used all the options available to him.

In fact, it became a standing joke that in virtually every match, sometime between the 55th and the 75th minute, Coppell would replace Little with Oster and Convey with Hunt, to the extent that in this Championship-winning season Hunt made just three league starts but came off the bench 35 times! As Hammond explains, it was all part of keeping up the team's intensity: *"If you look at the role that Stephen Hunt played that year with Bobby Convey – Convey would be sensational for 75 minutes, come off to a standing ovation, and Stephen Hunt would come on and run around like a screaming banshee."*

But it wasn't just the wingers who were integral parts of the midfield. In the centre the two ex-Arsenal apprentices Harper and Sidwell had formed a solid and effective partnership. Sidwell was the more dynamic and creative of the two, always ready to get involved anywhere on the pitch, and as Dave Harris explains: *"The lynchpin that every other player played around in many ways. He was everywhere, he would bomb forward – scored ten goals that season from only 29 starts, one in three. Not a bad ratio!"*

But while Sidwell got the publicity, he'd not have been able to play in this way without the industry and effort of Harper, who routinely covered more ground than any other player on the pitch but who was never fully appreciated by many of the crowd. But that's so often the fate of a team's water-carrier, the one whose efforts enable others to make their contribution but whose own contribution is often unnoticed by those who concentrate on what happens around the ball and don't see what happens off it.

Again, Harris sums it up nicely: *"People said 'Oh, he only plays it sideways – call him 'the crab'. So what? He picks up the ball off the back four, Sonko and Ingimarsson, who aren't there to be playing the ball and starting to set up attacks. He'd get the ball, he'd play it out wide, he wasn't a threaded ball-type player, he wasn't going to be playing balls across the pitch, it was 'pick it up and keep the ball moving; pick it up, keep the ball moving; pick it up, keep the ball moving'."*

"That's with the ball. Without the ball – for example if Graeme Murty or Nicky Shorey, as they were given licence to do, bombed forward and supported the attack, if the opposition picked up the ball, who did you see in that position? James Harper. Every time, James Harper. Convey, in the second half of that season, was given a licence to roam from that left-hand side and to a reasonable degree of success – if he roamed, who picked up that position? James Harper. A lot of the dirty work was done by James Harper."

This echoes what Coppell said about Harper's role and contribution at the August 2005 fans' forum, when he said that Harper is basically a defensive player, but the *"oil in the machine – if he is effective, the team is effective."* Coppell called Harper *"one of the most important pieces of our jigsaw"*, and *"our Claude Makélélé"*. Coppell also enthused about the third central midfield available to him, Brynjar Gunnarsson, who he said now gave the additional option of playing a three-man midfield.

In the end, Coppell didn't deploy this tactic, but Gunnarsson regularly stepped into the team in Sidwell's absence and proved a capable deputy, even scoring goals at crucial moments such as the brace that defeated Sheffield United in October. He's a perfect example of one of the players in the squad who didn't start as many games as they perhaps should have done, but who, as Downes says: *"Brynjar was terrific … never ever let us down"*.

In the attack, Coppell now had three in-form forwards vying for a place in the starting line-up in Doyle, Kitson and

Lita. As Coppell said in August 2005: *"In this league you need three or four good forwards in your squad"*. He now had those, and the performances of each raised the bar for the others all through the season in an on-going competition. As the cliché goes, the problem of which two out of three to select is a lovely problem for a manager to have! And of course it provides perfect cover for injuries – by some fortunate quirk of timing, in this season Coppell never had two of these three injured at the same. Each of them was injured at one time or another – and two of them out for significant periods of time – but it always seemed that an injury to one striker occurred exactly at the moment when another who'd previously been injured had recovered and was ready to play again. Plus, Shane Long was waiting in the wings as a potential fourth striker.

In particular, the discovery of Doyle was a seen by all as a masterstroke. To buy a virtually unknown Irish player for the paltry sum of £78,000, and to have them step straight into the team from the first match of the season, scoring nine goals before Christmas, was a phenomenal achievement by Hammond's scouting team as well as by team management and the player himself. At the other end of the financial spectrum, Lita had settled straight into the team just as well and was repaying his transfer fee. In particular, he'd proved that when the ball was played in front of him to run onto he was absolutely lethal – a recurring theme among the Lita goals scored, first seen away at Preston but repeated several times afterwards, was Sidwell threading a diagonal ball into the path of Lita for him to bury it in the back of the opposition net. Kitson, meanwhile, continued his rich vein of form from the previous season.

By the time of the match at Wolves on Boxing Day 2005,

these three strikers had scored 23 league goals between them, with the midfield chipping in 15 and the defence another three, a total just ten fewer than the team had scored in the whole of the previous season.

Nick Hammond summarised the importance of the strikers: *"When you look back now, there was consistency about team selection which was always one of Steve's traits – but your goal scorers were scoring and as soon as your goal scorers start scoring, you think you're in with a chance. You don't necessarily think you're going to romp away and win the championship, but you think you're in with a chance."*

But what we did that summer was – bearing in mind we took Kitson in the January before that – we took Kitson, we took Lita, we took Doyle. Now you didn't know that at the time, but we effectively put over 50 goals in the team, which as any supporter knows makes the difference."

CHAPTER ELEVEN

Take My Breath Away

THE FEAR THAT READING'S FINE form might be lost wasn't limited to pessimistic fans. It was felt just as keenly within the club and its management. Steve Coppell was asked about the regular 'mid-season dip' at a fans' forum and put it partly down to the annual deterioration of weather and resulting pitch quality affecting a team full of players who are comfortable on the ball on good-quality pitches.

But the difference between previous seasons and this one was the presence of Catalyst. Their 'pull not push' motivation had now been in effect for the best part of five months, and they had been having regular goal-setting sessions with the players since then, dividing the season into six-game 'cycles' and collectively setting targets for the next cycle.

Each of these session included a presentation from Catalyst to the players, constantly challenging them. The session before the Wolves match, facilitated by Mark Reynolds, took some players aback, though. With the team six points clear at the top of the table, undefeated in the league since the first day of the season, the message put across to the team was the need to improve. Reynolds pointed out to the team the run of really tough games coming up, starting at Wolves, and emphasised that improvement was required to see those matches out victoriously – as Reynolds said: *"If we had said 'let's keep going' I think that would have been the wrong message".*

But to add to this, Reynolds had a quite brilliant piece of motivation up his sleeve in the form of a video prepared for the players. Orchestrated by Downes but managed by Catalyst, this video came straight from Hollywood, where Vinny Jones, Downes's old Wimbledon team-mate and now enjoying a burgeoning career as a movie star, was preparing to make the movie 'Day One' alongside Jack Black. The video was a message from Jones and Black to the Reading team, which Reynolds described to me: *"Basically we scripted it for him. We said 'look we want these guys to get better'."*

Vinny Jones was blue in the extreme: "So don't you think you can sit down on your—! You have proved nothing yet! In the Wimbledon days we did this, that and the other. You know, we pulled it off – you haven't yet, all you've done is won a few games, na, na, na!"

And Jack Black would say 'is this American football?' Jack Black as you can imagine was hilarious. Really, really brilliant! [To the players] *'So – what are you going to do?' That was the build up to the Wolves game."*

Coppell also made a brave and unusual decision before this game, giving the players Christmas Day off. Ordinarily, players would be training the day before a big game like this, but Coppell again showed his respect for them as adults and his trust in them – trusting their responsibility to the utmost.

The story of the game is neatly delivered by Loyal Royal Neil Maskell, who told me about his memories of that day: *"Sweet thing about that game, we were in the pub beforehand – we were in a Wolverhampton pub and we've snuck in, we're not wearing any colours or anything like that, and the Wolverhampton fans really fancied beating us that day. 'What are Reading doing up there?' ... Reading never do well here … we always turn Reading over'. They must have been absolutely silenced because we really did them a 2-0 job. We dominated most of the game."*

Loyal Royal Dave Harris also remembers this game with great affection: *"Reading just took it in their stride, didn't they? Rocked up, snatched two goals, walked away with three points – thank you very much indeed. But the manner of the victory was brilliant. We took the game to Wolves straight away – we hit the post and bar three times in the same move in the first two minutes. And Glen Little's little dummy, just a simple drop of the shoulder that took three players out of the game, absolutely phenomenal!"*

That dummy and cross was another classic moment from this season that offered so many such moments. Just before the 30-minute mark, Little jinked to create space for himself and crossed to Kevin Doyle who he'd spotted at the far post. But before the ball reached the Irishman, Dave Kitson came steaming in to end a run that had started well outside the area by jumping between two Wolves defenders to head home. Aided by a second-half goal from Convey, Reading cruised through the match to not only secure their ninth straight league win but to also silence the doubters. As Harris says: *"A match we were almost expected to lose, it was seen very much as a real test of our mettle. We passed with flying colours, systematically dismantling a strong side and not really giving them a hope. Perfect away performance that had it all."*

As well as focussing on individual matches, Catalyst were also working to help Reading gain whatever competitive advantage they could – no matter how small it might be or however it was obtained. As Reynolds told me: *"We operated within the rules … the best example I could give of – let's say – sport manipulating its own systems is Formula One. It's Formula One's job, with the loads of money they've got, to produce a vehicle that is capable of going faster around that circuit than everybody else's. And if that means stretching or bending the rules or challenging the rules they did so. So as far as stretching/bending or challenging the rules we did them."*

Reynolds told me that this included, on occasions, changing the width of the pitch to suit Reading's game and to disadvantage an opponent's. All perfectly legal, as long as the pitch is within the required minimum and maximum width. He explained more: *"The only reason that clubs don't do it more often is the grounds man is lazy. So having painted a white line, in Reading's terms they were painting rugby lines for money. So why can't we paint a football line where we want it – as opposed to where we have to have it? Why do we have it there? Because the grounds man painted it there last time."*

Other innovations were more novel and unusual, and designed to help intimidate the opposition. Reynolds told me: *"We invested in stronger-smelling liniment. And Sonko was purposely oiled to look even more aggressive and intimidating than he did. So he looked like a black Rambo, he was just incredible! We toyed with the idea of raising our side of the tunnel by a couple of inches."*

One other innovation that seems to have been bought into by everyone – and was remarkably effective – was the use of the multi-ball system, permitted by the Football League at the time. This was where instead of having a single ball available, there were spare balls with the ball boys and girls around the pitch perimeter, so when the ball went out of play the nearest ball could be used in order to get play restarted as quickly as possible. Reynolds explained again: *"So as far as the ball boys were concerned we had an asset at home that was not being exploited. And that was if we get that ball returned quickly you can't be offside from a throw. And we had players like Doyle, Long, who were incredibly quick and we scored lots of goals from getting the ball boys to return that ball extraordinarily quickly by training. And that's not against the rules. We didn't afford the same service to the opposition but they have the ability to ask for it and they didn't – so we didn't."*

"And so if you got a corner the ball boy's job was to put that ball on the spot – and the player's job was not to jog over to the corner and take it whenever he was ready, but to take it on the fly. So typically Convey or one of the fullbacks, or Harper, would run up and take the corner on the fly. We got more goals from that because we didn't allow the opposition time to settle."

To make this happen, the teams of ball boys and girls were coached and trained to know exactly what they had to do and how to do it quickly – but I'd argue that this wasn't also offered to opposition teams. I think it was scrupulously fair – as it had to be, because opposition managers were very aware of the tactic and always looking for a reason to complain to the referee about misuse and to have multi-ball suspended for the rest of the match, as a referee had the power to do. But a ball boy or girl would throw the ball to an opposition player just as quickly as they would a Reading player, or would stand by an opposition player with the ball ready to give to them – but invariably that opponent just wasn't ready for the ball. In fact, the only game in which I remember multi-ball being suspended was when the ball boys and girls were too quick and efficient, and two balls came onto the pitch at the same time.

This use of multi-ball was just another factor of the pace that the team played with, and which Nicky Hammond described it as: *"A relentless team, that's what the team was, it was relentless. That's a good word, I like that – you just keep going, and keep going, and keep going."*

A flavour of what it was like to face is provided by Ady

Williams, who returned to the MadStad as part of the Coventry City defence in January 2006. *"I remember playing here, you did not get a breather, you did not get a rest. As soon as the ball went out, bang, it was back in play – even on the corners. They had a corner, the ball boy or girl would put it on the corner, Glen Little would sprint to it, Ingimarsson and Sonko sprinted up and he would just whip it in. You never had a moment's respite!"*

It was noticeable that Reading always started each match at a very high tempo, and then about 10 minutes before halftime they raised the tempo again – I asked Hammond whether this was a set tactic, and he explained 'the growler' to me. He told me: *"We had this thing, another thing that Catalyst did, called the growler. We looked at the goals and conceding of goals – and the season before we'd conceded a number of goals in that last five minutes before half time, so one of the things they did with the players, the developed this shout which was called growler. If Murty or one of the senior pros shouted 'growl', it was like a message for everyone to say 'come on, we've just dropped our tempo, we've just dropped our hand'."*

However, according to Reynolds, the growler was more about communicating any tactical change than just raising the tempo. *"When it came to challenging the coaching team to invent a communication system of how to change tactics on the pitch with a one-word message from the touch line, no whistles, no waving, no shouting, no screaming, just one word communicated from the bench to the player closest. The player closest had five seconds to get that word to every player on the pitch for the effective switch of strategy."*

"And the word was 'growler'. So if Wally typically shouted 'growler' those nearest to him – Convey, Sidwell, Harper – had five seconds to communicate it to every single player on that pitch. So the shout across the pitch just rippled across and within five seconds Reading had changed strategy in that game."

"We didn't set the strategy. We weren't saying all right we will play 4-4-2 diamond for the next 15 minutes, nothing to do with us. So when the coaching team said if we're one-nil up, nil-nil, one-nil down, what we want to do in the last 15 minutes of the first half is ... our involvement was okay if that's what you want to do, how do we execute? So we invented a system or we challenged the coaching team to invent a system. It was their idea to call it 'growler'."

The name 'growler', in case you were wondering, came from an incident involving Reynolds's youngest son. He had been playing in a local seven/eight-year-olds' match and, when being marked closely by a lad much bigger than him, had suddenly turned around and growled at his marker – disorientating him so much that he forgot his marking duties and allowed Reynolds's son to head in the winning goal and be a hero. Reynolds told that story in passing conversation to the dressing room, and from that day onwards his son, who attended matches with him, was known to the players and coaches as 'growler'. When a name was needed for this communication system, 'growler' was the one chosen.

With the predicted Boxing Day upset at Wolves well and truly avoided, the season carried on in the same style as it had before Christmas. Two days after the Wolves match, Reading beat Leicester 2-0 at home to achieve their tenth league win in a row. Three days later, though, the winning run came to an end with a 2-2 draw away at Derby, secured through an 88th minute goal from Shane Long, making only his second substitute appearance for Reading – a goal that, at the end of the season, Steve Coppell told a fans' forum was his favourite of the many scored that season, summarising it as an excellent move, an excellent cross and an excellent headed finish. He also commented on the real blend and variety of goals scored – team goals, individual efforts and set pieces, as well as the quality of many of them, in contrast to the previous season where there was hardly a goal scored 'out of the blue'. He was asked what in particular happened at halftime in this game to make Reading's second-half performance so much better than the first. He said that the players are always challenged to 'win both halves' of every game, and at halftime against Derby the mantra was to win the second half. He added that five minutes of the team's best football can win a game, and in this one the team produced 20 minutes of it – what he called *"some startling football which showed our capabilities"*.

Almost as a reaction to not having won that match, in their next match at home to Cardiff two days later Reading put in what was possibly one of their most outstanding performances in a season chock-full of outstanding ones. Showing stunning creativity, pace and fluidity they completely dominated Cardiff –eighth in the league – to annihilate them 5-1. It's not hyperbole to say that this scoreline flattered the visitors – this really was one of the most complete performances I've ever seen from any team – and certainly from Reading. Cardiff weren't bad and did threaten Reading at times, but just couldn't live with the pace and the sheer quality of Reading's play. The performance was even more unbelievable considering it was Reading's fourth match in eight days.

The season continued in the same style with a win over Coventry notable for some spectacular goalkeeping from Hahnemann as Coventry threw everything at Reading for a brief period to no avail. But that was part of the dilemma facing opposing managers setting up team against Reading – try to defend and you'd find yourself under almost continual pressure; try to attack and you'd find yourself being cut to pieces as Reading counter-attacked at pace and in numbers!

The same applied in the FA Cup that January, as a Reading team that was again much-changed, drew 1-1 with West Bromwich Albion at The Hawthorns and then won the replay 3-2, despite having been 2-0 down at halftime. Another fluid performance was topped off by a superb Leroy Lita hat-trick, and Reading had dumped a Premier League team out of the Cup, as well as having reassured many fans that they'd be able to hold their own at the higher level the next season – nine points clear at the top of the Championship, and an incredible 21 points clear of Leeds in third place – promotion was no longer being talked about as 'if' but was now 'when'.

Before January was out, though, there was another landmark game to face at Crystal Palace on a Friday night – of course, Sky TV had caught on to Reading and so matches rescheduled for TV broadcast with resulting inconvenience for travelling supporters were now regular annoyances. After the humdinger from a few months ago, this match was eagerly awaited, especially by Palace fans whose team was on a run of six straight wins.

In many ways this was a similar game to the away draw at Southampton, in that Reading spent most of the match soaking up pressure from the home team, but this game was different as it did have goals. Loyal Royal Alex Everson remembers this as his favourite match of the season: *"Reading played a tight defensive game against a Palace side fighting for a play-off spot with an in form Andy Johnson up front (who always seemed to score against us!). Reading battled away, and late in the game, about ten minutes left, Johnson smashed the ball into the stand before being bought down by Hahnemann. He tucked away a penalty and celebrated in front of a few thousand angry Reading fans."*

"The highlight, though, came a few minutes later when under the low roof we saw Glen Little play a ball forwards to Leroy Lita, who touched it off and played it off with a neat back heel to James Harper – who drove it past Kiraly into the top corner and saved the 28 unbeaten game streak. A moment to behold in the stands, and cue the Reading away fans going crazy in those terrible wooden seats!"

Dave Harris also remembers that turnaround with great affection: *"The Andy Johnson penalty ten minutes from time, they thought they'd won it ... but as is typical with Reading that season, it was almost as though the team were saying 'what the hell do you think you're doing?' and going up the other end and notching one themselves."*

Moving onwards, Reading won their next two league matches, scoring four goals in both, although the fluent, fast-paced 4-0 home defeat of Norwich was much more comfortable than the slight scare experienced in the 4-3 win over bottom-placed Crewe, who started the game 54 points behind Reading.

In February the FA Cup team – weakened even further as Coppell confirmed his view that the Cup was an unwelcome distraction this season – lost to Birmingham in a fourth round replay, having drawn 1-1 in the home tie. A 2-0 victory over Southampton and a predictably feisty draw at Sheffield United – where Dave Kitson missed an injury-time penalty – took Reading's unbeaten league run to 33 matches.

But just three days later – thanks to Sky TV's scheduling again – the run finally came to an end. Looking tired, and with Little and Sidwell rested, Reading faced a determined Luton Town team at Kenilworth Road and were beaten 3-2, despite Kevin Doyle giving Reading a first minute lead after being given the ball straight from the kick-off. It was an odd and scarce-remembered feeling to come away with a defeat – in fact it had not happened to Reading since 6th August the previous year, 194 days or over 27 weeks earlier. There could be no complaints, though – Luton deserved their win – and Reading were still 12 points clear of second place Sheffield United and 21 points ahead of Leeds in third place.

Dave Harris remembers that the next match, home to Preston, had suddenly gained an added significance: *"We'd just lost to Luton – second time we'd lost all season. People were thinking 'bang, Reading gone!' Preston were on their own 22 match unbeaten run and we beat them. They were looking good, took an early lead, immediately equalised by Preston – but another huge game that we needed to win and we did win. And generally, the huge games that we needed to win, we did win."*

Going into March, Reading went to Burnley and came away with a 3-0 victory, although this was marred by Lita departing the field on a stretcher with a broken ankle – the team's first really significant injury of the season. Two more draws – an inevitable 0-0 against Watford and 1-1 at home to Wolves – left Reading 20 points ahead of third-placed Leeds and 22 ahead of Watford a place behind them – teams that both had eight games left to play, a game in hand over Reading.

The majority consensus was that promotion would most likely be gained in the first week or two of April, but when Leeds lost their game in hand the following Tuesday evening, promotion the following Saturday – away at Leicester City – became a mathematical possibility. Tickets had already been on sale for a few weeks and few were left, but suddenly there was a scramble for tickets of Cup Final proportions as it became clear that the impossible dream was, at long last, in sight.

CHAPTER TWELVE

Do You Remember the First Time?

CATALYST CONTINUED TO USE ALL their skills and experience to help motivate the players through this period. But as the season went on, although there were still regular objective setting meetings with the group, the emphasis of these changed slightly to reflect how the team was performing and how the season was developing.

For instance, a month after the Vinnie Jones-inspired motivation message before the Wolves match, Catalyst's message was a simple one, designed to keep the team's standards up. Mark Reynolds talked me through the presentation given to the players, which as usual included statistics of the season so far, shown graphically. Those showed the progress towards the team's target of promotion and the Championship title – and this graph also showed the progress made by Sunderland when they set the record points total for this division of 105 points in 1999 – a remarkably similar line to Reading's progress.

The message from Reynolds to the players, as he repeated it to me, was: *"You're doing well. There is the target. So you're not doing as well as you think! So for us what we are saying is be careful – don't get cocky!"*

"We have got 73 [points], it was 70 was last season. This is what

Sunderland did. *This is how similar your performance is to their
performance. This is the previous winners of the league, can you beat
them? And that very quickly became: 'We want that!'."*

"*So well done – but now we want you to be ruthless. Because if you
in any way get comfortable there is a kind of flatline. People will say you
are doing well, you are invited out. Do you want to be a Premiership
footballer? If you do you are in the right place; if you don't leave the room
now. So we want you to intimidate. And there was a lot of debate about
this word 'intimidate', because there were various interpretations to it. So
what do you mean by that? You have got to frighten, you've got to be
unbeatable in your behaviour. You've got to prepare better, you have got to
warm up better, you've got to line up better. Those huddles in the middle of
the pitch need to become louder.*"

"*So intimidate, focus, perform, be your best you can be, nothing's
changed – win the next game. We have got to win three points. You have
come this far, finish the job!*"

For the next match, against Norwich, Catalyst also organised a surprise for the players. When they came out for the
game, they were greeted by all the Reading fans in the
stadium waving 'Bring It On!' placards and chanting the same
message. Predictably, opinions in the crowd were mixed – for
everyone who thought it was a novel way of supporting the
team, there was someone else, perhaps a more 'traditional'
supporter, who hated the thought of anything organised. And,
as always happens, some of the more vocal took to the internet
to share with the world just how 'embarrassed' they were by
this – although can anyone with a properly developed sense of
perspective really be 'embarrassed' by anything a football club
does?

The memories of Loyal Royal Neil Maskell, who was one
of the volunteers helping out that day, demonstrate vividly the

split in supporter attitudes: *"STAR* [Supporters' Trust At Reading] *sent an email to members asking for help on behalf of the club with a pre-match campaign. They were unable to give specific details so curiosity killed this particular cat and I volunteered. We met a couple of hours before kick-off and were ushered into the Lower West where we met a rather corporate-looking and serious type who told us we would be handing out 'Bring It On!' placards to each of the 18,000 Reading supporters expected to attend that night."*

"My heart sank at what I assumed was another club gimmick – those of us of a certain vintage will recall the club's attempts at manufacturing a pantomime atmosphere with the short-lived introduction of 'Rumblestix'. The corporate chap insisted that walking out to a sea of placards and a crowd chanting 'Bring It On!' would give the players a huge boost ahead of the run in. So I took it as seriously as I could."

"I handed out placards to spectators as they arrived at Gate Eight. Most took them with an air of inquisitiveness, many asked what it was all in aid of. A minority refused to take them – more than a handful rather brusquely so."

In the event, I don't think many of those up in arms appreciated that the 'Bring It On!' slogan wasn't one that had been thought up by the club's marketing team or by the Supporters' Trust. Instead, it was a slogan the players used in their warm-ups and a theme developed with Catalyst, but the desire to surprise the players meant there was no pre-match publicity and so the origin of the slogan was never well publicised to many supporters.

But although this may not have been fully understood by most supporters, it was certainly appreciated by the players, who reacted in great style with an effortless, high-quality 4-0 victory. In the words of Reynolds, as a reaction to this and the challenge issued to be careful and not to be cocky: *"Going into*

February, they pushed on."

'Bring It On' was just one innovation involving the crowd that Catalyst was involved in, working with both the Stewards and the Supporters' Trust. Reynolds told me about work involving the stewards to manage away crowds: *"The stewards – bless them – were guys that managed the ground. Reading's crowd was abhorrently silent apart from, oddly, one section of the crowd in the East Stand. Normally the crowd is at either end. The away support was gifted the whole of one end. Why do we gift all that space and let them sit back? Why don't we just bung them in the top corner like Newcastle do or like Manchester United do? So we recruited the stewards to manage the crowd in a different way. We didn't pay them more money. We just said 'we are trying to win games here, you could help'. They liked to help and they said 'we would love to'. So we engaged the support of some of the most committed supporters anyway – the stewards love what they do. We just cut them into the plan."*

This crowd management included measures like controlling where away supporters were positioned in the away end, although of course this could only be done when the away club's ticket allocation was not fully sold. Reynolds also took credit for the introduction of the drummer in the stadium (another 'marmite' innovation that supporters either loved or hated) and other attempts to get the crowd to make more noise: *"There were loads of things. We had the drummer organised by the stewards; we had the 'Bring It On' campaign; we had 'loud and proud'. And if the stewards felt that the crowd could do more we asked the stewards to help get that crowd up and going."*

"And we managed to turn Reading from a quite polite, almost church-like environment to a noisy place, and it got easier when we were winning. But the more we won the louder we got. And when we weren't winning they were just as loud, if not louder. If I had played you a soundtrack in

the previous season with a similar number of points and the same period the volume was about 100 percent better."

On this point, as a member of that crowd, I'd take issue with Reynolds. Yes, the crowd was loud for most of that season, and sometimes extremely loud, but I'm not convinced that this was down to outside attempts to get them to create noise. Instead, I think it was the quality of the football, the drama and the passion and the sheer emotion of seeing the team doing so well that created atmosphere – seeing the players completely committed to the cause will always have the same effect in a football crowd, and I'm sure this atmosphere came far more from the team than from anywhere else. It's a misnomer to say that Reading's crowds are always quiet, as they can be extremely noisy, but they just need to be roused by something, and generally a sense of righteous injustice does this perfectly – they were as loud as I've ever heard them when Sheffield United's 'keeper Paddy Kenny wasn't sent off in the top-of-the-table clash in November 2005. Conversely though, long before Catalyst arrived, way back in May 2001 when Nicky Forster transformed the play-off semi-final against Wigan, the atmosphere was electric and the noise from the Reading crowd deafening.

I think, as well, that in trying to organise the crowd to be noisier, Reynolds (like many others before and after him) failed to appreciate the fact that those in a football crowd who are likely to make the most noise and to show the greatest passion are precisely those who go to football because they're attracted to the spirit of rebellion of the game – and attend matches as a way to escape routine, everyday life and authority. They are therefore precisely the ones least likely to conform to any attempts to 'organise' them – for them, spontaneity is everything!

When speaking to Sir John Madejski, I asked him how important the supporters' contribution at this time was: *"Oh enormous, because the fans are the number 13 shirt* [a reference to Reading allocating a squad number to the fans], *the fans are so instrumental if they can be positive. We can't orchestrate that but they've shown their mettle ... I think the fans have to appreciate that they do play such a role in the fortunes of Reading because when they get behind their team it makes all the difference. I've always found it very difficult really because having known the Northern clubs and how enthusiastic they are, we are a bit timid in the South, especially the South East. But to persuade them to be vocal and get behind the team was quite challenging. You never get the fans to do what you want them to do, it has to be spontaneous – if you give them songs it's worked a few times but largely thinking they have to think of it, which is great ... but I suppose when the team's doing well it just comes naturally – but sometimes you'd like them to be a bit more vocal, a bit more helpful to the team and back them up because they can make a huge difference."*

By the time the objective-setting session for cycle seven of the season, it was 6th March and Reading had a 20 point cushion from the third-placed team, and the target for promotion had been coming down all the time as Reading picked up points and the clubs chasing them failed to. It would have been so easy for the team to ease off and coast to promotion, but again there was a drive to keep the team aiming high and giving everything.

Reynolds told me about the presentation he gave to the players that day to help ensure that happened: *"In the end that promotion target came down all the time, of course, but even before promotion the target had changed to the 106. And as the team got on that it became achievable. So – no apologies – we dangled it."*

"We said 'you said – and you obligated yourselves – to deliver. You have set the objectives this season, we haven't. We have asked you to set the objectives. You said you wanted to create history. Well, that is 17 points – or you are full of shit. Eleven points will get you promoted, nine games left. Fourteen should see you be champions mathematically."

"But you said you wanted to create history. You don't have to! So here is your sheet of paper."

Wally Downes explained why these targets for each cycle of the season were important: *"That [March] was when we could have really eased it off, but they had the targets of a 100 goals or a 100 points or whatever it was, and the Championship virtually secured by then – but you still had to keep going."*

"Everywhere I went, all the people I know in the game, staff and coaches and managers were saying – even sort of October/November time – good team, you're going to do it'. But then come Christmas they were saying 'you've done it, it's going to take a proper melt-down for you to knock this up' – and you start looking at it and think perhaps they're right. That's why you have to keep those short-term objectives and goals with the players – because it's there, but it's easily fucked up, if you know what I mean. Everyone's looking at you to see if you can maintain this."

But it wasn't just inside the club that people weren't counting their chickens. This is Reading, after all – the club that finished second in the table and didn't get promoted, and the club that lost their only two play-off finals from where they looked home and dry. So despite their team's comfortable lead at the top of the table, many Reading fans had their own theories about bizarre ways in which things might still go wrong – my own personal dread, which ten years later sounds ridiculous, was that the bird-flu epidemic that tabloid papers had been trumpeting for the best part of a year would finally strike, with the fear of contagion causing the rest of the season to be abandoned and all results expunged!

Despite all these far-fetched fears, on 25th March 2006 the team went to that match against Leicester City, in what was then The Walkers Stadium, with the declared target of 106 points and 100 goals. With 3,000 Reading fans in the away corner of the ground – and several hundred more, at least, incognito and sitting on their hands all around the home areas of the ground – there was a real air of expectation but also of nerves. Those nerves showed in the players, who had drawn the previous two matches, and who were largely outplayed by Leicester in the first half and went in at halftime a goal down after an unstoppable long-range goal scored in the 38th minute.

On the concourse at halftime, the 'if it can go wrong it will go wrong' attitudes of Reading fans came to the fore again, with a subdued atmosphere and many looking shell-shocked that Reading were 1-0 down – for only the third and final time that season – and might not seal the deal on that particular day. As Neil Maskell told me: *"I remember feeling that the atmosphere at halftime that day felt just like post-match Wembley 1995 and Cardiff 2001 play-offs. My own heart sank. I felt like slapping myself for being a drama queen but given all the disappointments before there was an anxiety that the job needed to be done ASAP. All this contrasted with pre-match, which had a carnival atmosphere in the concourses and people openly celebrating already! Reading fans fearing the worst shocker!"*

The second half started in the same way, but Reading gradually got more into the game, and after a number of substitutions, especially the arrival of Stephen Hunt ten minutes from the end, were exerting more and more pressure on the Leicester defence. After 85 minutes, the latest in a series of corners was taken by James Harper, flicked on by Ivar Ingimarsson, and Kevin Doyle rose to equalise at the far post before sprinting to celebrate in front of the exultant Reading fans. Once again this season Reading had left it late to turn around a game that was itself fairly mediocre and uneventful. The final whistle went, the players trooped off to the dressing room and everybody waited.

It was a bizarre couple of minutes – although in my memory it seems like ten or 15 minutes it was probably just one or two, but no-one knew what was happening. Anyone there will probably remember a raucous shout of *"just give us the fucking results"* – and that single demand summed up the wishes of every one of the 3,000 in that period as rumours and counter-rumours circulated wildly but no-one actually knew the crucial scores of the matches involving Leeds and Watford.

After that age, over the PA came five immortal words that all Reading fans will remember for ever: *"congratulations Reading on your promotion!"* Sheer, undiluted joy erupted among the Reading supporters, and the Leicester supporters still in the ground broke into genuine applause. I can't start to capture on paper the depths of emotions reached that day – the joy and over-powering elation, the tears, the hugs with strangers, the whole stadium shaking as 3,000 Reading fans leapt and danced in unison – it really was one of those events where you had to be there.

Shortly afterwards, the team and coaches came out and celebrated on the pitch and with the fans, spraying champagne and throwing items of kit into the crowd. At the same time, those Reading 'lurkers' gravitated from the home sections of the ground to the corner that was the focus of celebrations – all credit is due to the Leicester ground authorities for allowing them to do this, and their tolerance and flexibility for allowing the celebrations to carry on unhindered until they reached their natural end, a good hour after the final whistle.

Before returning to the pitch, though, the players and coaches had suffered the same hiatus of uncertainty as the supporters, while they waited to hear if promotion had been achieved. Ron Grant shared with me what it was like to be in the dressing room that day: *"The real highlight was that we'd actually gone in the dressing room, not knowing if we'd got promotion – and then they said we are promoted so we were back out there on that far side to see the Reading crowd up in that corner. My son – he'd got a ticket, but he wasn't with the Reading crowd, but he was on that side, and he actually was down the front, and the Leicester crowd had almost gone, but he'd gone down the front and he said to the steward 'I've got to shout to my dad' and he gave me a shout. But also at that time the players had done their traditional dives on the deck and forward. Also what stands out was Steve Coppell had a coat on and he said 'is it alright if I throw this in the crowd' to me? I said to him 'do what you like with it' and he threw it up into the crowd and one of the supporters got it and probably still guards it to this day. I mean, he didn't have to ask permission, did he? But that was the respect he had for the gear, the kit and the club."*

Everyone who was there that day has a story to tell; Loyal Royal Linda Dubber, for instance, recalls most of all: *"The pure joy on everyone's faces, the stand actually moving due to us all jumping about – it was the best moment and one that will never be replicated unless we win the Champions League."* Michele Mead remembers most of all: *"The moment after the results were announced at Leicester from the other games, making my friend cry because I had refused to sing 'we are going up' at all throughout the season and seeing me sing it made it real to him, much more than anything else had."*

Dave Harris also remembers 25th March 2006 vividly:

"The raptures in that stand, I'll remember them all the way to my grave. At the end it was all a bit of an anti-climax, no celebrations, just anxious waiting around to find out what Watford and Leeds had done. Then – jubilation. Sheer, unbridled jubilation! Tears from people I thought I'd never see cry; jumping around, singing and chanting abound. An hour later, on the way back to the car, a burger van was still selling. Hungry from all the exertion of celebrating I bought one, then immediately identified a car of Reading fans, got them to wind down the window, pointed to the burger and said 'This … is the world's first Premier League burger!" – chomped down on it to horn beeping and cheers from inside the car. Then proceeded to have what is almost certainly the most unanimously good-natured night out in town ever, ending in the Purple Turtle. John Madejski, no less, pissed as a fart on Kronenbourg, serving; one of my best friends crying in the beer garden. Wonderful memories – memories I am certain I will tell my children and grandchildren. My family knows what Reading Football Club means to me, and I'm so, so proud to be able to say when Reading were first promoted to the Premier League 'I was there!'."

Although John Madejski nearly didn't make the game himself. He explained to me: *"I was in India and I got a phone call from my then PA, Paula, and she said 'we're playing Leicester at the weekend, if we win or draw we'll then be promoted to the Premier League" – and I was in India. So anyway, I cut short my holiday and left my friends there and just got back in time to go to Leicester to see that fantastic 1-1 draw, which was probably the highlight of my tenure of Reading Football Club, the sheer joy … that was my mission completed, really, I mean my mission statement had always been to get promoted, to play the top flight in this country and that season I was able to achieve it, so to me it was job done and to do it with such style, such panache, such a way, was just the cream on top of the cream."*

One of the other main architects of this team, though, wasn't at Leicester. Nick Hammond had been off scouting players when the results all unexpectedly combined to mean promotion happened sooner than expected. Hammond told me: *"I'm 99.9 percent sure I was coming back from Cardiff and I was driving down the M4 and I put Radio Berkshire on and I just remember coming down and I had tears coming out of my eyes thinking 'wow!' Because it was history, wasn't it – and I wasn't there. And that's sort of my way a little bit, to keep a little bit away, but as you say it was the way the results conspired but I always remember driving down the M4 thinking 'wow!' Don't quote me on the crying …"* Sorry, Nick, but if I have a few tears in my eyes from remembering that day then I think that's perfectly reasonable to share.

It was striking, the reaction from other clubs and other sets of supporters, who almost all responded with magnanimous congratulations – there was something about this Reading team, the way they played and their attitude that meant they weren't disliked in the way that successful teams often are. Countless Reading fans tell stories about receiving praise and best wishes from supporters of other teams whose paths they crossed in motorway services on the journey back, while I had an experience after the match that for me sums up just how much the football world took Reading to their hearts that day.

Before the game we'd parked in one of the less affluent parts of Leicester, and heading back to it at well past 6.00 pm, still shell-shocked from the experience and the elation of promotion, we saw a group of around eight or ten teenage 'wannabees' in Leicester shirts. They'd obviously seen us in our Reading shirts, and were planning something between them, so when we got closer we were bracing ourselves for some 'banter' – or worse. Instead, they lined both sides of the pavement in a spontaneous 'guard of honour', applauding as we walked between them! A completely unexpected and almost surreal gesture, and one of my fondest memories from over 40 years of watching football.

At the end-of-season fans' forum, Steve Coppell also spoke about salutations received, saying there had been a flood of congratulations, the first from Rafa Benitez at Liverpool and with compliments on the team's style of play received from Alex Ferguson. Coppell said that in the Championship it was possible to lose a third of your matches and still have a successful season, so the team was receiving considerable respect for only losing two matches all season. He also told the meeting that the most poignant letter he received was from his doctor when he was a young boy back home in Liverpool, who'd been asked by Coppell's mother to prescribe something to help him grow.

As Harris has outlined, the celebrations went on long and loud all through Berkshire and the surrounding area that weekend – again this is where all supporters have their own particular promotion story to tell.

But as well as the celebrations there was a profoundly emotional aspect to promotion, too. Immediately after it was confirmed, a very moving thread appeared on the leading Reading fansite '*Hob Nob Anyone?*'. The author of this thread started it in memory of their father, who'd introduced him to watching Reading many years earlier and with whom he'd always gone to matches, but who was no longer alive to share in the joy and celebration of promotion. In the days that followed many more posters added to this, with heartfelt and emotional tributes to family and friends who'd supported the team all their lives, but weren't able to witness the miracle of promotion. Scrolling through the entries on this thread was a deeply moving experience, showing just what football means to people and how closely it's linked to friends and family. All the surveys among supporters show that the single biggest factor that introduces fans to the team they support is being introduced to it by family members, especially, or by friends – and this thread proved that, and how deep the emotional roots linked to football go, in the most poignant way possible.

But despite Reading being promoted to the Premier League on 25th March – the earliest this has ever been achieved – there were still six matches left in the season and a record points target to chase.

CHAPTER THIRTEEN

Once in a Lifetime

IF THE STORY OF THIS season were to be written as a Hollywood script, the writer would probably have come up with an idealised but saccharin storyline where just seven days after the away fans got to celebrate promotion at Leicester, the home fans got to celebrate the Championship being won at the MadStad. The script would probably have been rejected as just too contrived and too schmaltzy, but reality didn't care about such niceties, and that's exactly what happened seven days later on April 1st 2006 the when Reading played Derby at home.

Their first half performance was slightly slow and visibly more nervous than usual, but once James Harper broke free and scored just before the hour mark, they relaxed, started enjoying themselves and simply swept Derby aside. Scoring five goals in 24 minutes, they upped their performance to a level their visitors just couldn't compete with. Kevin Doyle scored his 17th goal of the season, John Oster scored his first and Shane Long came off the bench with 18 minutes to go in the game and scored twice in 11 minutes to complete the rout. It was a stylish, confident display, one that Wally Downes nominated as one of his highlights of the season, calling it a 'terrific performance'. The three points it gained took Reading up to 95 after 41 games – and ensured the Championship itself as Sheffield United had drawn 1-1 at home to Stoke and were now 16 points adrift of Reading.

At the final whistle, the players dashed off as a veritable flood of humanity appeared to flow across the pitch from the East Stand – a dramatic sight and one that must be frightening to see from pitch level. The joy was just as unrestrained as the previous week in Leicester, except this time there were 20,000 fans celebrating instead of 3,000 or so. The celebrations were just as raucous, and centred on the balcony of the directors' box, where all the players appeared after a short while. John Madejski, who was also on the balcony, recalled: *"I'll never forget when we had the pitch invasion when we won 5-0 against Derby and it was just – the whole place was electric, you could just cut the atmosphere with a knife, it was so darn good."*

With five matches left, Reading needed 11 points out of a possible 15 to break Sunderland's all-time points record, and with both promotion and the Championship they secured this target, plus the accompanying target of 100 goals were all Reading had to play for the following week as they travelled to Cardiff. For Dave Harris this game is one that really stands out. He recalled: *"After we'd beaten Derby to tie up the Championship, many people in the press and across the fanbase and across the footballing family were saying Reading were going to be taking their foot off the gas. We go to Cardiff and what do we do? Notch five!"*

As usual, Coppell put out his strongest team for this match, and they delivered another fine performance. Although two up by halftime, and three ahead just seven minutes later, Reading did allow Cardiff to score twice in the second half. So Reading did what this Reading team tended to do when someone had the impudence to score against them – they went down the other end and scored two more to win 5-2. This was the fifth league match in which they'd scored five goals, one of the previous instances also being against Cardiff who they'd beaten 5-1 at the MadStad in January.

For Loyal Royal Rob Langham, this game was an eye-opener: *"Bizarrely, the moment when the penny dropped that this team was so good didn't come until a 5-2 win away to Cardiff City in the final weeks. Prior to that, so much of the underlying narrative from fans of other clubs and the press was that this was some kind of fluke – from Sunderland supporters I overheard on a London tube train, from Nigel Quashie stating that he knew Southampton were better than us after a hard fought 0-0 draw in the autumn, from Rowan Vine tying us up in knots in that second league defeat of the season at Kenilworth Road, I just didn't believe the team had that much quality. Of course there were momentous performances aplenty. But to go to one of the toughest grounds in the division, a location where Reading had always found it tough, and to blow away the opposition to the tune of five goals, with nothing riding on the result – well, that really made me sit up and take notice."*

One interesting fact that was first noticed towards the end of the season was that every single regular outfield player in this Reading team had scored a league goal, with one exception – Graeme Murty. As a result, whenever the ball came close to Murty, wherever he was on the pitch, the crowd would urge him loudly to 'SHOOT!!!!' – and at the fans' forum the same week as the Cardiff match Coppell was asked if Murty would ever score and what he could do to make this happen. His response was to say that Murty tends to have a shot once every ten games – a shot that is *"normally from long range and normally well wide of goal"* and when asked if he would consider playing Murty up front to help him get that elusive goal, he said he would never do that as he felt it would be disrespectful to the opposition.

A week later, away at Leeds on Easter Saturday, was a 1-1 draw, rescued by a late Stephen Hunt header, with Wally Downes telling the press after the game that staying unbeaten for the rest of the season was more important than beating Sunderland's 105 points, a target by now much talked about. Reading now had 99 points with three games left, and 93 goals scored. That draw, incidentally, ensured that Leeds could no longer catch up with Sheffield United, so Neil Warnock undoubtedly suffered some real mixed feelings at the knowledge that his team's promotion was finally made certain by the actions of his arch rivals!

Two days later, with Stoke the visitors for Reading's penultimate home match, Coppell rotated his squad – partly to give many of his first-term regulars a rest after playing on the Saturday, and partly with the aim to allow some of the fringe players a chance to participate in front of the home crowd. Murty was one of those rested, and so didn't get a chance to get his name on the scoresheet – but John Halls, signed from Stoke the previous January and playing his first and only league match for Reading, did, scoring the third in a comfortable 3-1 win that took Reading to 102 points and 96 goals.

Five days later, Reading fans were rapturous as they celebrated the season at Sheffield Wednesday with their traditional horde of inflatables – anything that could realistically be blown up and thrown around was blown up and thrown around the Hillsborough away end. On the pitch, things were less memorable, though, and Reading only picked up a single point after another 1-1 draw – and they only managed that through a dramatic goal line saving header from John Oster late in the match.

The team now just needed a win from their final match to break Sunderland's record, and three goals to reach a century of points. This match was against Queen's Park Rangers, and STAR, the Reading Supporters' Trust, had for a number of weeks been planning an event at this to celebrate promotion – this was to be 'Raise the Hoops', an initiative to have fans hold up coloured plastic banners before the match to fill the stadium with blue and white hoops. By a quirk of fixture-compilation fate, even the visiting supporters could participate in this display with a clear conscience!

In the days leading up to the match, which was on the Sunday afternoon of a bank holiday weekend, Reading was the centre of press attention. Predictably the chase for the points and goals records was a topic of much interest, but just as much focus was on the on-going question of whether Murty would put the ball in the net. All season, as captain, he had been a perfect press spokesman for the team and the club, and well known in the media as a result so this question was almost tailor-made as a matter of press interest. In his many inter-views, one message came across loud and clear from Murty – if he did score, then *"that lion* [Kingsley, the team mascot] *was going to get it!"*

On the day of the match, STAR's 'Raise the Hoops' worked like a dream, creating a memorable spectacle around the ground as the teams came out – and a fair proportion of the visiting QPR fans did join in, so at least some of the hoops went all the way around the ground.

The game itself was just as entertaining, with Reading playing well in the first half and Dave Kitson scoring a 40th minute goal that was created by a lovely interplay down the left from Convey and Shorey. But the home team failed to extend this lead and with 18 minutes to go QPR equalised and threatened to spoil the party.

But this is where that Hollywood scriptwriter who special-ises in idealised and saccharin storylines took over. With time running out, a Shorey cross from the left hit the arm of Rangers midfielder Langley in the box. Whether it was deliberate or not is a moot point, but the referee gave the penalty anyway, and there was no question in anyone's mind who was going to take it! If the ball hadn't been given to Murty, there would likely have been a riot. After what seemed an interminable delay while the referee dealt with the protests of the away players, Murty put the ball on the spot and stepped forward to take the penalty that, if scored, would give Reading the all-time points record of 106, as well as give him his first goal since March 2001, five year and two months and 236 matches ago. No pressure!

The silence that enveloped the ground as he approached the ball turned into a tumultuous roar as, cool as anything, he blasted the ball into the net and turned to head after Kingsley. But seven-foot tall lions wearing fake football boots are no match for professional footballers in a race, and soon Murty had bundled Kingsley over, shortly to be joined in a pile by his ten teammates as the whole ground went wild.

The game was over shortly afterwards, and after the match Murty's next role was to hold up the Championship trophy in the presentation ceremony that followed the game, and subsequent laps of honour. Then the euphoria continued the next day with an open-top bus parade from the town centre to the MadStad and further laps of honour and trophy-lifting around the stadium – all of this watched by over 80,000 people to the strains of Neil Diamond's 'Sweet Caroline'. At a training week in Marbella in the first week of April, celebrating promotion and the championship, Glen Little's enthusiasm for this song had infected the rest of the squad, and it had now become an unofficial 'theme song' of promotion and the championship.

The team had beaten the all-time points total of 105, and had scored 99 goals – not scoring just one more represented the only 'failure' to hit an objective of the season, but under the circumstances of everything else achieved no-one was too devastated by this. But some of the other statistics of this season are quite phenomenal. No sendings off and no suspensions all season; just a single booking each for both of the centre-backs, who also played in every single league match; just 18 players started for the team all season with an additional four who substitute appearances – and of the 18 starters, eight players made 40 or more appearances, while 16 of the 18 players scored goals, four of them scoring ten times or more. Truly an all-round team performance. The margin of victory was astounding – 16 points ahead of second placed Sheffield United, and an incredible 25 points ahead of Watford who finished third. Although mathematically promoted on 25th March, hindsight shows that Reading actually had won enough points to ensure promotion in the second week of February, when they drew with Sheffield United (of course!).

It was a wonderful time to be a Reading supporter. As if to prove just how fondly the football gods were smiling down on this part of Berkshire, just as Reading were moving up to the top tier for the first time ever, local rivals Swindon Town were being relegated to the bottom tier of the league while Oxford United were being relegated out of the Football League altogether. Yes, it really was a wonderful time to be a Reading supporter!

CHAPTER FOURTEEN

Making Plans For Nigel

THE THOUGHTS OF ALL FANS by now had turned to the next season and to the Premier League, but within the club planning for this had been going on for many months. Nigel Howe told me that planning had started by February when it was clear that Reading were on track to go up. He told me: *"So as CEO, when I realised we were going up I'd already started to plan for the summer – this is where people don't realise what CEOs do. I'd already started to think about what I thought we needed to get the team established in the Premier League so with the likes of Nicky Hammond and Steve I was saying to them 'What are we going to do to …?' and I suppose the bits that everybody will remember from what happened were the changes to Hogwood, the spending money on putting together a better environment. That really didn't evolve until later but Catalyst were one of the early people who wanted things down the training ground improved."*

Nick Hammond also talked about planning for the step-up, and revealed that some in the club shared the fears of supporters that something would go wrong: *"I think everyone sort of knew, it was like 'don't talk about the war' almost. Because the club hadn't been there in its history it was like 'No, no, it's not going to happen …'"*

But the planning did happen, of course, and one of the

most significant developments in this area was a presentation from Catalyst delivered to the board in early March – effectively a business plan for Premier League survival, considering both the football and the financial aspects of this. Supported by an 88-page PowerPoint presentation, this provided a full analysis of revenue and expenses of Premier League clubs, especially those who had been promoted and survived, as well as those who had been promoted and not survived. Packed full of statistics, this started bleakly, pointing out that since the Premier League had started, 19 promoted clubs had stayed up while 19 clubs had gone down at the end of their first season: 'therefore your chances are 50-50!' But this strategy's stated purpose was to 'significantly increase your odds'.

In terms of the players, the proposals identified where strengthening was needed – this small squad had achieved so much but it was recognised that to face a Premier League season the squad had to be bigger. Noting that the average squad size of the teams Reading would be competing with for survival was 36, compared to Reading's squad of 30, the strategy also said that: 'based on current performance of Reading's 30 players … only 18 are premiership-capable players!'

Although there are fewer games, they are more intense and the squad was painfully short of cover in some positions – for instance at centre-back and in central midfield. It was also recognised that the careers of some of the players in the squad were nearing their end, and so this plan included replacements for those players – it was effectively a shopping list for the summer, but not one that named specific players to be purchased; instead it listed the positions to be filled. Included in the financial model underpinning this was a recognition that wages would have to rise to Premier League levels.

At that time the average Premier League player's wage was 4.54 times the average Championship player's wage, and while Reading might not have matched that level, which is skewed by super-stars at the biggest clubs, any rise to Premier League wage levels would mean a substantial increase in wage levels. This strategy presented by Catalyst pointed out that: *"on average a promoted side sees a wages and salaries rise of 59 percent"* – but the accompanying increases in revenue meant that increasing wages to these levels was perfectly feasible, while also maintaining a wages to turnover ratio under 55 percent – what Mark Reynolds called 'wages best practice'.

Catalyst's strategy noted that the average net transfer spend of clubs who survived their first season in the Premier League was just over £11.5 million, and so this level of spend was factored into the financial aspects of the strategy. However, as football economists Simon Kuper and Stefan Szymanski have demonstrated there's no direct correlation between transfer fees paid by a team and its league success, but there is a demonstrable correlation – of 92 percent – between a club's total salary bill and its league position. This is contrary to what most supporters think – the common assumption is that the club that pays the most for players does the best in the League. But despite this lack of direct correlation, there is still a need to purchase the right players, hence the inclusion of this figure.

Performance analysis objectives for the team in 2007/08, their first Premier League season, were also laid out, with the comment that the Premier League is an inherently unfair competition, with a financial structure designed to disadvantage smaller clubs. Splitting the teams in the Premier

League into four 'tiers' (those who qualify for Europe; those who compete for European place; those who are below them and safely mid-table; and those in or around the relegation places), the target was to finish in the top half of tier three, in a safe position well clear of any relegation danger. The targeted points average of 46 points needed to achieve this would result in an average league position of 13th.

The financial proposals in this presentation were also very interesting, and were based on the playing objectives being met, and so a certain level of prize money being achieved. Fully costed out, and based on a potential increase in group revenues of 180 percent, the strategy was designed to enable the football club to effectively be self-sufficient, without needing an annual input of cash from the owner – or a player sale – to keep the books in balance, stating that: *"Benefaction from a wealthy supporter does not need to be an intrinsic part of the business model."*

However, this model needed some changes to make it happen, which would boost the club's overall revenue. Stating that an average promoted side increases its revenue by 146 percent from £14.6 million to £35.9 million, the strategy pointed out that to compete with tier three clubs Reading needed to do more than that – increasing revenues by a further £6.5 million.

This would be achieved through increases in all three of the club's crucial revenue streams: broadcast, matchday and commercial. 'Broadcast' was income from TV and radio, and mainly consisted of the Premier League prize money (calculated based on this 'top of tier three' position), the club's fixed share of the League's TV revenue, as well as facility fees for participating in live TV matches. Although the number of these was expected to be relatively small, there was a minimum facility fee value paid by the Premier League to all clubs. The total of broadcast revenue was fairly predictable, varying only with league position.

'Matchday' revenue related to tickets sales, programmes, catering etc., and again was fairly predictable, based on 100 percent occupation of the stadium. As half-season tickets had gone on sale the previous Christmas and had been snapped up like proverbial hot cakes, this figure was again fairly predictable, and comparatively low because of the fixed capacity of 24,200 at the MadStad – only Portsmouth and Watford in the Premier League the next season had lower capacities. There was also considerable debate about whether season ticket prices should rise, and innovative options such as a two-year season ticket were explored. The Catalyst proposal suggested there was no need for prices to rise, as long as extra revenue came in from elsewhere. In the end, though, they did rise by around £100 a year.

The third revenue stream was 'commercial' – income from sponsorship, advertising, corporate entertaining and similar activities. This is where Catalyst identified the biggest shortfall and the biggest opportunity. As Reynolds explained: *"The corporate world is an unexploited asset"* – located in the heart of the Thames Valley, Reading was ideally located to force commercial partnerships with some of the world's largest and most affluent companies, especially in the technology sector. It's easy to reel off a list of such companies – for instance Microsoft, Oracle, WorldCom and Symantec in Reading, Vodafone in Newbury, Hewlett Packard and 3M in Bracknell, O2 and Blackberry in Slough and so on. Reynolds saw these as a wonderful opportunity to expand commercial revenue, saying that he felt that as soon as the club was promoted the marketing manager of each of these companies was almost certainly waiting for a call from the club.

However, these proposals to boost corporate revenue were more involved than simply selling advertising or corporate hospitality, although one strand of the proposals did include focussing on selling perimeter advertising to multi-national brands rather than to local ones – after all, why sell a local business to the 24,000 local people who might actually buy its products or services, when the same advert could be seen globally by millions? I detected some signs of resistance when discussing this topic – understandable signs of the dilemma faced by those asked to consider dropping (if not directly then indirectly by way of massive price increases) local businesses and long-term supporters of the club in favour of more wealthy and more lucrative advertisers and sponsors.

Instead, it was recognised that although the MadStad boasted an award-winning conference centre and hospitality facilities, these were too limited to bring in the commercial revenue Catalyst believed was necessary. Instead, the vision involved working in partnership with global corporates to provide them with entire suites – for instance the 'Microsoft Suite' or the 'Vodafone Suite' – a facility not just to be used to watch a match from but would also be a showpiece for the company's technology, potentially all through the week. So instead of having an executive box for 12 to be used for a meal and a game of football, a company would be able to entertain 20 or more potential customers while demonstrating their products in a state-of-the-art technology suite.

It's a seductive vision, and I've no doubt it would be suc-cessful and extremely lucrative – but at the time there was no way the stadium and conference centre could accommodate such facilities. Among options discussed was actually selling the MadStad to their rugby-playing tenants, London Irish, and moving to a new, larger, ground south of the M4 motorway at Mereoak, but instead plans to expand the current stadium and conference facilities were formulated. This planned expansion, increasing the ground capacity to 36,900, was announced in October 2006 and formally applied for in January 2007.

Other parts of this strategy included looking at ways to provide extra facilities for supporters – and extra ways to separate them from their money. This included what Reynolds calls 'the fans' journey to the game' – looking at, for instance, the time supporters spent sitting in the car park and providing refreshment or other entertainment facilities for these times. This concept included giant steel umbrellas as protection from the rain for fans while eating or drinking or watching TV.

Although radical, this strategy was accepted by the board, and a similar strategy, targeted to the players, was shown to them at their late-season break at Marbella on 20th April. Telling the players that to 'survive in the Premier League was not enough' but that instead they should aim to 'thrive in the Premier League' this was accepted by the players – who endorsed the targets set – including the primary objective of tier three in the Premier League. The players were also set individual targets to achieve in preparation for the forthcoming season. Reynolds called this the 'entrance fee' – something that had to be paid by each player to demonstrate that they wanted to be a successful Premier League footballer. This took the form of a personalised binder containing a tailored set of fitness and physiological goals to be met over the summer in order to ensure the player came back ready for pre-season training for the Premier League. The player recruitment plans for increasing squad size and providing cover – and replacement players – were also shown to the playing squad and accepted objectively, even by those destined to find themselves replaced in the starting 11 by new arrivals.

But in the end there turned out to be precious few new arrivals – in fact just three significant signings – that summer. These were Korean winger Seol Ki-hyeon from Wolves, central defender André Bikey from Lokomotiv Moscow and full-back Ulises de la Cruz from Aston Villa. Player acquisition has always been a thorny subject for Reading, but it seems that this relatively small number of arrivals was down to a number of factors.

The first of these is the age-old problem Reading has always had when it comes to attracting players – as teams go, Reading is just not a 'sexy' team for potential players to join. Their first obstacle is one of geography and doesn't favour them – inevitably young men in their late teens or earlier twenties are more attracted to the bright lights of a city than they are to a provincial town. Other players are attracted to a club by reputation, by size of crowd, by history, by atmosphere or by any of the other things that make up a club's 'footballing pedigree' – and in all these factors a smallish club with largely unremarkable history, a relatively small ground and a famously quiet crowd is hardly likely to get a player's contract-signing muscles twitching with anticipation.

Of course, in today's game there's one factor that trumps all others – money! Any club that outbids others in terms of player wages is likely to overcome opposition in achieving the majority of their desired signings. But again, this is an area where Reading is often beaten by other clubs. Historically, the club has always been run in a prudent way, refusing to 'live the dream' and always maintaining an affordable wage structure. Although this wage structure may not be one that actually allows the club to break even, it has been one that has meant that the annual cheque presented to the chairman to sign to cover that year's losses isn't too eye-watering – and has meant that losses might reasonably been covered with player sales. This is known both inside and outside the club as 'The Reading Way' – something that polarises supporters. Some, who want to see Reading compete on equal terms with richer clubs whatever it costs, are hypercritical of this financial approach, while others feel that it's the only practical approach for a club the size of Reading in a financial environment where all the chips are stacked heavily against them. Included in this 'Reading Way' is a long-term refusal to be 'held to ransom' by players' wage demands – Nick Hammond and the manager will place a value on a player in terms of both transfer fee and salary and they will not pay over that figure. This is maybe another example of how Madejski's approach to financial management is different from that of many others in football's mainstream.

Of course, the financial straightjacket can be relaxed at times – and was in the summer of 2005 – but despite that there's no doubt that when it comes to straight financial battle to sign players Reading will frequently lose out to a club with a bigger or looser chequebook.

As Reading looked to strengthen for their first Premier League season, player recruitment was made even harder by many of the football pundits – who almost without exception wrote the team off as relegation certainties. Not the best advertisement to entice players to join a club!

But although it was clearly a hard sell attracting players to Reading, it was never an impossible one. Some players are attracted by other factors – for instance Leroy Lita was attracted by Coppell's reputation as a manager – and there are other aspects that can be used to help persuade players to sign. An obvious one is the promise of playing games and having the opportunity to be in the first-team showcase, which might not be possible at a larger club – while one that the club tried to maximise was ensuring that the player's facilities and the whole environment for players was as favourable as possible. This dovetails nicely with the 'pull not push' ethos that Catalyst had been working on, and their efforts to upgrade the Hogwood Park training facilities. So in furtherance of this aim, Nigel Howe explained more about the problems of player recruitment: *"The whole dynamic of Reading really was always perceived as a little parochial club that spent its history in League Two or League One and worse and basically had hopped along for a hundred years. And its facilities! Everybody remembers Elm Park because it was there for so long – it was a right old toilet. But a lot of players had evolved their careers by at some stage visiting Elm Park and they had that awful feeling that 'God, if you visited Elm Park, you really knew you'd been there'. Then the training facilities had evolved in the same way, we were doing it piecemeal and there was a feeling that to recruit the right players we had to be able to sell ourselves. So to improve Hogwood, to spend money on the changing rooms, to spend money on the canteen, to make things better, the gym and stuff like that, was going to help – and that's what we did."*

I also spoke to Nick Hammond about planning for the Premier League: *"The Catalyst people were very good in that respect so I began to write plans in terms of Premier League, Championship, just actually showing that we were looking at both possibilities. But it's very difficult because the club had never been there before – getting their head round what did it actually mean, what did it mean in financial terms because it's hard to do the projection. We worked on the premise at the start of every season with the board and Sir John – it's a great way for a board to work because I had Sir John, I had Nigel and I had Ian, and we'd worked together over a period of time so you knew exactly what the dynamics were of a board meeting and how to run it – but we hadn't been there before so you don't really know what it means."*

"So you start to talk about plans for the summer but the truth is – and this is how it panned out – its slightly changed now but at that time, when you're a team going into the Premier League for the first time in your history, it's very, very difficult to buy players. Sorry, it's very, very difficult to buy the right players! It's changed a bit now, but it's still difficult to buy the right players but we were planning … we were still a bit blind to it and it's not like 'we'll go and get a deal done early' because it just wasn't feasible. No player you'd really want at that stage, worth his salt, was going to be committing to Reading in April/May. So yes, we were planning, yes we were looking at possibilities."

But those possibilities only involved signing one or two players, as Hammond continued: *"So plans were in place but we weren't able to get things early … in terms of Steve that summer, his mind-set was very clear – as was mine. In terms of the football squad, [it] was to add little, to not disrupt. Continuity, team spirit, loyalty – all words that were synonymous with Steve were going to be important. So we were looking for only two or three players probably – and primarily he wanted to bring another centre-half to bring some support there, not because he had any lack of faith in the two that he'd got, but he thought that was an area that we definitely needed strengthening."*

The player identified as the ideal centre-half signing was Joleon Lescott, then with Wolves. But despite protracted negotiations, dating back to the beginning of March, and a reported offer of £4 million, which would have almost quadrupled Reading's transfer record, the signing never happened. In an almost perfect illustration of the problems Reading have in player recruitment, when faced with a choice between Reading and Everton, Lescott opted for the more famous and established Premier League club. Hammond told me: *"I had worked hard that summer on that* [Lescott] *– I really worked hard on that, and it was one of those – you always knew was just there and you couldn't get it – but he was our main target and what a great boy he was, respectful … but anyway, we didn't do that deal."*

So despite the limited transfer aims, and the presence of real money (by Reading's standards) transfer dealings that summer were not wholly satisfactory. Perhaps it's best to leave the last words on this subject to Coppell himself. When asked in April 2006 what the transfer policy in the summer would be, he told a fans' forum that there is a limited field of players available, and that he felt it would be wrong to ruin the current mind-set in the squad by bringing in people 'who are on the gravy train'. He added that players are not always willing to come to newly promoted teams, and that he did not want to bring in someone who would be on bigger wages than the players who actually achieved the promotion. He said that agents were already in contact, and that the club had contacts abroad through the good work of Nick Hammond and Brian McDermott. He also felt that the team as it stood then had no discernible weaknesses, and that he'd love to give the current squad ten games to prove themselves in the Premier League, but the transfer window puts paid to that idea. He said that when he was managing at Palace and his team lost 9-0 at Anfield in September, his chairman panicked and threw money at the situation immediately, but that that was something that could no longer happen.

So Reading went into their first ever Premier League season with their players superbly prepared, but with precious few reinforcements, and with the whole of the football world expecting them to be the top league's whipping boys in their single season eating at this exalted table.

CHAPTER FIFTEEN

Even Better Than The Real Thing

HOW DO YOU FEEL WHEN your team is facing its first ever Premier League season? It's a real mix of extreme emotions. On one hand, there's the excitement of mixing it with the big boys, and of the prospect of visiting famous grounds for the first time. But there's the opposite extreme – a fear of humiliation, of the team not being able to bridge the chasm of class between the leagues and the dread of spending a season following a team that you desperately want to do well but is hopelessly out of its depth at the higher level.

Loyal Royal Neil Maskell recalls his feelings that summer: *"There was that excitement and trepidation and what else – everybody thinks we'll only last one year. It was exciting, it was all fresh, it was all new, 'we're going to be on Match of the Day!' Grown men – not including myself – men older than me saying 'I'm going to get the Panini sticker album' without any hint of irony."*

But the negative aspect of being in the top division was the hostility of the press. Maskell remembers one piece that particularly infuriated him and other Reading fans: *"I remember the pre-season pull-outs you have in the national papers where the tabloid journalists have been covering Premier League games all season and there was one, in* The Sun, *where Antony Kastrinakis said Reading were certainties for relegation in a particularly acerbic way. At the same time, he* tipped *Sheffield United to stay up – the team who'd finished 16 points behind us!"*

Sir John Madejski also recalled being written-off by the press: *"That's what they do. There's so many of those pundits who don't even like clubs like Reading being at the top – they feel that we're muddying the water or disenfranchising it. But I think there's something about being the underdog and the thing about all this is it's not just about the players on the pitch … I've got people who have been working here for 20 years or more, a solid team of backroom people who are vital to the running of the club and those people like yourself, the fans that have been loyal throughout."*

These negative feelings weren't shared within the team and coaching staff, although Nick Hammond did confess that before the first match his feelings were: *"All the things you would expect, I guess. Excited, nervous, apprehensive – you know, are we going to get battered every week?"*

Instead, there was a feeling of optimism, as Wally Downes explained: *"We were 18 points and 25 points better than the two teams who were coming up with us so theoretically you've only got to beat one team – and you've got to deteriorate massively not to be better than the two teams you've come up with. So I'm looking at the league thinking there's no way we're going down – it was impossible for us to go down. Someone would not do well and as long as we maintained what we were doing, onwards and upwards, great. I had no qualms about us doing well in the division."*

Ady Williams agrees with Downes's analysis, saying: *"Well, I've always said the line is thin. People think that you're going into the Premier League and playing against Arsenal and Man United and Chelsea, you're talking about the very best there. There's still quite a few teams in the Premier League that aren't going to excite me too much and there were a few at that time and I thought 'you know what, you keep that*

*momentum going, you add a little bit of something to the squad ...' Would
I have said they'd finish eighth, no I wouldn't have, but I'd never thought
for one minute they'd get relegated."*

The long-awaited first match of the season, at home to
Middlesbrough, on 19th August 2006, turned out to be truly
memorable – and a defining moment of the season. But it
started in the worst possible way, with all the worst fears of
Reading fans apparently being realised as their team stared the
match looking every inch like rabbits caught in the headlights
and nothing like the team that was so successful the previous
season. Defending nervously, passing poorly and just generally
failing to compete in any aspect of the game, Reading seemed
clearly in awe of their opponents, and soon discovered just
how quickly mistakes were punished at this level, as the
Teesiders strolled into a 2-0 lead within the first 21 minutes.
The home crowd, so excited before kick-off, sat in a stunned
silence, while the away end rang with *'This is the Premier League'*
and *'Are you Sunderland in disguise?'* – a reference to the team that
had set a record-breaking low points total of 15 in the Premier
League the previous season.

Based on Reading's performance in that first 20 minutes, it
would be fair to say that Sunderland's record might well have
been in some danger, but shortly afterwards came a single
moment that changed the match and, I'm convinced, the
whole season. The ball was played out to Nicky Shorey on the
left, Reading's most usual outlet the previous season. Just a few
minutes earlier he would have pumped the ball forward in the
hope of finding Kitson or Doyle up front, but this time he cut
inside and went on a run, beating a couple of players and
playing a clever pass to Doyle who in turn forced a save out of
the Boro 'keeper.

Writing this the best part of ten years later, it seems ludicrous, but this single move seemed to absolutely galvanise the team – it was almost as if someone took the players and inflated them. Heads were raised, chests were pumped out and the whole demeanour of the players changed. It was as though Shorey's run had demonstrated to his teammates 'we can do this, you know' – and the old confidence almost visibly flowed back into the team. All of a sudden passes were accurate, the ball was kept, the defence was much tighter and Middlesbrough were being denied any time and space on the ball. The team of the previous season – unchanged except for Seol, replacing the injured Glen Little – was back on the pitch.

The crowd saw this transformation and it inspired them to noisily back their team, and the whole emphasis of the game had completely changed – it was now Reading taking the game to their opponents. Seol was playing well in his debut, and after 43 minutes he beat his full-back and crossed for Kitson to score, and Sidwell scored the equaliser just a minute later. Middlesbrough were clearly rattled, as Riggott took out Dave Kitson with a horrible tackle that looked to be wholly borne of frustration – but which inexplicably only received a booking.

The atmosphere was now unrecognisable from that just 25 minutes earlier, and it carried on in the second half as Reading continued to dominate the match, while Middlesbrough, an established Premier League team, faced the same problems that so many Championship teams had faced the previous year – being unable to cope with the pace, guile and defensive solidity of the Reading team. There was only ever going to be one winner, and that was confirmed just ten minutes into the second half as Lita, on for the injured Kitson, slammed the ball home from another fine Seol cross.

For Reading fans, this was a breath-taking match – where all their worst fears were confirmed and then those fears were blown away by the team's sudden revival. In many ways the turnaround made this sweeter than victory in a game they'd dominated from the start would have been – and the pleasure in spending most of the second half reminding the visiting supporters that, yes, *"this is the Premier League"* was total. Just to round off a perfect day, that match was first up on Match of the Day that night, although it was glaringly noticeable just how little knowledge Messrs Lineker, Hansen and Shearer had of the Reading players.

I asked Downes for his recollections of this game. He told me: *"I wrote something up on the wall beforehand about what we'd done and what we wanted to achieve, and 'this is for your families' and 'be proud of yourself, enjoy this thing, this is a massive game for all of you, make sure you enjoy it, make the people who've been with you all your life proud of you' – and they did. 2-0 down after how long was it? Then they didn't lie down and we didn't give Middlesbrough time to start passing it around … Their attitude didn't change – the important thing is we didn't have to wait till half time to get into it, they did it themselves. Two-all at half time? And they could see as soon as we got the goal we were up and running. That was it, the season had started, they weren't bothered anymore and they sussed then that they could do to the Premier League teams what they'd done to the Championship teams."*

The Premier League season was off and rolling, and the confidence was carried forward to the team's first away match at Villa Park four days later, where the team was 1-0 up in the fourth minute of the match – although M6 traffic problems mean that many Reading fans arrived late and so missed this high point of the game. Just after half an hour, Sonko slipped when chasing back after Villa's Moore, bringing him down in the process. Although this clearly wasn't deliberate, it resulted in a red card and a penalty, which was converted. Reading heads stayed high and continued to compete well with Villa, but despite a resolute performance the ten men conceded in the second half to lose 2-1. But this didn't feel like a defeat and was hailed as a gutsy performance full of positives.

Despite a narrow 1-0 defeat to Wigan in their next match, Reading's season continued to prosper, and after five matches the team was in fifth place in the table, having recorded wins over Manchester City and away at Sheffield United – another comprehensive outplaying of Neil Warnock's team. The first, much-anticipated test came against Manchester United at the end of September, and the team excelled, taking the game to their illustrious opponents throughout and competing fully with them in a fast-paced and pulsating match. United looked unable to break down a superbly well-organised Reading defence for much of the game, and Wayne Rooney – then at the height of his game – wasn't given a look-in all day by Sonko. Ahead just after halftime following a penalty for Gary Neville's handball, Reading weathered the resulting onslaught well, but were undone by a moment of class from Cristiano Ronaldo in the 73rd minute. The Portuguese winger cut in from the left to wrong-foot Murty and placed his shot just inside the far post. The score remained level, but it was Reading who claimed the plaudits for a wholly committed and perfectly judged performance in which they held their own against the likes of Rooney, Scholes and Ronaldo.

A week later they were away at Alan Pardew's West Ham, and picked up their second away win of the season in a game played in the pouring rain. Ahead after just two minutes from

Seol's long-range rocket, the three points were secured by a resolute defensive performance for over 88 minutes, including a superb full-length saving header at the death from Steve Sidwell.

For Nick Hammond, the contribution of Seol at the start of the season was critical to the team's success. He told me: *"He was our only perceived signing of that summer, but his impact and his input probably only in the first two, two and a half months of the season was actually crucial – and then after that he sort of faded away really and didn't push it. But his contribution in the very start of that season was actually crucial – and imperative in terms of getting some momentum ... it was a good lesson that a player can, for a period of time, fulfil a role."*

Just one week later, Reading were embroiled in one of the most controversial and memorable matches ever held at the MadStad, when they hosted Premier League champions Chelsea. Just 20 seconds into the match, Stephen Hunt, making his first Premier League start following injury to Bobby Convey, chased a loose ball as Chelsea 'keeper Petr Čech came out to claim this. The subsequent collision between Hunt's knee and Čech's head, which resulted in Čech undergoing surgery for a depressed skull fracture and wearing a protective skullcap ever since, was something that would set the media agenda for the club for months afterwards. John Madejski's comments on how the media regard smaller clubs in the Premier League were shown to be prescient, as a media circus ensued to demonise Hunt for what Chelsea Manager José Mourinho said was *"not an accident."* Columnist Oliver Hunt called Hunt 'a feral thug' and suggested the collision was deliberate, while the Chelsea official website hosted a discussion forum on which Chelsea supporters from around the world heaped bile and opprobrium on both Hunt and Reading. Hunt received numerous death threats and suffered an attempted break-in at his flat, purportedly from a disgruntled Chelsea fan, and Mourinho raged to the media about how poor Reading's medical facilities were and how his player might have died while waiting for an ambulance "for over 30 minutes" – hyperbole shown to be a fabrication by South Central Ambulance Service's logs, which showed a seven minute response time to the call.

Things were further complicated in the match as Čech's substitute, Carlo Cudicini, also departed injured after a last-minute collision with Sonko and so John Terry finished the game in goal for Chelsea, and there were two sendings-off – one for each team, including Reading's André Bikey who had only come on as first-half substitute when Reading lost Graeme Murty to injury. In true Mourinho style, his fury and the resulting controversy masked the fact that his team of champions had been thoroughly outplayed by 'Little Reading', and had only secured the points by a cruel deflection from a free-kick that cannoned off the wall and into the Reading net via Ivar Ingimarsson's legs. Despite constant second-half pressure, though, Reading were unable to secure the equaliser their performance deserved, and the sense of injustice and outrage among Reading's fans was only compounded by watching Chelsea's players celebrate a 1-0 win over Reading, secured via a deflected own-goal, with a fervour that wouldn't have looked out of place if they'd won the European Cup, and then further inflamed by Mourinho's ravings.

All these years later, it's amazing that the controversy still lingers and still hangs over Hunt's heads in the eyes of some – although even Oliver Holt, seen by many at the time as

'Mourinho's chief rabble-rouser' in the media, finally met with
Hunt in January 2015 and has since retracted much of what
he alleged at the time.

From the perspective of Reading fans, this was a genuine
accident blown up out of all proportion, and a consequence of
a thoroughly honest and wholehearted player, Coppell's
perennial substitute, at last getting a Premier League start and
putting everything he had into grabbing it with both hands. As
Hunt himself said, if he hadn't gone into that challenge as he
did he would have had the coaches screaming at him for lack
of commitment.

Talking about Hunt, Nicky Hammond told me: *"The great
quality of Stephen Hunt was his desire. His heart was so big that having
played second fiddle in the Championship, he became number one player in
the Premier League – and I use him as a great example to our young
players about where character and desire can get you because he had it in
abundance. I mean he could play as well."*

In many ways this match also marked a 'changing of the
guard' on the Reading left wing. As Hammond says, Hunt
became the number one choice, with Convey – so inspirational the previous season – only making one further start and one
more substitute appearance for Reading that season, with
Hunt Coppell's first-choice left winger started only missing
three more Premier League games. Part of this was down to
injuries, particularly a knee injury that required surgery, which
Ron Grant feels meant he was never quite the same player as
before – but Hammond feels that Convey had trouble
accepting the rise in stature of Stephen Hunt, telling me: *"And
actually then Bobby sort of couldn't – psychologically couldn't – deal with
it. He didn't really deal with that, that Hunty had then gone past him,
having been a little bit of a superstar at the level we were operating at the*

previous year, but he did have a sensational season, Convey, as did the whole midfield because we scored goals across the whole midfield."

Loyal Royal Roger Titford sums up very well the feeling of many Reading fans at this time, as he recalls that Chelsea match as one of his highlights of Reading's first Premier League season: *"The game started in twilight with Petr Čech in their goal and ended in floodlit frenzy with John Terry in the gloves and the East Stand baying 'You should have brought three keepers'. Although we lost – 0-1 to a jammy deflection – I really felt we stood toe-to-toe with the Premier League champions that day, both on the pitch and off it. We nearly got a late equaliser. International controversy followed Čech's unfortunate injury but our club handled the Mourinho-inspired furore very well. The home game before we had drawn with Manchester U. but that felt like a cup-tie we didn't quite win. The Chelsea match had me thinking we were really involved in the meat of the Premier League now. It was about that time I caught sight of a forthcoming fixtures ad on Sky Sports. It read from the top something like: 'Liverpool v Manchester U.; Reading v Chelsea; Barcelona v Real Madrid'. And Reading wasn't in small letters or with asterisks or anything. Wow."*

Another greatly-anticipated match was Reading's first ever visit to Anfield at the start of November, although fate, in the form of the draw for the Third Round of the Carling Cup that gave Reading supporters an opportunity to visit Merseyside ten days earlier, to watch a frenzied match in which Coppell's team featuring mainly fringe-players lose 4-3 after being 3-0 down after 50 minutes – the manager was still committed to using the cup competitions as a chance to give his less regular starters valuable match experience.

Despite also losing the league match at Anfield, Reading then won four straight games, beating Tottenham, Fulham, Charlton and Bolton, so that in the first week of December

2006 they were in sixth place in the Premier League, with 25 points, and behind Liverpool on goal difference.

Nigel Howe recalls this period when Reading were winning consecutive matches and being taken seriously with great fondness. He told me: *"Every minute of that season I loved. I loved going to the Premier League meetings, I loved going to the Premier League clubs. I hated the Premier League meetings when we first went there – their approach was 'enjoy your year with us!' – condescending! I think in some ways there's more highlights and memories from that season than from the one before because it was all so new and we were going to places that we haven't played at for 50 years or so."*

One aspect of the club that came to the fore in this period was what was known as the 'Royals Families'. We've already seen how the club had an unusually good team spirit and togetherness, and this extended to the wives and girlfriends of the players as well. The 'Royals Families' was an initiative to put the publicity exposure of the Premier League to good purpose by harnessing this coverage and channelling it towards charity fundraising. A stark contrast to the industry stereotype where most football 'WaGs' are known most for their shopping and leisure activities, this was something that caught the imagination of the media and helped mark Reading out as being something special – something not quite the same as any other football club.

This initiative evolved spontaneously from among the WaGs, primarily organised by Karen Murty and Amanda Hahnemann, rather than something consciously created from within the club, and was just another illustration of how close everyone in the club was. As Nick Hammond said when I asked him about this togetherness: *"Yeah, and it's not uncommon. My opinion is in a more general way – you've got a club that's together, you've got a lot more chance of being successful. You've got a club that's split, you've got no chance of being successful. I really, really believe that and I think that was a group of people who were all together and you had the support from the non-playing staff, the academy staff, bearing in mind at that stage we weren't getting any academy players through but the support for Steve and the team from the academy manager and the people that he – I guess his lieutenants – was absolutely 100 percent."*

John Madejski looks back on this initiative with particular fondness: *"Well, we had the WaGs and all that sort of lovely stuff and the Royal family came down to talk to them – the Countess of Wessex, Sophie came down. I remember that day very well, they all came to the Royal County of Berkshire to greet her and so on. I remember when she left, I took her round to the press compound and opened the door and she was driving herself. We've always tried to keep a great family atmosphere here and there's always been that feeling of punching above their level which I particularly like doing. So yeah, that was really – it was the best season ever."*

That season continued into December and a return match with Chelsea at Stamford Bridge on Boxing Day – which was always likely to be over-shadowed by the ongoing Hunt/Čech furore. For this match Hunt was rested, and Reading twice came from behind to draw 2-2 – with a particularly spirited second-half performance taking the match to Chelsea. The equaliser – scored just five minutes from the end – was particularly satisfying, an Ashley Cole clearance pinging off Michael Essien into his own net. This was a performance that Reading fans were universally proud of – they'd matched Chelsea in their own backyard, and in the end it was only an inspired solo performance by Didier Drogba that carried Chelsea. The next match was also a big one – away at Old Trafford, and again Reading refused to be overawed by their opponent's reputation, putting in a fighting performance that saw them lose by a single goal out of five.

Having scored four goals in two matches against the two most successful teams in the Premier League, spirits were high for the home match on New Year's Day against West Ham. The Hammers were in disarray in the relegation zone amid rumours of dressing room turmoil and they proved to be easy meat for Reading's fluid and confident attacking play. At 4-0 ahead by halftime, Reading were slightly profligate in their shooting in the second half and only added two more, when it could have been plenty more – it was a joyous game for Reading supporters, as their team tore apart their famous opponents, literally looking likely to score every time they attacked. For me, this was a landmark match, a 6-0 demolition of a club that just three years earlier was seen as a much better bet and a much bigger club by everyone as they lured Alan Pardew away as manager. The only cloud, albeit a tiny one, in an otherwise bright Royal blue sky was that Pardew wasn't with West Ham to experience this drubbing in person – he's been sacked by the club three weeks earlier.

John Madejski felt the same as any other fan during this match, naming it as one of his highlights of the Premier League season: *"New Year's Day, because I'd been out New Year's Eve, celebrating as you do and about halfway through I thought 'am I dreaming this?' I was slightly inebriated and I thought 'shit, is this really happening?' – because it really was, wasn't it?"*

This fine run of form continued, as Reading won four of their next five league matches, drawing the other, to return to sixth place in the Premier League table in mid-February – while the 'cup team' won FA Cup third and fourth round matches before being given a fifth round draw away to

Manchester United at Old Trafford.

One of these league victories was a hugely impressive 2-0 win at Manchester City, with both goals coming in near identical fashion from Leroy Lita. With 11 minutes to play Sidwell passed a through ball behind the City defence for Lita to run onto and score, and ten minutes later Harper played a similar ball for Lita to repeat the finish. This victory, in the first week of February and with 12 games still to play, gained Reading the nominal 40 points that is reckoned will ensure Premier League survival.

But despite the on-field results, not everything was going Reading's way. Two weeks earlier Reading had won 3-1 in a highly-charged match against Neil Warnock's Sheffield United (who else?) – a match that saw United's Keith Gillespie come on as substitute and head straight across to Stephen Hunt and unaccountably launched an elbow at him! Immediately sent off, Gillespie had been on the field for less than ten seconds, none of it while the ball was in play. This match also saw Warnock making kicking gestures to his players which were interpreted by Downes and just about everyone else nearby, including me, as an instruction to maim. Wally Downes waded in and that punch-up led to him and Warnock both receiving red cards. Warnock denied that his gestures were any such instruction – but then he would, wouldn't he? Steve Coppell told an end-of-season fans' forum that Downes had received over 100 texts congratulating him for hitting Warnock after that incident. While this may just be a product of Coppell's dry sense of humour, it was wonderfully received by the assembled Reading fans.

However one incident in this match of greater long-term significance was an injury to talismanic centre-back Sonko, who fell awkwardly in the first half and limped off, only to receive some treatment and return a few minutes later. But he was clearly injured, and within ten minutes had to be replaced by André Bikey. This injury turned out to be to Sonko's knee ligaments, and this was his last match of the season. The player dubbed 'Superman' by fans the previous season, and who had been a virtually ever-present part of Reading's defence since joining the club in July 2004, would be ruled out for ten months and, to many observers, would never be the same player again.

In the FA Cup, Reading gained a creditable 1-1 draw at Old Trafford, despite Coppell still not playing the team that would be his first choice in the league. The replay was a bizarre match, with Reading starting shambolically and finding themselves three goals down within six minutes, the first when 'keeper Adam Federici allowed what should have been a routine shot from Heinze to go under his body in the first minute. Three down and looking dead and buried, Reading slowly clawed their way back into the game, and after Kitson – only recently back from that injury suffered in the opening match of the season – scored in the 23rd minute it was 'game-on!'

From that point it was all Reading, with Manchester United pinned back and soaking up the pressure. Six minutes from the end Lita scored a second, and with a TV audience almost unanimously willing Reading to get an equaliser, a last minute piledriver from Brynjar Gunnarsson beat Edwin van der Sar in the United goal but crashed back against the crossbar. Reading came so very close to taking the match to extra-time, but as so often in this season even when they lost, they lost with heads held high and in a manner their fans could be proud of, competing to the end and refusing to let football's pecking order intimidate them.

Roger Titford sums up how many Royals fans felt at this incredible time, with Premier League survival assured and ten games still to play: *"January and February 2007 was as good as it ever got and I didn't feel by then there was any reason it should end so quickly. West Ham on New Year's Day, 6-0. At the end the bloke next to me had the biggest grin you've ever seen on a grown man – 'I've got it recorded on Sky+, I've got a case of Stella and the missus is out all day – Happy New Year!' We crushed Villa, were disappointed to get only a point at Everton and had two great and close Cup matches with Manchester United when only the crossbar saved them from an extra-time pummelling."*

Out of the cup, but just three points away from achieving Catalyst's target of 46 points – and still in February – the feeling of wonder and incredulity Royals fans had felt all season was no less diminished.

CHAPTER SIXTEEN

The Final Countdown

AS MARCH BEGAN, WITH TEN Premier League matches remaining, many supporters wondered where Reading would go from here. Premier League survival was already assured, and with their team sitting sixth in the table and UEFA Cup qualification a real possibility, Reading supporters more and more frequently broke into a chant of 'we're all going on a European tour'.

But while the fans relished the idea of a trip to Europe, something else in that incredible season that would have been completely beyond the bounds of imagination just a few years earlier, within the club the prospect wasn't viewed with such optimism. Steve Coppell publicly stated that he wasn't in favour, telling a late season fans' forum that qualification would create the need to bring in three or four extra players more than already planned in order to deal with the extra games. As well as not having the budget for this, it would also make the squad more congested, which would not be healthy.

I asked Mark Reynolds about the possibility of European football, and whether this had any bearing on the objective-setting sessions facilitated by Catalyst, which were still going on ahead of every cycle of matches. He told me: *"Steve didn't want to* [qualify]. *Let's face it, the UEFA League is not a popular competition to qualify for. Steve's reasoning was entirely logical and very sensible."*

"We didn't have the resources to play away in the back end of Eastern Europe on the Thursday and perform again on the Sunday. It didn't seem to anybody at that particular time, ten years ago, that it was a worthwhile competition for the smaller teams to go into. I think as a Premier League team you need two to three solid Premiership seasons under your belt in order to have the strength and depth of squad to be able to do that."

"The bottom line was we had got an exceptional performance out of a small squad – out of a small number of players – and we had done extremely well in the various cup competitions, the FA cup, the league cups. To add another burden to that camel's back would have been one step too far. It would have been very interesting to try and justify recruiting another five, six, seven or eight players – or even for a manger to want to. You can fill up your squad with two or three players in a window – but to bring in another quarter, a third of a team, quickly and expect it to perform?"

"So was performance manipulated downwards? No. Was it expressed as an objective to finish sixth or whatever we had to do to qualify? No. No, our objective was to maximise the performance of what we had. The objective was to finish thirteenth. We had achieved the objective."

Others inside the club had different views, though. Nigel Howe would have welcomed European qualification: *"Yes, of course. I wasn't one of these CEOs that say 'you can't play in that league because you don't make any money', I'm all about brand, so I thought it would be great."*

Wally Downes had mixed feelings. He recognised the strain qualification would put on the team but his heart welcomed the opportunity: *"I wasn't of that opinion because I thought it was an adventure, it was a journey and Reading had never done anything like that. But I didn't have the burden and responsibility of the sack like the manager. That's where, whenever we had conversations, I'd put my piece forward to him but then invariably anything I thought, he'd already thought the week before."*

Back on the field, though, the season continued, with a narrow 2-1 defeat away at Arsenal. This result was a pleasant surprise for Reading fans who travelled fearing the worst – Arsenal had looked simply superb at the MadStad the previous October, beating Reading 4-0 in a match that Loyal Royal Dave Harris particularly remembers: *"In many ways it was an emotional match as it was the first match my brother had not been to that season, and it is one of my life's regrets that he was not there to witness the exhibition of football on show that will live long in my memory. For Arsenal fans this match will probably not even register on the radar but for me, well, I've not seen a display like it before or since. From the moment Thierry Henry swept Arsenal in front on 50 seconds (the first goal to be conceded by Reading at the North Stand end of the ground in well over a year) Arsenal settled into a rhythm that we simply couldn't match. In the end goals from Hleb, van Persie and a further Henry penalty settled the mismatch."*

"After about half an hour and 2-0 down, I had settled into accepting that there was almost no chance of getting anything from the match so turned my attention to just enjoying what is probably the best performance of any team at the Madejski Stadium. It was an absolute pleasure to watch, passing and movement of the highest order, and was the first and only time in which Reading were comprehensively outclassed that season. In many ways this represents a lot of what is bad about the Premier League, with complete mismatches between the top few select clubs and the rest, in what is supposed to be a level playing field, but I didn't see it at the time as we had matched both Manchester United and Chelsea within the previous four–six weeks. So my applause at the end was not only one for the efforts of my own team, but for the sheer quality of Arsenal's

performance in outclassing a side that was, pre-match, seemingly capable of going toe-to-toe with them. Brilliant."

Having been completely outclassed by Arsenal on their own ground, to lose by just a single goal at The Emirates, where Arsenal were still unbeaten in their first season there, shows the progress and the growth in confidence of the Reading team at this time.

This period in early 2007 also saw the introduction into the team of the two players that Reading had purchased in the January transfer window – Michael Duberry and Greg Halford. Duberry, aged 30 and with the best part of 300 games under his belt, was signed from Stoke for £800,000 as a supposed like-for-like replacement for the injured Sonko – although it was questionable whether he would ever fill that role adequately.

Halford, though, was at the other end of his career. The six-foot four-inch 21-year-old was signed from Colchester for £2.5 million, a sum that smashed Reading's transfer record. At a fans' forum that April, Steve Coppell explained the purchase of Halford, saying that the player sees himself as a right-back but has the ability to play anywhere. Coppell said he would have preferred to wait until the summer to sign him, but as there was considerable competition from other clubs the deal was done as quickly as possible.

But this time, however, Halford was the subject of some controversy – although the record-breaking signing, he'd only started twice, the second time against Tottenham when his handball gifted Spurs a penalty for the only goal of the match. Asked about Halford, Coppell said that the player had a great reputation and that his time will come, but there is a lot of competition for the right-back spot and no player will be played just because of their price-tag.

But just three months – and one start – later Halford had left the club, sold to Sunderland. Nick Hammond explained to me: *"Greg Halford was a chance – we actually ended up selling him to Sunderland for half a million more than I bought him for so he wasn't the worst deal we'd ever done – but there was always a question mark around Halford in terms of his position. Actually not so much in terms of personality, because he was a quiet boy and he came into the group and I think he found it difficult. Nice boy, very nice boy, but quiet and I think he just found it hard to settle. But at the time he was a reasonable take because he was multi-functional – huge long throw, which obviously Steve liked; good on set plays; big chap and could play centre-forward, right-midfield, right-back, centre-half. So in the overall scheme of things he wasn't a bad take at the time, he just didn't work out and we sold him for half a million pounds more than we bought him for."*

Wally Downes was slightly more specific, telling me: *"Gotta take some responsibility for that. He had a poxy start, he handballed the ball at Tottenham, Steve took him off and that was the end of him."*

Ron Grant also spoke to me about Halford: *"I actually had the pleasure of actually greeting Greg when he arrived at the club with his mum, when he arrived at the stadium. Nice guy, pleasant mum and what have you, we had a chat. He was relatively young coming into – I wouldn't say an old squad, but a very mature, playing-wise, squad and of course he did have to wait his turn, didn't he? He had his moments but I don't think he ever reached the standard that we wanted, didn't give us what we wanted from his playing."*

Clearly, sometimes transfers just don't work out – and every transfer is a gamble, big or small. One transfer that had worked out spectacularly well in January 2003 was the acquisition of Steve Sidwell, inspirational midfielder and the closest that this 'team without stars' had to a star player. But all through Reading's first Premier League season Sidwell had been the lowest paid senior player at the club, having declined to sign a new contract – his current contract expired in the summer of 2007 and the likelihood was that he'd leave on a 'Bosman' at the end of this season.

In such a situation where a player in his last season is not signing a new contract, there's often rancour and a drop in performances – but not in the case of Sidwell. All through this season, his performances and his desire and commitment were exemplary – as Ady Williams, still an interested observer throughout this period, said: *"Siddy ran through a brick wall until the last game."*

I spoke at length to Nick Hammond about Sidwell that season, and how his contract situation was managed. One of the first questions to be decided when Sidwell wouldn't sign was whether to try to sell him straightaway. Hammond told me: *"So Siddy, going into the last year of his contract – this was a big discussion because obviously he'd come to Reading prior to me becoming Director of Football and then I became Director of Football, so his contract had a year to run. Steve* [Coppell] *was very, very keen to keep him; I was very, very keen to keep him; the board, as always, were just going to be supportive of what we were proposing."*

"They were supportive but asked the pertinent questions – and the pertinent questions were 'is he going to be motivated?', 'are we going to get an offer?' The absolute correct questions to ask and Steve and I both felt that because of Sidwell, the way he was in character and personality, he'd be okay, it wouldn't be a problem. We had the deal that was in place, there was a large sell on to Arsenal – don't ask me exactly what the percentage was, but it was a large one. So I knew the market place, at that point in time, Steve Sidwell may have been £3 million, but if you took the money that you were then going to pay on to Arsenal out of that, what were

you going to come out with? So that was a fairly big part of the decision-making, allied to the character of the player and allied to what the players wishes were. And I think Siddy got a good agent, Eric Walters, and they both made it clear to me that 'listen, in 12 months' time I will be leaving on a free transfer and it's the club's prerogative …' But he's such a good man, Sidwell, so we made a recommendation to the board that we wanted to keep him and the board supported it."

"*I think he played it perfectly in that there was definitely a loyalty to us, to Reading … I don't always believe the perception that players necessarily do earn more money on a free transfer, my experience doesn't actually back that up – but in 12 months' time he would have options and one of the options might have been to stay at Reading. But I think, you know, he always felt that he was leaving … at that point he would make the move, that would be the right timing. Sometimes in these situations it goes horribly wrong – in this particular situation I think it worked really well for all parties.*"

"*My discussion with him and with his agents as the season progressed was where he was going.*"

Coppell reinforced this view when he was asked at a fans' forum in September 2006 whether Sidwell would be a Reading player the following season. He responded that it depended upon how the team did in that first season. He commented that in the same position he would do what Sidwell was doing, since the player was confident in his ability to play for a top five club and so could become very rich very quickly. But he also pointed out that Sidwell now had to play well to attract the best teams – although as far as he was concerned: "*Siddy is still a part of us on a daily basis.*"

On the pitch, as March turned into April, that defeat to Spurs followed by a 2-1 home defeat to Liverpool meant Reading dropped to ninth in the table, a position consolidated with a goalless draw at Charlton, and the chance of European football seemed to have gone. But then three straight wins reignited those hopes – for supporters, at least. Two 1-0 home wins over Fulham and Newcastle were sandwiched around a dramatic 3-1 win at Bolton's Reebok Stadium.

Reading were largely ineffective for 75 minutes, and their only notable act in this period was to concede an unlucky own-goal through Nicky Shorey. But with 15 minutes left, and with the match looking destined to fizzle out into a defeat to that single goal, Coppell brought on Harper, Seol and Long – and the match was turned on its head. Suddenly Reading were inspired, playing with pace and vitality, and when Doyle was taken out in the 84th minute he equalised from the penalty spot. Many teams would have been happy with a draw, but that was never Coppell's style, and his team continued attacking, with Doyle scoring a winner five minutes later and Hunt adding a third just 60 seconds after to ensure that by the time the final whistle went the Reebok had virtually emptied and joyous Reading fans outnumbered the few Bolton fans who remained to the end. For many a fair few who'd shed tears at the play-off defeat to Bolton at Wembley in 1995, this late turnaround was doubly satisfying.

These victories were achieved despite Coppell tinkering with his starting line-ups, trying out some of the fringe players – this is in line with what he told the April 2007 fans' forum when asked about the team's performance that season. He told the meeting that he and his coaches were philosophical at the start of the season and so gave the players realistic goals – which have been regularly achieved. There had been a fear at the start of the season that the team would be battling against relegation, but in the situation they were in he could tinker with the team 'in the heat of battle'. How much of this tinkering was related to the chase – or lack of – for a UEFA Cup place is open to conjecture, but despite the changes the team kept winning.

The final home match of the season, against Watford – bottom of the table and already relegated – was a match that not only were Reading expected to win easily but which was planned to end with celebrations and an end-of-season lap of honour. In the event, though, it was a massive anti-climax as Reading had a real off day. Although they had the bulk of the play, they were undone by a spirited away performance by Watford, who triumphed 2-0 – and whose victory leant heavily on an outstanding virtuoso goalkeeping performance by Ben Forster, in his second loan period with Watford from Manchester United. The lap of honour was something of a damp squib, which many disappointed fans failed to stay for – very unfortunate, for this was to be Sidwell's last match in a Reading shirt.

Winning that game would have put Reading on 57 points, in sixth place behind Everton on goal difference – and surely in pole position for European qualification, since UEFA Cup places were awarded to the sixth and seventh placed teams this season as both FA Cup finalists, Chelsea and Manchester United had already qualified for the Champions League while Chelsea had also won the League Cup. Instead, they went to the final match, away at Blackburn, in seventh place, a point behind Bolton, and realistically needing to win to have any change of the fans' desired 'European tour' the following season.

As befits such an epic, memorable and dramatic season, this was an epic, memorable and dramatic match. Reading fans were in great spirits, celebrating the end of a quite remarkable season – and their end-of-season inflatables were more numerous and more lavish than ever before.

Despite going behind three times, and despite losing Marcus Hahnemann after 23 minutes with a broken hand – incurred as Blackburn scored their first goal – Reading fought back three times to equalise in a breathless match that showed the spirit in this team and Coppell's determination to go for a win in every match. The final equaliser, scored 13 minutes from the end, came from Brynjar Gunnarsson who blasted home a loose ball after a Leroy Lita free kick had hit the Blackburn wall.

The draw turned out not to be enough for a trip to Europe, as Bolton had also drawn, and so Reading finished their first ever season in the top-flight in eighth place – a position a million miles away from that predicted by all the pre-seasons pundits, a position that exceeded the expectations of even the most optimistic Reading supporters and a position that was achieved with minimal investment and the core of the team that had stormed the Championship the previous season.

Considering the resources available, Coppell and his coaches, aided by Mark Reynolds and his Catalyst team, had achieved miracles, and was named the League Managers Association Manager of the Year – the only manager ever to have won this award two seasons running.

As Reading supporters took stock at the end of this incredible season, the same feelings of disbelief and 'where would it all end' that we'd felt for the past two season were still there. Walking away from this Blackburn game I made the comment "it'll never get any better than this", which kicked this whole book off, while Loyal Royal Neil Maskell had similar thoughts.

Recalling this match, he says: *"One more match that I've got to say encapsulated the spirit was the last game of that season, the three-all at Blackburn, where we were behind three times and we could have won and qualified for Europe."*

"But that would have been the cherry on top of it – the Bullseye *speedboat! And it would have been something else, because we had the goalkeeper injured, we had the sense of injustice, battling back – and then the goal for three-all when it banged into the wall and the Blackburn fans jeered, then it came back to Gunnarsson and a fringe player scored the three-all. And at that point an inflatable JCB flew past my eyes, I thought 'this can't get any better' – and do you know what? It didn't, actually."*

CHAPTER SEVENTEEN

You Can't Always Get What You Want

IN HINDSIGHT, IT'S EASY TO see that this last match of the 2006/07 season, away at Blackburn, was very much the high point for Reading. Within half an hour, in his post-match interview on Radio Five Live, Coppell confirmed what many had long expected – that Steve Sidwell had left the club. Nine days later Sidwell had signed for Chelsea. Nick Hammond told me that he felt that Sidwell would be better going to a club where he was more likely to play, but that there was a real pull to Chelsea for him: *"Obviously the lure of Chelsea and the confidence in his own abilities, his father was a Chelsea supporter and I think that was just, sort of too big for him really … that lure."*

Many were surprised by the size of the club Sidwell had signed for, which would potentially limit his opportunities, and as it turned out Sidwell only started seven Premier League matches for Chelsea. But that confidence in his own abilities that Hammond spoke about is critical – it's a characteristic of the vast majority of professional footballers that they have total belief in their abilities, as much as anything else because they need that drive and confidence to get through the many years in the academy and to prove themselves worthy of a professional contract in a profession where an estimated 99 percent of the kids who enter clubs' academies fail to make a living as players.

Nine months after Sidwell left, in the week he wasn't named in Chelsea's Champions League squad, Kevin Doyle was asked whether he felt that his ex-teammate had made a mistake in signing for Chelsea only to sit on the bench. His answer was very revealing about the mind-set of professional footballers, as he said that he felt sure Sidwell would have gone to Chelsea with a firm belief that he would succeed there – that although he might not get his chance straight away, one day it would come and at that point he would have the ability to grab it and to be successful. Tellingly, Doyle added that one of the worst fears of footballers would be to look back on their career in its final days and think 'what might have happened if I hadn't turned down that big move when I was offered it?'

With that in mind, and considering the contribution he'd made to the club over the previous four and a half years, I don't think anyone can seriously criticise Sidwell for leaving at this point. John Madejski feels no bitterness, telling me: *"Steve Sidwell was one of the finest players we ever had and I was very sorry to see him go, but he did and obviously to better himself, no doubt, but he was a first-class guy and there's not much more I can say about him."*

For many supporters, one of the Coppell's greatest achievements of this season was to get such a consistently high standard of performance and commitment from Sidwell for the whole season, despite the situation with his unsigned contract. But he had now left, and would leave a massive hole in central midfield to be plugged.

As Ady Williams told me: *"The thing with Sidwell was the gaffer knew he was going, we all knew he was going. So the clever managers and coaches, they knew that he wouldn't be there the following season so you've got to make sure to replace him. Did they have enough time to replace him? I imagine they did because they had the closed season and everything else – but a huge loss and at the end of the day it didn't work out at Chelsea for Siddy, but what an opportunity – I don't think any Reading fan begrudged him going."*

But the story of the search for a replacement for Sidwell is perhaps symptomatic of the perennial problems Reading face in player recruitment. The 20-year-old Hibernian midfield starlet Scott Brown had been lined up as a replacement for Sidwell, and a deal had been agreed with his club. Nick Hammond takes up the story: *"Of course we had to replace Sidwell and in fairness I'd done a deal with Hibs for Scott Brown. The deal was done, the deal was agreed between the clubs – but we couldn't get the player to come to Reading. He was a player that I really liked, he was a player that Brian really liked, he was a player that we'd got Steve to go and see him up in Edinburgh. We literally couldn't get him on the plane, we couldn't get him interested and actually it was very disappointing at the time – but on reflection he had no interest in coming to England, full stop."*

"He went to Celtic and he's had a very good career and good luck to him for that, so that would have been a natural replacement and the deal was done so there was no lack of support from the club from a financial perspective. But there was also other deals that materialised – possibly more expensive and I think we lost an opportunity at that point in time. I think Steve was in a bit of a quandary as well in terms of the group that he had and how well they'd done – there was a change in dynamic in the group, but understandably so because they had proved to be capable players in the Premier League so therefore they did want to be rewarded for that, which you could completely understand."

"If you finished eighth in the Premier League and played in every game, why would you not expect an improvement in your contract if your existing contract doesn't reflect that? So that is understandable – so there

was a change in the group. I think Steve was concerned – and again I'm not going to talk for him – but I think he found himself in a little bit of a quandary as to where the salaries were going to be for the three or four players that we would bring, that was definitely a concern for him."

"I think he's said this publicly before so I don't think I'm betraying a confidence, but there was a concern on his part that if you've got a core group of players earning this much money, what happens if you bring a player in earning twice as much money? And he was always of a view that the players will accept a superstar who's making the difference, whose earnings are considerable, they'll accept it – but if there's a more standard player, a more journeyman player, whatever term you want to use, and he's earning significantly more, that's a harder sell ..."

The player finally purchased as a 'Sidwell replacement' was Emerse Faé, purchased from Nantes for £2.5 million. As Hammond told me: "So Emerse Faé was a result of not replacing Sidwell with Scott Brown and not replacing Sidwell with a couple of others that were more expensive and I couldn't get done – whether it be Steve or upstairs – deals that we should have done in my opinion. Emerse Faé came late, we knew him from France, Steve [Coppell] didn't know him, Brian and I knew him. He was a talented boy, he was a good footballer, he was actually a fairly decent like-for-like replacement for Siddy in terms of he could get around the pitch, wasn't as aggressive as Siddy, but he was a bit more progressive in terms of his ability to run forward. So we got to a stage where we needed to bring one in so we brought him and he was a player who probably needed to go straight into the team and play and find his way in the team – and he didn't."

Wally Downes expanded on the dilemma facing Coppell, Hammond et al when I asked him if Coppell had been too loyal to his core group of players: "Perhaps, but you have to be. The players that you're given through your recruitment have to be significantly better than the ones you've got. Now we were buying players, I think

Emerse Faé was £3 million, Greg Halford £2 million. Now our players were all worth more than that so the players we're getting in weren't a significant improvement on the ones we had. So if you buy players in who aren't better than the ones you've got – and you're offering them a lot more money than the ones you've got – then you're going to have trouble."

Asked at the end-of-season fans' forum where he thought the squad needed improvements, Coppell said that he felt they were lacking three or four match-winners, as well as to improve and maintain their defensive strength and also to be more proficient up front. He also pointed to a lack of cover at left back.

That certainly ties up with the 'three or four' players that Hammond was talking of. He remembers going into that summer with some optimism: *"So it was a remarkable season. Again I've a clear recollection of the summer because I think we'd put ourselves in a position – I don't like the term 'take the next step' – but the season had been strong enough where we'd given ourselves a bit of profile, a league position in the Premier League of eighth and therefore a greater ability to attract players to our club, that's what I thought."*

Coppell also seems to have been optimistic going into this summer, telling the April fans' forum that he felt the club now had 'more options' due to their league position, and while identifying target players is easy, the difficult task is to identify those that the club can afford, which normally means finding fresh talent from outside the UK. He also pointed out that he needed players who were Premier League-ready, as he no longer had the time to develop players, citing Sidwell who'd been developed at the club for three and a half years.

Downes also told a fans' forum a few months later about the difficulty in recruiting players to Reading, saying that teams like Reading can only get the players the bigger clubs

don't want – talking in terms of 'crumbs off a table'. But he felt
that Reading's players at the time were as good as those they'd
looked at outside the top four clubs, and they needed to find
players who wouldn't upset the balance of the squad, something that can be very difficult.

Kevin Dillon told the same fans' forum about a new method the club was using to try to sell the club to potential players,
involving sending out DVDs to agents of players the club is
interested in. This showcased the stadium and the local area:
"It's quite a nice area, affluent, good houses and nice country-
side."

But despite all the efforts, in the end, that summer saw just
one other signing apart from Faé – that of right-back Liam
Rosenior from Fulham, who came in as part of a player swap
that saw Seol leave for West London. Several of those I spoke
to felt that the thriving Korean community of New Malden –
home of Fulham's training ground – was always Seol's
ultimate destination, and was one of his reasons for joining
Reading in the first place.

I asked Hammond if the failure to secure the players he
and Coppell wanted was down to a lack of overall budget or
an unwillingness to bid enough for individual players. He
replied that it was a lack of overall budget, adding: *"We'd
finished eighth, so was there a desire to spend an enormous amount of
money. Because the one thing that you can guarantee is you can spend – I
guess I'm talking more and more up to date now – you can spend £15–
20 million and make your team no better in my opinion. It might be
wrong, but that's my opinion – in fact you can make it worse."*

*"So it was a tricky summer, I certainly wanted to push on and I
thought we had good targets that we had a realistic chance of signing – but
for all sorts of reasons we didn't."*

Apart from players, another change was to happen this summer to take away another component of the machine that made Reading function so well both on and off the pitch. After just two years of them working so closely with the club, retained each time on a single year's contract, the engagement of Catalyst as performance consultants came to an end.

In many ways this was inevitable, since, as Reading were Catalyst's first sports customer, they were engaged on very low rates to allow them to prove their worth – in a similar way to the way a supermarket sells baked beans below cost price as a 'loss leader'. As Mark Reynolds told me: *"We didn't ask for more than one season for the simple reason the Reading deal was a very good deal. And we were able to achieve a factor of about nine times the reward from our next client – as opposed to our current client. So if Reading had asked for a two-year deal – which they didn't – we would probably have said 'No' anyhow. We might have said 'Yes' but it wouldn't have been on the same terms – and that would have resulted in an ultimate 'No'. So, just like many of the contracts in the club at that time, it was a one-year deal. And that suited us."*

Reynolds told me that there was discussion at some length about that second Premier League season, but that he saw the way forward would be for the skills and techniques that Catalyst brought to be taken up inside the club, or, as he told me: *"If you are steering an ocean liner, you use a small pilot ship to get you into dock. You don't use the pilot ship to cross the Atlantic. So the skills set, the ideas, the plans, the strategies had to at some stage go inboard. And I am bound to say they didn't go as quickly as inboard as they should have done."*

There appears to have been no rancour or bitterness, and Catalyst simply moved on to their next, far more lucrative, engagement, as is the nature with consulting assignments. I asked Reynolds if he felt that Reading would have survived if Catalyst had been retained for another season. He told me: *"Yes – for the simple reason that we never failed. In every club that we worked for we achieved the objective. So our client in 2007/2008 were promoted. A little less emphatic than the way that Reading went up but nonetheless promoted. Less resources; less talent in the squad; lesser frenetic, electric environment than we managed to create in Reading – but a lot of the same techniques and tools we applied. And our client succeeded."*

"So if Reading had retained us for the following season we would have succeeded. Or, more to the point, if Reading had proposed and we would have accepted we would have accepted. We would have succeeded or we wouldn't have taken the retention. We have to be very careful. Nobody wants to employ a consultant who failed. Nobody wants to pay a huge amount of money to not succeed. So we couldn't take a project where we wouldn't succeed. We never failed in any of the objectives or any of the contracts that we took on. We never failed."

One of those I spoke to likened Catalyst to a magician, and said, disparagingly, that after two years at the club people were starting to 'see how their tricks were done'.

This clearly rankled with Reynolds, whose response was to point out that: *"I thought the idea was we were all learning to be a magician."* But it's beyond doubt, to me at least, that Catalyst's magic tricks benefitted Reading massively. The question now was whether the club would be able to perform any more magic tricks all on their own.

CHAPTER EIGHTEEN

I Think We're Alone Now

FOR THE START OF READING'S second Premier League season, without Steve Sidwell, without Catalyst and without significant new signings, the fixture compilers had not been kind. Reading started with an away trip to Old Trafford to face Manchester United, followed by a visit from Chelsea three days later – the two top placed teams in the league the previous season.

Despite Reading's eighth place finish the previous season, they were still towards the top of most pundits' lists of likely relegation candidates, and the most frequently heard buzzword of the time was 'second season syndrome' – but when asked about this at a fans' forum four months earlier, Steve Coppell had reacted with scepticism, questioning its existence and saying that he intended to talk about it as a challenge to motivate the players to improve as a team.

And, facing the champions on their own turf in the first game, Reading equipped themselves well and confounded the critics again in a match where Coppell's tactical nous came to the fore once more. With five men in midfield and with Kevin Doyle alone up front, Reading denied United time and space, marking them man-to-man whenever near the Reading area. This type of defensive performance is physically exhausting at any time, but in this case made even harder for the last 20 minutes when Dave Kitson was sent off within a minute of coming on for a lunge on Patrice Evra – careless, yes, and probably worth a yellow card, but one of those cards that inevitably turns red at grounds like Old Trafford. But this gritty, organised, backs-to-the-wall performance earned Reading a creditable 0-0 draw, and on a day when every Reading player put in a real shift, the way that Graeme Murty made Ryan Giggs look unexceptional all afternoon is particularly worthy of mention.

Back at the MadStad against Chelsea, again Reading produced a creditable performance against a team much bigger and richer. Dominating the first half, Reading went in for halftime just one goal ahead despite creating numerous chances – a goal scored by Andre Bikey with his very first touch, having come on to replace the injured Michael Duberry. This was a tap-in after Čech had dropped the ball from a corner – his first match at the MadStad since incurring that fractured skull ten months earlier.

With the Chelsea midfield misfiring badly, it was no surprise that José Mourinho made changes just after halftime – taking off Paulo Ferreira and Sidwell, the latter making his first for the visitors after two substitute appearances – and the game changed almost immediately. First Lampard broke from midfield to score, and just three minutes later a superb turn and shot from Didier Drogba, from the edge of the area, put Chelsea ahead. Reading worked hard to get back into the game and tore forward at every opportunity, but it wasn't to be, especially after debutant Kalifa Cissé, purchased from Boavista for £600,000 the previous May, was sent off for a second yellow card with 18 minutes left – the team's second red card in their first two matches.

A match in which Reading received plaudits for a brave, hard-working performance, but got nothing from! It's perhaps a good indicator of the difference in class between these teams that Reading had plenty of chances but scored only one goal, while Chelsea had far fewer but scored twice.

The season did get properly underway against Everton the following Saturday, with a 1-0 home win secured by a neat goal just before the interval from Stephen Hunt. But with Murty limping off in the first half to join an ever-growing injury list, with Seol playing his last match before departing for Fulham and with Kitson and Cissé suspended, the lack of depth in this squad was starting to become apparent.

And this was really exposed for the first time in the team's next match. Nicky Shorey was also injured, and replaced by Scott Golbourne – a young prospect signed as defensive cover in January 2006 but making his only League start for Reading in this match. The team was comprehensively outplayed by Bolton, losing 3-0. This match was really the first warning of what was to come this season – Reading had lost plenty of matches since the start of this incredible period, and had been outplayed by teams many times. But in all of those matches they'd never lost their incredible desire and sprit. But at the Reebok Stadium this day they looked defeated as soon as the first goal went in, as if they didn't really have the stomach for the fight. Bolton manager Sammy Lee, 'Little Sam' who took over in charge of Bolton after the departure of 'Big Sam' Allardyce, was sacked in October 2007 after only winning one match out of 11 – this match against Reading was that one victory, which shows just how poor the visitors' performance was that day.

Things were no better as the season moved into September, with a dispiriting 3-0 home defeat to West Ham in the first week (partial revenge for the Hammers' 6-0 drubbing eight months to the day earlier), followed a fortnight later by a 2-1 defeat away at Sunderland that saw Reading drop to 18th in the table.

Sunderland were desperate to win this match as a tribute to Ian Porterfield, their much-loved 1973 FA Cup winning legend, and also manager of Reading for 18 months from 1989 – and therefore the first manager ever sacked by John Madejski! Despite facing this extra motivation, it was impossible to escape the conclusion that something was missing from this Reading team – not just the spirit and the desire, but the defensive organisation that had served them so well for over two seasons.

Prior to Ibrahima Sonko's injury in January 2007, he and Ingimarsson had formed an unchanged central defensive partners for all but one of 71 consecutive league matches spread across three seasons. The only match either missed in this 21-month period was the one-match suspension Sonko received after his red card at Villa Park in their first away Premier League match. Although Sonko's return from injury was imminent, his absence was conspicuous for all to see, and his was a vacancy Duberry was unable to adequately fill. He'd had a long and distinguished career elsewhere, but it was drawing to a close now, and he wasn't a like-for-like substitute for Sonko in terms of pace, of power – or of sheer physical presence.

Ady Williams, a central defender all his career, expanded on the impact Sonko's injury had on the team: *"Duberry was coming to the end of his career. Sonko was a different player to Duberry although they were both big physical men, but Sonko had that pace and I think you need that pace in the Premier League so without a doubt I think him getting injured changed that back five – when I say 'five', I mean Hahnemann as well, and if you've only got one link that comes out of it and someone relatively new comes in then it's going to affect the balance and it's going to affect the performances."*

To emphasise this fact, and the loss of defensive organisation, in the nine starts Duberry made in the first half of this season, Reading shipped 21 goals. However, these numbers may be skewed by one single game – a bizarre and shambolic afternoon on the South Coast that is still the Premier League's highest scoring match ever.

Away to Portsmouth, Reading were two goals behind after 37 minutes, fought back to level the scores and then conceded a third. Given an immediate chance to equalise again from the penalty spot, Shorey fluffed it. After that it was one-way traffic as Pompey scored three more in an 11 minute period, in which Reading got just one goal before adding a late consolation. If you've lost count of the score by now, that's exactly what it was like being at the game – a 7-4 defeat that saw one goal after another fly in with the Reading defence looking like stunned strangers chasing shadows in a darkened room, with a midfield in front of them offering no protection. Both supporters and players came away from the game shell-shocked, and in subsequent matches the impact on the team's confidence was plain to see.

Loyal Royal Dave Harris shares his recollections of this horrible match: *"Look at their side, look at ours – they're bigger than us everywhere, 6 foot-plus players all over the park. The defence couldn't handle Benjani; the wide men couldn't handle Utaka and Kranjčar; our four-man midfield were hopelessly overrun by the trio of Davis, Muntari and Diop. Couple that to individual errors we made all match – Benjani free at the back post for the first; backing off Banjani for the second; Hahnemann's error for the third; Pompey's smallest player winning a header for the fourth; complete miscommunication for Benjani's hat-trick and Pompey's fifth; an unfortunate deflection for Davis's sixth; and the flailing hacks at Kranjčar when giving away the penalty for the Pompey swansong. A team devoid of confidence that couldn't handle the pace, power, movement and ability of Portsmouth. And let's not forget we missed a penalty at 3-2 down! All in all a day when if anything could possibly go wrong it did!"*

Despite this defeat, Reading did win their next match 1-0, with Kevin Doyle scoring his first goal of the season in his eighth match. However, if they hadn't their fragile confidence would surely have been shattered, for the visitors to the MadStad were Derby, who had already achieved their single win of the season and were en route to becoming officially the poorest Premier League team ever. But away at Blackburn the following week, Reading again shipped four goals. Three down after half an hour, though, they improved after Coppell changed the team around, saying after the match: *"It's me, it's my fault. I chose the wrong way of playing, 100 percent. I fiddled around with the team and the consequences were all too evident."* Whether this is the absolute truth or an attempt to take the blame in an effort to shore up his players' plummeting confidence is open to debate, though. Notable for the return from injury of Sonko, this was not a great performance from the Senegalese defender, with him conceding a late penalty. However, Reading fans were happy to recognise his talismanic status and give him the benefit of the doubt after such a serious injury.

The season continued in a similar vein, with a home win over Newcastle and a much improved performance – which

Coppell called 'just like seeing an old friend' followed by another morale-sapping defeat. This was away to Fulham, in the match dubbed 'El Middle-Classico'. Fulham were looking prime relegation candidates with just one win, over Lee's hapless Bolton, from their first 11 league matches, although they'd also drawn seven matches. For Dave Harris this was one of the defining matches of the season, with Reading: *"Unable to beat a Fulham side desperately short on confidence, despite dominating the game."*

This was definitely points thrown away in a match that Reading could easily have won, but one that highlighted how inconsistent the Reading midfield had become. In the centre, James Harper was obviously missing the partnership with Sidwell, a partnership that went back to January 2003, and played alongside a series of central midfield partners. The de facto, last-turkey-in-the-shop 'Sidwell replacement', Emerse Faé, had started just three matches, so Brynjar Gunnarsson had found himself alongside Harper for the bulk of the season so far.

Gunnarsson had made only ten starts the previous season, and at the age of 31 sadly wasn't the player to replace Sidwell on a match-by-match basis. Sidwell's game had been all about getting up and down the pitch, helping out in defence and attack and driving the team on. Although a marvellously versatile and combative player, much loved by every Reading fan for his industry and indomitable spirit, that wasn't Gunnarsson's game. Combative and technically very skilled, he didn't have the ability to cover enough ground for 90 minutes in a four-man midfield at Premier League level. Loyal Royal Neil Maskell puts it succinctly: *"It was a bit like replacing your iPod with a Walkman. It did exactly the same job on the face of things but less effectively."*

As well as these damaging changes in the centre of the midfield, there were also devastating changes on the flanks – the areas that had been so vital to Reading's attacking play over recent seasons. Glen Little, on the right, had not played since the previous April with an Achilles tendon injury, an injury that always seemed to be on the verge of recovery, but which in the end lingered on and on. Asked about it at a fans' forum at the start of this season, Wally Downes said that Little's Achilles was improving and he'd just started walking on it, but that things had to be taken slowly and he'd not yet returned to training – adding that he'd rather the famously talkative Little was suffering from laryngitis instead! But as the season went on there was no improvement, and despite reportedly being treated by a Swedish specialist who injected honey to help the healing process, Little's only contribution this season was two substitute appearances at the very tail end of it.

With Seol now gone to Fulham, John Oster was Coppell's first choice on the right wing. As Ron Grant says of Oster: *"He was a good player … one of the things with John was he'd have two or three good games then have a bad game, he wasn't as consistent as what you were looking for, but he could be a match winner."* But as football fans tend to do, many Reading supporters noticed the bad games more than the good games, and there was a general resentment against Oster among many for the simple fact that he wasn't Glen Little, so his mistakes tended to be criticised more loudly than was reasonable – something unlikely to increase the ratio of good to bad games.

On the other side of the pitch, although Convey had re-covered from his long-term injury his impact was much less that he'd had two seasons earlier. The previous season Stephen Hunt had become the first choice left winger, and, as Nick Hammond has told us, Convey found it difficult to cope with this change in status. But Coppell found himself with far fewer options on the wings than he would have liked. Two seasons ago he'd had the luxury of four fit and in-form wingers throughout virtually the whole season, and so invariably brought on fresh players on both wings in the final stages of a match – now there were matches where he had only two wingers available to him, and sometimes not even that many. Right-sided midfielder Liam Rosenior, who had arrived from Fulham in exchange for Seol, was not a conspicuous success – especially during the heavy defeats at Portsmouth and Blackburn, and at Blackburn it was only when Coppell took Rosenior off and reverted to an orthodox four-man midfield that Reading started to get back into the game.

These injuries had a greater effect than just the loss of the players on the pitch, though. Nigel Howe highlighted the impact that losing players like Little and Sonko had upon the dressing room – Little for his part in camaraderie and overall team spirt, and Sonko's loss as an on-field leader. Nick Hammond agreed, saying: *"Yes. Strong characters, good characters. I mean Glen was Glen but Sonko was a real solid individual, didn't speak very often but just by his stature, the way he carried himself, he was a leader. Glen just talked rubbish most of the time, but he was great and if things are tough or your day's difficult, he's the one who gets them going again."*

This defeat at Fulham was the first of three straight defeats. The second, to Arsenal, was not unexpected, but the third, at Manchester City, was a painful one. Reading defended well and despite going behind to an early scrambled goal they fought back to equalise from a lovely volley from Harper just before the break. Soaking up the pressure right until the end, they looked to have secured only their second away point of the season until a spectacular long-range wonder goal in the 92nd minute from Stephen Ireland took that single point away. Yes, Reading were odds-on to lose this match, but they had played so well and fought so hard it was gutting to come away with nothing in the end. As Neil Maskell says: *"It would have been a massive fillip to get something against a side that had spent so heavily under Sven-Göran Eriksson."*

Despite the mixed results, and the clear crisis of confidence, Reading were in 12th place – still comfortably mid-table – as December came. Although they'd suffered some seriously demoralising defeats, they were still picking up enough draws and the occasional win to keep them out of the melee at the bottom. It was a season notable both for the number of poor teams in the league and for the dominance of the biggest teams, which left those towards the bottom fewer points to fight over and increased the significance of the games between them.

Another draw came in the next home match against Middlesbrough. In a drab game, Reading again looked disheartened and low on confidence, with only Kitson and Hunt showing any real quality. Kitson scored Reading's goal with a neat chip, but the visitors equalised (as most there expected them to) seven minutes from the end – the days of Reading's invincibility, with the crowd confident they would hold onto a lead and would always create chances to score, were by then a distant memory. Atmosphere had declined accordingly, too.

This game, however, was notable for another sign that the old Reading team spirit wasn't what it had been just a few months earlier. Midway through the second half, a poor back-pass from Sonko put Marcus Hahnemann under pressure, and the 'keeper rounded on the centre-back. Neither of these players had been playing as well as they had in the two previous seasons, and they were now showing the kind of indiscipline that was anathema to Coppell's side. Team spirit and togetherness had been crucial factors in their phenomenal success, so this kind of public confrontation was totally out of character – the first all too visible sign of cracks in Reading's famous unity and team spirit.

After failing to beat a Middlesbrough team in the bottom three, a week later Reading's up and down season continued with their first ever win over a 'Big Four' team – a 3-1 home victory over Liverpool. With Coppell's 'old friend' back, every Reading player rose to the occasion to out-play a full-strength team featuring Gerrard, Crouch, Torres, Mascherano and Carragher in their prime, a team that had yet to lose a league match all season. A great performance, and a great day for Reading supporters – although, of course, the media's take on it wasn't how well Reading had played to beat Liverpool, but how Liverpool had allowed themselves to be beaten by a team like Reading.

Away at Birmingham, in Alex McLeish's first match in charge of The Blues, another point came with a creditable and hard-working – if unspectacular – 1-1 draw. Again, Hunt and Kitson were Reading's standout players, and Reading had a glorious chance to take all three points in the final minutes when Shane Long, on as an 86th minute substitute, tried a

spectacular scissor-kick when the ball broke to him in front of
goal – when almost any other method would have given him a
better chance of scoring. In the words of Dave Harris: *"We
should have come away with three points but for Shane Long trying the
spectacular when ruthless composure was the order of the day."*

Another home victory followed, three days before Christmas with Sunderland beaten 2-1 in a tight game with a
dramatic 90th-minute winner, scored by Stephen Hunt. This
was awarded by the linesman who overruled the referee's view
that the ball hadn't crossed the line, and came eight minutes
after Sonko had given away a penalty to allow the visitors to
equalise. All this late controversy was too much for Roy
Keane, who lost his cool and lashed out in Coppell's office
after the game. In his 2014 autobiography, Keane cites this
incident as the only time in his football career that he truly lost
control – but he lays the blame wholly at the feet of Kevin
Dillon, who he says was abusing him throughout the match
and again when he arrived at Coppell's office post-match.

Clearly all the teams towards the bottom of the table were
feeling the pressure, but surprisingly Reading weren't among
them. A hard-working match on Boxing Day at West Ham
saw Reading lose Brynjar Gunnarsson to a straight red card
with less than half an hour gone but hold on for a 1-1, their
fifth match unbeaten. So at this halfway point of the season,
the traditional point where pundits take stock of progress and
decide likely relegation candidates, Reading were in 12th place
with 22 points. Eight points and five places below them came
Sunderland, just ahead of Fulham, also with 14 points, and
Wigan followed with one point fewer. Derby propped up
everyone else with just seven points. Although the season had

been marked by inconsistency and a noticeable drop from their standards, Reading had eight teams below them in the table and looked safe enough as they tackled the second half of the season.

CHAPTER NINETEEN

What's the Story, Nicky Shorey?

TWO SEASONS EARLIER, IT HAD been an acknowledged truism that Reading's form dipped after Christmas – hence the special motivational efforts from Catalyst, including the video performance by Jack Black and Vinnie Jones, to ensure this didn't happen again.

After two seasons where their performances had hardly dipped after the New Year it may have been considered that this particular ghost had been exorcised, but in fact it came back with a vengeance to haunt Reading all over again. After those five unbeaten matches, and the draw at the Boleyn Ground, Reading's next league point came nine matches later on 1st March.

This run started at White Hart Lane on 29th December, in the second match this season where Reading scored four goals away from home and lost. But unlike Portsmouth, where the damage was wholly self-inflicted, on this occasion there were some mitigating circumstances. At Fratton Park Reading had always been playing catch-up, but here they matched Spurs goal for goal, taking the lead three times after going a goal down after seven minutes. But Spurs equalised each time in a spirited and committed performance where every attack from either team looked like it might create a goal.

But with the scores at 4-4 and with 12 minutes left to play, Sonko brought down Robbie Keane in the area to give away another penalty, which Keane took himself. This was saved by Hahnemann but the rebound was scored by Jermaine Defoe, who'd encroached so much that he was alongside Keane as he took the kick. Mysteriously, this was unseen by the officials and the goal stood – and effectively knocked the stuffing out of Reading. With heads down, and concentration replaced by outrage, they conceded Dimitar Berbatov's fourth goal of the match four minutes later to make the final score 6-4 and saw Spurs move above them in the table.

A year later I attended a presentation given by a Referees' Assessor from Professional Game Match Officials Limited, demonstrating the use of video technology in his role. One of the case studies presented was this error by referee Keith Stroud and his assistants – described as one of the most egregious errors made by a referee that season. Having seen Reading's fight and spirit throughout the match, and the way the game had fluctuated for the previous 78 minutes, I'm sure they would have carried on competing to the end if that decision hadn't kicked them in the guts. Although after the match Coppell said that the penalty should have been retaken, the correct decision in that circumstance should have been an indirect free kick to Reading. If that had happened, without the incorrect goal – and with the players' minds still focussed on the match and not on the officials – I'm sure the final score would have been quite different.

The performance at Spurs meant confidence was still high, and the New Year's Day home match against Portsmouth was a quick chance to get the season back on track – but instead it veered badly off course almost from the start. Just three minutes into the match Sonko was caught out by the pace of Benjani for the second time – he dived in, giving away a clear penalty and receiving a red card. The penalty was missed, but Reading had another 87 minutes in the match with only ten men and with all other game plans out of the window.

They failed to get anything from this game, losing 2-0, and in many ways two things became obvious from it – neither of them positive. The first was the sad truth that Sonko post-injury was not the same player as Sonko pre-injury. Something had gone from him. He'd lost none of his bravery and commitment, but his game had always relied on an extra yard of pace and acceleration to allow him to overcome quickly any positional weaknesses. Now that pace and acceleration was slightly diminished and he found himself increasingly out of position and being beaten by attackers. Not used to being beaten so easily, as a result he found himself increasingly out of position and unable to recover, mistiming tackles when he got to the ball later than he once would have done.

This penalty was the third penalty he'd conceded in his last four matches. The man dubbed 'Superman' after making an unbelievable diving goal-line block to stop a point-blank shot against Ipswich in October 2005 had now turned into 'Blooperman'. Everyone sadly agreed that the injury had taken something vital away from Sonko's game – or at least nearly everyone. Nick Hammond said, with a glint in his eye: *"Actually I can't say that, 'cos I signed him to Stoke!"*

But Reading's defensive talisman, described by Ron Grant as *"like a pedigree racehorse – the most powerful and impressive central defender I've ever seen at the club and one who was such a key component of the perfect team and its almost impregnable defence"* – would make only three more starts for the club.

The other worrying sign was the form of Nicky Shorey, another defensive stalwart but also someone whose distribution from the back was a vital component of Reading's attacking play. His recent performances had been noticeably below those of previous years – a level of performance that had seen him become the first Reading player to play for the full England team when he won his first cap in his country's first match at the new Wembley stadium the previous May. A second cap was won against Germany three months later.

The drop in performance, and an apparent change in attitude, was highlighted in this match when he was easily beaten to a routine ball by John Utaka to allow Portsmouth's second goal. Coppell said after the match that Shorey was completely washed out after being ill and vomiting for the previous couple of days – but fans who'd seen his demeanour over recent games weren't particularly convinced.

Loyal Royal Neil Maskell remembers this game well, saying: *"Shorey was done for pace. He wasn't the quickest and there was a bit of an air of 'well, you know …' He didn't seem to really care. I remember looking across, he was on the far side of the pitch. It was hands on the hips and a shrug and back to the centre circle. And that seemed a bit … not what we were about to be honest."*

Loyal Royal Dave Harris adds: *"It was clear he was just lacking that extra little bit of heart required. His performances the season before were simply stunning, and while nobody ever expected him to maintain such a high level of performance it was roundly disappointing to see him so visibly below the level we knew he could maintain."*

Ever since Shorey had missed the away match at Bolton at the end of April, rumours had abounded that an offer from West Ham had come in for him that had been declined, and that Shorey was now, in the terminology of media pundits, 'unsettled'. Accompanying this were rumours that this yearning for greener grass elsewhere had been compounded by spending time with the England squad where all the players earnt considerably more than him, as well as by the close friendship between his wife and Sidwell's.

I asked Nick Hammond about this time. He told me: *"So we'd had an enquiry from West Ham, we had an offer from West Ham – in football parlance it was a 'derisory offer'. It certainly was a derisory offer, I can't remember how much, it might have been £2 million, £2.5 million – something like that. The upshot was after that West Ham disappeared – never came back! Nicky was under the impression that West Ham were chasing, chasing, chasing him. They weren't!"*

"Maybe they should have been because he was an outstanding footballer, but I've known the family ... Stevie [Shorey's father, Steve] *still works for us ... I've known the family for many, many years, so I had to sit down and say 'look, this isn't happening. There was interest at a certain level – pushed back on that. Would have expected something else to come – it never did'. What I believe now is that it was a deal that was starting to be driven by upstairs* [at West Ham] *but not really by Alan Curbishley. That's my recollection."*

Hammond agreed when I asked him whether Shorey's performance levels dipped: *"Yeah, that season they certainly did. For a player of such high quality, yeah. There was no doubt in my mind that that wasn't anything to do with his ability and 100 percent that wasn't a thing on his part. It's just the psychology of a player and how things work – but another great player for us over that period. Fantastic player!"*

Nigel Howe, though, is more forthright. Speaking with hindsight, he believes that the club made an error in not tackling this head-on the previous summer when the tentative 'offer' came in: *"Shorey should have gone. We tried to keep him and he just started playing like ... that was the mistake, and we went into the next season with a disenchanted Shorey. There was a nasty smell in the changing room all the time and it should have been dealt with. The club made a mistake. I don't blame any individual, it was a collective thing that we weren't going to have our hand forced ... but on reflection ..."*

With Shorey below par, and without Little and Sonko, it's no wonder that overall performance levels had dropped. Other players who had done so well for the previous two seasons saw their form drop as well, such as Bobby Convey. But one of the real enigmas is the form of Leroy Lita.

Before the season started, Lita had a very successful European U21 Championship as part of the England team that lost in the semi-finals, and he was named in the tournament's 'UEFA Dream Team'. But his performances for Reading had dipped notably, and this striker – scorer of seven goals the previous season and 11 the year before that – scored just one goal this campaign in the very last minute of the very last game of the season. Kevin Doyle worked tirelessly but was only on the scoresheet six times, while Shane Long was developing but still a little too raw to carry the burden of impact player.

The bulk of Reading's goals were coming from two players who were having superb seasons, two players who many said had 'carried the team' in this season so far. The first was Dave Kitson, scorer of eight goals in the first half of the season, and the highest-scoring Englishman in the Premier League at the time. Kitson was subject to a serious level of attention from the football media – not just because of speculation that he was on the verge of a call-up to Steve McClaren's England but also because he was in many ways the antithesis of the average Premier League footballer, something that will always be of interest to the media.

The other in-form player was Stephen Hunt, who in two seasons had turned himself from perennial substitute to one of the first names on Coppell's team sheet each week. He was now the most threatening and most prolific part of Reading's midfield – and indeed often the only threatening and prolific part of it, with five goals to his name compared to a combined total of four from the other midfielders.

While the combined efforts of Kitson and Hunt were spearheading Reading's efforts to stay safely out of the relegation scramble, there was the opportunity to strengthen the squad in the January transfer window. Two players arrived in the form of Malian winger Jimmy Kébé, signed from Lens for £400,000, and Czech midfielder Marek Matějovský, who came from FK Mladá Boleslav in the Czech Republic for £1.5 million. Emerse Faé, the planned Sidwell replacement, had made just three starts and three substitute appearances, so for many Matějovský was the missing link that was needed in midfield.

But events were to conspire to disrupt the successful streaks of both Kitson and Hunt. In the second week of January, Kitson was arrested and charged with failing to provide specimens after being arrested on suspicion of drink-driving. Several around the club have told me that they are convinced Kitson was the victim of some kind of 'trap' or 'set-up' specially laid for him, but Kitson was found guilty in court a week later. After this incident he scored just two more Reading goals that season.

Hunt's great form, meanwhile, had been noticed by other clubs, particularly Sunderland, possibly because of his match-winning performance against them just before Christmas. All through January there were reports of ever-increasing offers from the Stadium of Light, with three separate bids reportedly being made. The highest of these reportedly stood at £5 million and would have made Hunt the highest paid player at Sunderland.

But at the end of January Hunt signed a new contract with Reading, and almost immediately his performances seemed to drop, which of course led to many leaping to the conclusion that he'd played well to earn the contract and had then 'taken his foot off the gas'.

This was something else I spoke to Nick Hammond about. He told me: *"As I've said, Hunty is a fantastic player for me in terms of attitude and work and it's really interesting because obviously he got to a point where he played really well for us and there was talk about interest from this club and that club ... the simple truth is Steve Coppell didn't want to sell him. He was under contract, Steve Coppell didn't want to sell him – so I think he got himself quite wound up about it, Hunty, and he blamed me – which he always did."*

"And of course I have to take the brunt, because I have to keep it away from the manager ... I think he got himself to a point where he thought the club were being restrictive in terms of his career and all the things that go around that – and they certainly were in the Sunderland instance, and he was under contract. But beyond that they weren't, so it sort of manifested itself in his own mind in terms of where that went ... but he was such a great boy, Hunty, and when I see him now we have a laugh and a joke about it. He's done fantastically well and, as I said, always a great example."

Ady Williams, however, puts Hunt's apparent decline down to a more straightforward reason – that the player had been over-performing to such a degree that it was inevitable that this could not continue. Williams told me: *"It's weird, strange, when things like that happen, because its happened with one or two other players and people think 'hang on – once they've extended their contract they can take their foot off the pedal'. But Stephen Hunt, particularly – he loved playing football, he was dogged, determined, he was a grafter, he never let anybody down. So coincidence or not, I don't know – but there was no way he could carry on doing what he did in the first part of the season because if he was playing like that week in, week out, he wouldn't be going to Sunderland, he'd be going to Chelsea!"*

The team played – and lost – three league games in January, but this wasn't seen as a major cause for concern as they were defeats to Aston Villa – at that stage flourishing under Martin O'Neill and on the way to European qualification – as well as to Manchester United and Chelsea. Reading also went out of the FA Cup after a third round replay defeat to Spurs – Coppell was still playing some of the 'fringe' players in the cup competitions, although with the size of the squad and the injuries suffered the lines between the first choice and fringe players was becoming increasingly blurred.

But if January had been poor – and pointless – February was where the wheels really came off. Dave Harris comments: *"I think for me it all started to feel wrong when we lost at home to Bolton in February. Up until that point I think we'd been far from brilliant but secured enough results and put in enough decent performances to suggest we could survive fairly comfortably. On the face of it we were in the middle of a bit of a slump, we'd suffered five defeats on the spin but for me I wasn't too concerned because the defeats came against teams that we were perhaps unlikely to beat. That's not to excuse the defeats but against Spurs, Man United and Chelsea in particular we played to the best of our ability and were somewhat unfortunate, perhaps naive, but the performance level was generally of a standard that suggested we'd be more than a match for the teams around us when we played them. Then the Bolton match. They'd not won an away match for a year, I think, and they rock up and*

*deservedly take all three points. An insipid display, we were usually strong
at home – so to lose in such a fashion was deeply concerning."*

That match at home to Bolton, Matějovský's first start
after two substitute appearances, really was a horror show that
still makes me wince all these years later. It was a poor game
from two poor teams, but Bolton won easily – although
Reading tried hard, there was minimal guile beyond pumping
endless hopeful balls into the box. Although his class as a
creative passing midfielder showed, Matějovský disappointed
many in other aspects of his game, especially when he lazily
left a leg out for Bolton's Grétar Steinsson to fall over in the
box. Hahnemann saved the resulting penalty, but it was a brief
respite with stand-in centre back Kalifa Cissé thoroughly
exposed by the height and power of Kevin Davies. Cissé had
filled that role well against Manchester United, shutting out
the relatively small duo of Wayne Rooney and Carlos Tevez –
but in this physical and aerial battle with Davies he was
horribly exposed. Bolton won 2-0, and the MadStad crowd –
or at least the 10,000 remaining at the final whistle, sensed
that something significant had happened on this grey day.

Reading needed to pick up points from teams around
them, and before the match Coppell had called on them to
step up – but once on the pitch they singularly failed to do so
and instead surrendered meekly. Deeply dispiriting for all, and
one of my most vivid memories of that depressing day, was of
the post-match queues to leave the car park, where behind me
a routine disagreement about who got to a junction first
turned into full-blown road-rage incident, complete with
fisticuffs. Fair play, I understood the sentiments completely – it
was that sort of day, everyone felt like lashing out!

That defeat dropped Reading down to 17th, with opti-

mism starting to evaporate, and this was exacerbated further
as they also lost their next two matches – away at Everton and
at home to Aston Villa. That made it eight straight league
defeats since Christmas, with the only goal in the run coming
in the 90th minute of the eighth match via a Shorey free kick.

Now down to 18th, the team had at last reached the relegation zone – just a point behind Birmingham but still three
clear of Fulham. The strain had been telling on everyone
throughout these depressing months, and it was clear the
team's confidence was at rock bottom and that they were no
longer enjoying what they were doing. The smiles of the
previous two seasons had been replaced by grimaces, the
rugged determination by nervousness and the confidence by a
reluctance to take responsibility of the ball. The old unity and
togetherness, the bedrock of their success, was also absent
much of the time, with persistent rumours of dressing-room
unhappiness and even the occasional clash. Nick Hammond
didn't dispute this, agreeing that there was *"a difficult atmosphere
around the group at that stage."* But he qualified it by explaining
that: *"A team who is losing games rather than winning games – the
issues become a little bit more magnified. But I had enormous confidence
and faith in the manager because he was the one constant and again that
was one of his great strengths …"*

Personally, although the team's league prospects looked
dire, I was confident Reading would stay up. I remember a
conversation with Nigel Howe and others at the end of
February in which I declared I was confident Reading would
stay up – as long as they finished above Birmingham. With
Derby's points total still in single figures, and Fulham playing
as badly as Reading – they'd not won away all season – after
Bolton had leapfrogged Reading it looked like Birmingham

were the only other competition for the single remaining
relegation place.

And once that nightmare February was gone, things
picked up considerably in March with the team managing
three wins, a draw and just one defeat. The first eight days saw
two crucial wins, at Middlesbrough and home to Manchester
City, and then a narrow 2-1 loss away to Liverpool. This
match at Anfield featured one of the best goals ever seen from
a Reading player, a stunning half-volley from outside the area
after just four minutes from Matějovský. And although
Liverpool triumphed in the end, it was another much improved performance from a team that looked so much more
like their old selves.

No one had expected any points against Liverpool, but
there was an expectation of – and a yearning for – a win in the
crucial home match over Birmingham. And for once in such a
crunch match the team didn't disappoint. In a scrappy game
they did enough to win 2-1 through two headed goals from
André Bikey, who was now a permanent fixture in the
Reading defence.

The previous season much of Reading's league success had
been down to good wins over clubs in the bottom half of the
table, but this season that ability had virtually deserted them,
so it was a real boost see them win such a proverbial 'must-
win' game against a club in such close competition to them.
This was followed by a tense 0-0 draw at home to Blackburn,
marred by some odd refereeing decisions including two yellow
cards for Matějovský for sloppy tackles.

That excellent March had relaxed everyone, and Reading
were back up to the heady heights of 14th, with 32 points.
With just six matches left to play, they were six points clear of

the final relegation places, occupied by Bolton who had slipped back into the thick of things. Two points behind Bolton, eight behind Reading, came Fulham, and at the bottom Derby had just reached a double-figure points total.

March had been a wonderful month with the Reading of old back, but another page on the calendar somehow meant another Reading team turned up, and away at Newcastle the team started brightly enough but were soundly beaten. Undone by their inability to convert the chances they did create, and soundly punished by the clinical finishing of Newcastle's attack of Michael Owen, Mark Viduka and Obafemi Martins, they were beaten 3-0 with spirits visibly declining the more the match went on. But they remained in 16th place, two points ahead of Birmingham and still eight ahead of Fulham, their next opponents.

If ever there was a vital game it was this one, as Fulham visited the MadStad without having won away from home since September 2006, playing without any confidence and firmly placed at 19th in the league. They proceeded to murder Reading!

In an almost completely one-sided match, Fulham's 2-0 win massively flattered Reading, who offered nothing and looked completely disjointed and could have conceded many more. Coppell's team selection mystified many, with Kitson on the bench and Long and Doyle up front – and with the extent of Reading's attacking play again being to repeatedly pump high balls into the opposition area, these two smaller strikers didn't get a look in. Glen Little made his long-awaited first appearance of the season, from the bench, but he was largely ignored as the aerial bombardment continued, and Fulham were allowed the freedom to play with belief and confidence.

They also hit the Reading woodwork three times.

Leaving this match felt much the same as leaving the disastrous Bolton game two months earlier – that Reading had hit the self-destruct button. But the opponents and the proximity to the end of this season made it feel ten times worse.

Although they remained in 16th position, the team was now just one point ahead of Birmingham, three ahead of Bolton and five ahead of Fulham, with five matches remaining. The first of these was a routine and thoroughly expected defeat at Arsenal, while Bolton won to again climb above Reading, this time on goal difference – all those heavy away defeats ensured that this would not be the club's friend if called into play.

The next match, away at Wigan, was a workmanlike 0-0 draw with no significant action. The most memorable events of this game, in fact, came from elsewhere – 21 miles away, at Manchester City, Fulham were trailing 2-0 at halftime and virtually relegated. With just three games to play they'd have ended the day seven points behind Birmingham and eight behind Reading, but remarkably they turned the game right round to win with three goals in the last 20 minutes, including a last-minute winner from Diomansy Kamara in the 90th minute. Instead of being eight points behind Reading they now trailed by just five, with three matches left.

By now, the stress and unhappiness in the camp was an accepted norm. After the Newcastle game Shorey didn't endear himself to very many by being quoted in the press that Reading had played 'like a pub side' in the second half, and there was further angst as Faé and Sonko were suspended for two weeks for what was called 'an internal disciplinary measure', after refusing to play in a reserve team match. This dispute escalated in the local media, with Faé calling Coppell 'stupid' and 'weak', and saying he never saw Coppell at the training ground.

This was clearly unwelcome distraction for Coppell and his coaches, and absolutely not the best preparation for two vital matches to try to ensure the team's Premier League survival. Before the first, at home to Spurs, Coppell was predicting that his team would need at least a win and a draw from this and the final match, away at Derby, who'd already been relegated for weeks.

The Spurs match was in many ways a microcosm of Reading's problems that season. The MadStad crowd was up for the game and the team was up for the game, but their energy and positivity was nullified by inconsistency and silly errors. Spurs had less of the ball but were often gifted it without being made to work hard, and in possession their superior technique showed the difference between the two teams. Ahead after 16 minutes, Spurs never looked back, and although Reading huffed and puffed they couldn't get an equaliser – the sixth match in which they'd not scored.

Fulham, however, had continued in their great escape, beating Birmingham 2-0 at home, and had for the first time moved above Reading in the table. It was also the first time that Reading's fate was no longer in their own hands. Birmingham in 19th place were on 32 points, with both Reading and Fulham one point better off, but Fulham's goal difference was six better than Reading's. Although Reading could confidently expect a win away at dismal Derby on the final day of the season they needed to either better Fulham's result, or to turn around that goal difference of six in order to survive.

To compound matters, and to make Reading fans feel that

those football gods who had been so kind to their team over recent seasons were now playing a cruel trick on them, Fulham's final match was away to Portsmouth. The same Portsmouth who were sitting comfortably in the top half of the Premier League and who would, seven days later, turn out at Wembley in the FA Cup Final – their first final appearance since 1939. To say doubts were expressed about just how committed they'd be to this last league match would be an understatement.

As if to confirm the worst suspicions of Loyal Royals, Fulham beat Pompey 1-0, with their goal coming when 5 ft 9 in Danny Murphy easily outjumped the entire Portsmouth defence to head home after a free kick. Meanwhile Reading won 4-0 at Derby and could, possibly, have scored more, but those four goals just weren't enough. Reading were relegated. They'd finished ahead of Birmingham, but with goal difference three goals worse than Fulham's.

Nick Hammond shared his particular memories of that afternoon: *"I went to Derby. I didn't know quite what to do and I had Tim Coe, who's now the Chief Scout at Crystal Palace who was working for us, and I sent him to Portsmouth. And I was sat next to the Chairman as I do when I go to away games – very rarely – and we played well and I remember them jumping up. I mean, I never jump up anyway, but I'm just sitting at Derby and I remember the Chairman jumping up. That's why I love the Chairman, he was just in the game and enjoying the game, but almost oblivious to the actual relevance of it."*

"And I never forget the phone vibrating in my pocket and I get it out and I see it's Tim and he'd rung me to tell me that they'd scored – Fulham. And the Chairman ... the Chairman was like 'come on, Nick, its four!' and I was like 'Chairman, this game's done, this game's not relevant'. I remember saying it to him, but again he was just ... the

Chairman was brilliant."

As for the Chairman, again his thoughts reflect very much the feelings of the supporters. He told me: *"And so we got relegated and it was very, very, very tough. I remember I took that part badly because when you win the game and the other two teams have never played whatsoever ..."*

The period of dreaming was over. Three incredible, unbelievable, wonderful seasons – even if the third one was slightly soured – ended on a sunny Sunday afternoon in Derby. The perfect team was perfect no more.

Reading fans, who'd brought with them optimism in spite of all the odds, together with the usual end-of-season inflatables, trudged home feeling as let down as the countless punctured beach balls scattered in front of the away end at Pride Park.

CHAPTER TWENTY

Here's Where the Story Ends

COULD READING HAVE STAYED UP?

The answer has to be a resounding 'yes'. Relegated by such a tiny margin, there are many examples where just one tiny change to a single instance would have meant survival.

If Shane Long had done the simple thing and scored instead of trying the clever scissor-kick away at Birmingham, Reading would have stayed up. If Stephen Ireland had not produced a miracle strike from distance in the match at Manchester City, Reading would have stayed up. If referee Keith Stroud and his assistants had not blundered in allowing Defoe's encroached penalty goal to stand, Reading would have stayed up – although that's partly supposition on my part. These are just a few examples of individual incidents that would have or may have made a difference.

In the same way, if Reading had managed not to lose their defensive heads to such an extent at Portsmouth, Blackburn and Tottenham, and had conceded just one goal fewer in each of these games, they would have stayed up.

It's easy to play this game of 'what if?' – especially when looking at a season decided by such a small margin. But what essentially did for Reading was their results in key matches against the teams they were competing against for survival.

While the highlight of the season was almost certainly the resounding victory against a full-strength, unbeaten Liverpool team, the harsh truth is that if Reading had lost to Liverpool and swapped that victory for one against they would have stayed up.

Not only was that match against Fulham a classic 'six-pointer', but the manner of Reading's defeat, allowing Fulham to pick up their first away win in over 18 months, played a major part in Fulham's sudden revival as they won their last three league games to ensure survival. Before that match everyone, including probably themselves, had written them off as already relegated.

Wally Downes told me about the preparations for this match and in particular a difference of opinion with Steve Coppell on how it should have been approached: *"Not falling out but my perception of the Fulham game was that we should have gone 4-5-1 and got the draw, because I'd been and watched Fulham the week before. They were crap, they got beaten 2-0 by someone, and I came back and thought 'all we've got to do is stop them getting three points and they're down'."*

"But – Steve's philosophy: 'This is how we play, we've got where we are, we're not going to change for one game and we play how we play'. If we'd drawn with Fulham they'd have been gone."

It's hard to argue with that, and it raises a number of other 'what ifs?'. What if, for instance, the team hadn't been so unremittingly attacking at all times? In both of the matches against Fulham – the 3-1 away defeat in November and the 2-0 home defeat in April – Reading's attacking intent, pouring forward and leaving space at the back, allowed Fulham to score 90th minute goals. It's agonising, with the benefit of hindsight, to consider that if Reading had just shut up shop and settled for 2-1 and 1-0 defeats then they'd have stayed up.

The question of formations also raises other questions. When Coppell experimented with 4-5-1 away at Blackburn in October, it was a disaster. This game was probably a reason for his reluctance to change Fulham, but what if he'd stuck to his principles then and not experimented? After reverting to 4-4-2 Reading looked the better team – would they have won, or drawn, or not conceded four, if they'd been 4-4-2 throughout?

This kind of 'Monday morning quarterbacking' is irresistible but pointless now – as is wondering what would have happened if Portsmouth hadn't reached the FA Cup final. Would they have fielded a team against Fulham that wanted to win, rather than one that seemed primarily concerned with avoiding injury? In the same way, could Reading have scored seven at Derby? Many think they should have been even more attack-minded there, and should not have eased off and trusted to luck and Portsmouth once they'd gone three up, as they seemed to do.

Those are the questions about single incidents that are easy to speculate about. But there's a whole other set of questions about changes and differences that affected the whole season. For instance, just how much of a loss was no longer working with Catalyst, the performance consultants who'd been so integral to their success in the two previous seasons?

I'm convinced that the combination of Steve Coppell and his coaches, with Catalyst and Mark Reynolds behind them, and with Nick Hammond as mentor and dealing with player contracts, recruitment, etc., was an absolutely perfect one for this team at that time. Coppell is a superb manager and tactician who engenders phenomenal loyalty in his players. But with Catalyst there to help improve communications and motivation, the effectiveness of Coppell's management was substantially increased – those players who would 'run a mile naked for Coppell' now knew exactly in which direction he wanted them to run.

This working relationship seems to have flourished right from the start, with Hammond and Coppell immediately 'getting' what Catalyst could bring, and there was clearly a shared respect and understand. We spoke earlier of teams within teams on the pitch – just as much, with Catalyst involved, there was a perfect team off the pitch, providing the sort of synergy that is, after all, what this book is all about. Reynolds has a tremendous respect for Coppell, telling me: *"He is undoubtedly – I've worked with a lot of them – one of the best managers this country has ever had. He is not as good at Brian Clough, he is not as good as José Mourinho, he is not as good as Alex Ferguson. He is nicer than Alex Ferguson – he is less manipulative than Alex Ferguson. He is as ruthless as José Mourinho can be."*

The drive and motivation of the players was phenomenal, and much of this was down to the regular goal-setting session Reynolds had with the squad. Before each session, he would brief Coppell on what he planned to say to the players, and Coppell: *"... would approve or disapprove – and I would say he approved it 99 percent of the time. He would encourage us to be more aggressive, more assertive with the players. He would encourage us to ask the players questions that I have never heard any other club ask – and the players were smart enough to realise this is possibly the best chance they were ever going to get. So to the players' credit they seized it."*

"I don't think they realised at the time, but I am sure they will tell you since: they were given more accountability – I wouldn't say responsibility – more accountability then they probably ever had been in their careers, and they had a great time. They enjoyed every minute of it. And it

was their pull that changed it, not being pushed. In this instance the X-factor was the pull we created from that playing group."

This 'pull' motivation created by Catalyst in the two years they were involved was vital to the success of the team, and it's noticeable just how strong and united the team was in the period and how good the team spirit was – leading to such innovations as 'The Royals Families'. But it's also noticeable just how quickly the cracks in this unity started to appear in the second Premier League season. These tensions may be inevitable in a tight-knit squad of highly committed players who are failing to play to the standards they know they can, as Hammond suggests – but I can't help but feel that Reynolds and his Catalyst colleagues would have had some effective strategies to reduce these tensions, or more likely would have worked to create an environment in which those tensions wouldn't have erupted in the first place.

It's hard to quantify just how much of the team's decline was down to having lost Catalyst. But the role of consultants is to deliver short-term assignments to their clients – and Reynolds has shared with us the commercial reality that now the football world knew what Catalyst could do through their cut-price assignment with Reading, any retention would cost nine times as much – a figure well outside Reading's budget.

Mark Reynolds has told us he's confident that Catalyst would have ensured the team's survival if re-engaged, if only because he wouldn't have agreed to this re-engagement if he didn't believe that they could survive. And he told me: *"Don't get me wrong, we wanted to carry on, emotionally it would have been a pleasure for me personally to carry on. The terms would have had to have changed. There wasn't going to be an exclusivity. And there had to be an acceptance and approval of certain investments – club and playing side –*

that needed to take place to maintain the momentum that we had built up."

Even if it had been financially viable to re-engage them at nine times the cost, it made no sense in the long-term. Like a child learning to ride a bicycle, Reading had to wobble off on their own at some stage, leaving the stabilisers of Catalyst behind them. And this is something that patently didn't happen.

Coppell said at the time: *"We've deliberately kept quiet about the involvement of Catalyst … not because we are ashamed or embarrassed, but because we think we've got an edge."* I wonder if that secret was kept too well from those higher-up in the club, whether key people appreciated just what Catalyst did and how much difference they made.

As to the 'certain investments – club and playing side' that Reynolds would have required, these are central to the relegation of the club.

Downes summed up one of the problems succinctly, saying: *"We should have recruited better."* Reading lost three key players – Glen Little and Ibrahima Sonko to injury, and Steve Sidwell to Chelsea, while the performances of several others dropped due to unhappiness with their wages or being held to their contracts. It's clear that players were identified and every effort possible was made to sign them, but as with Joleon Lescott and Scott Brown among others, for whatever reason – maybe money, maybe because Reading just isn't a 'sexy' club – they didn't sign in the end.

And those players they did manage to attract to the club all failed in one way or another. The most expensive of the five signed this year, Emerse Faé, had had a disastrous season. He made just three starts, his availability complicated by a spell at the Africa Cup of Nations in Ghana and a bout of malaria contracted while there. By the end of the year he was under a cloud, suspended for refusing to play reserve-team football and calling Coppell 'stupid'. Within a few weeks, Coppell would tell the press: "*I have to accept that Faé was not a good signing for us. He is not the right person. He did not come at the right time and he is not the right fit, but I am sure there will be a lot of French clubs who would be ready to take him.*"

Hammond, who sold him back to Nice, speculated: "*Could he have been the right fit if he'd have gone straight in the team and played? Because he was a talented footballer, but it sort of degenerated really – and in the end we had to cut our losses on that one.*"

Kalifa Cissé had played more games, but often as emergency centre-back instead of in midfield position, and had been thoroughly exposed in that position by Bolton's Kevin Davies.

The other big name signing in January 2008, Marek Matějovský, polarised opinions. Loyal Royal Neil Maskell gives his opinion on the Czech midfielder: "*He wanted far too much time on the ball. He clearly had some quality but wanted to play in slow motion all the time. His goal at Liverpool was technically one of the best goals we have ever scored – but most of the time he was harassed out of possession and frankly displayed the heart of a pea!*" Although this is harsh, it also has a grain of truth. While undoubtedly immensely skilled, the Czech was a yellow card waiting to happen when it came to tackling – and often his skills didn't mesh well with the others in the team. Perhaps he'd succeed in a midfield five, but in a four he was a luxury player that Reading couldn't afford in the midst of a relegation battle.

Hammond explained to me the purchase of Matějovský: "*Again, Steve wanted a creative player in that type of position and there was certainly a pressure in the January that we needed to be seen* [to be buying], *and that's always a difficult one. And I do believe – people always say this, but I do believe – that January is a more difficult market. In terms of where we were, we needed to be seen to be doing something, and Matějovský was a talented player, but again maybe just from a fit perspective, wasn't quite the right fit … Matějovský needed to play with a team that had the ball a lot and were confident and would give it to him and give him licence to play, because he could play – and obviously he came into a team that was struggling, confidence was low …"*

"He probably needed to go to a team that were higher up the division. He went back to Sparta Prague, a big club in the Czech Republic and had a career and so when I look back, obviously Matějovský and Faé were two of the very few players that we've lost money on. Halford didn't work, but we made money. When you look at the trading we did, I think we lost about £1.5 million on Matějovský and Faé, which in these days isn't the end of the world – we sold them both back for reasonable money back into France and Czech Republic. But when you're languishing in a January, it's very difficult …"

Jimmy Kébé's time for Reading would come a few years later, and the other signing of this season, Liam Rosenior, was another who failed to shine. Bought as a right-sider midfielder he failed to impress there, and when Murty was injured he moved to right-back. But, as Loyal Royal Dave Harris says: *"When you're a full-back your first job is to defend. Rosenior for me just didn't cut the mustard there – positionally poor, heart for a relegation battle lacking, always ready to have a go at another player."*

Downes summed up these new signing by saying: *"Not as good as the ones we had. Steve hadn't seen these players, I don't know where they came from, he might have had a look at a couple of DVDs, but the budget we were on they might have been the best you could have got for*

£3 million or whatever it was."

Before I started researching this book, I subscribed to the rather glib school of thought that said 'Coppell was too loyal to his core group of players', and believed that new players weren't brought in so as to not upset that group of players.

And I was told about one example where Coppell did veto a transfer that was all setup, and even the bank draft for payment of the transfer fee had been raised. This was the proposed purchase of midfielder Gary O'Neil, who joined Middlesbrough from Portsmouth for £5 million in August 2007. Nigel Howe told me about this: *"He [Coppell] was the one who said 'let's get Gary O'Neil. He'll make a difference'. Then it's: 'oh, £6 million, I'm not really sure…' I'm going: 'I tell you what Steve, I'll sign him and you can tell the fans it was my fault … don't you worry, tell the fans I was pushed into it…' and he'd go, 'no, I've changed my mind, I don't want to'."*

Coppell's loyalty to his players was probably one of the reasons that they were so committed to him and would run that naked mile – but the more people I spoke to the more I came to realise that things here are slightly more subtle than they first appear. As Hammond told us, players can always accept a superstar on higher wages, or indeed any player better or who would add something extra to the team. But what is harder for players to accept was a new signing coming in, inevitably on better wages, who was no better than those already at the club – in this case players who'd just achieved eighth place in the Premier League.

And that, as with so much else in football, brings us to the moot point of wages. This is a point of real contention, and I spoke to people with views at both extremes of the argument.

Wally Downes explained the view from within the playing

and coaching side, telling me: *"When you get into the Premier League and you stay in the Premier League, the players should be rewarded – and we were very obtuse when it came to wages, very reticent to pay the players their worth. Lost Sidwell, he goes away and gets big money elsewhere, the rest of them think 'I've stayed, I should be rewarded' … as I said, it hadn't gained the momentum, it hadn't followed through on the momentum that we delivered to the board and the Director of Football. We'd delivered and if they wanted to move it on and do better they had the opportunity to do it – and they didn't do it."*

At the other extreme is Sir John Madejski, who told me: *"The first season, it was sublime, because the team punched way above their level. We hadn't really spent that much, we were holding our own and then we almost got into Europe, it was mind-blowing. I'll tell you what was very strange about that season, in my humble opinion, was the fact that there we were – the new kids on the block – most of them hadn't played in the Premiership before, they thought 'wow, this is new' and 'this is fantastic' but they all punched way above their level again and continued to do so. However – this is just my spin on this – the season after that, they all became – you know – 'we know what it's all about' and they just lost the plot, and that's how we ended up getting relegated."*

Mark Reynolds, always a shrewd observer, takes a line somewhere in the middle, saying: *"Some of the players found themselves in the position that they couldn't have dreamt of two or three years earlier and were extraordinarily lucky to be in that position – and, I think, it is right to say that with other clubs they would have struggled replicating the success they enjoyed in that club. So it is no surprise that the second the size of the trough goes up so does the number of pigs trying to feed in it. So I don't regard that as a problem. I think some of the requests were probably justifiable. Some required the liberal dose of 'piss off' and 'if you don't like it go somewhere else'. And the club was eminently capable of handling those conversations."*

The question of wages was one that has occupied many conversations, and I probably gained enough material about wages and Premier League money and the state of the club at the time of relegation to almost write another complete book.

But it's clear to me, from all I've been told, that the club didn't react well to the change in scale of being in the Premier League, and the sums of money that were the norm for Premier League players. But that's not a criticism, because the club certainly tried to scale up to Premier League standards, and, true to Madejski's original mantra, invested some of the Premier League income in infrastructure in the form of a new Premier League-standard media centre and improvements at Hogwood.

And while players' wages did increase, and increase substantially, it appears they didn't increase enough to meet the players' expectations. Whether this is 'greed' or whether this is an inevitable consequence of Premier League level of money is a matter of opinion. Or perhaps there's a corrosive effect that, sooner or later, tarnishes every club that joins the Premier League – a league awash with money but structured to ensure that the richest clubs get an ever-bigger slice of the pie, and organised as much as a money-making machine as a sporting competition.

For there was one big inhibitor that stopped Reading fully adopting the Catalyst plan that was presented in March 2006 – the strategy that set out a blueprint and a financial structure for Reading's survival in the Premier League. This plan showed how it could be done, but it depended upon all three of the revenue streams – broadcast, matchday and commercial – to be in sync.

But they weren't in sync, and didn't look like they would be for a while. The 'commercial' revenue stream had failed to increase to meet the strategy – as much as anything because much of it was predicated upon a new stadium, with 'corporate technology suites', etc. The global price of steel, at record highs due to demand in China at the time, had stalled the stadium development, and after relegation it was eventually postponed. Although they'd sold every available ticket when in the Premier League, it made no economic sense to expand the stadium to host football at a lower level.

As Reynolds acknowledged, this was easier said than done, although telling me: *"I think the stadium expansion was very easy for a consultant to come in and say 'oh, you should expand your stadium'. But actually it – these things – don't happen overnight."*

I share the view of Downes, who told me: *"One of the big things that affected us was, I don't know if it was that year or the year after, they had permission to extend the stand, didn't they – to go up a tier and for some reason they didn't do it. I think that had a much bigger effect on people because there was momentum, we were doing well, we were told about the plans to make it bigger that would have got more revenue, which meant we could have kept possibly players like Sidwell – not saying we would have done, but extra revenue gives you a bigger budget to keep better players – and once we heard that wasn't happening we sort of thought 'why?'"*

For me, this is one of the saddest outcomes of relegation, that the club failed to take this opportunity to set themselves up with a stadium and a revenue-generating platform that would have set them up to compete on a more equal footing as a Premier League club. For me, this is what 'ambition' in football means – not the clichéd fans' 'ambition' of buying ever more expensive players, but the real 'ambition' of building a foundation for the club to develop and move on up the leagues – a natural progression of the whole process that Madejski started when he rescued Reading and set about moving them from ageing Elm Park to the brand new Madejski Stadium, and subsequently invested in Hogwood as a high-class training facility and the academy as a way to mitigate Reading's perennial difficulties of player recruitment.

But the team was relegated in May 2008 by such a small margin, and the opportunity was lost. Nearly eight years later it still exists, although current development plans focus more on the land around the stadium than on the stadium itself.

But for the supporters who experienced these three incredible seasons all we have are a few souvenirs, photographs and wonderful memories – although as time goes by I find myself more and more shaking my head and asking myself: *"Did that really happen? Were they really that good? Was the team really that special?"*

It was. It really was.

And that's why I felt compelled to write this book, to put it all down on paper before the memories fade.

To Sir John Madejski, to Steve Coppell and to everyone involved in this story of the Perfect Team – thank you for giving Reading supporters a team that in just three years gave them more highs and more wonderful memories than many other supporters experience in a whole lifetime.

Postscript

FULHAM'S WIN AT PORTSMOUTH ALSO relegated Birmingham City, who finished one place behind Reading. After their match, thousands of Birmingham supporters remained at St. Andrews, loudly calling for the sacking of the manager, Alex McLeish.

The day after Reading's relegation, rumours appeared in the local press that Steve Coppell was about to resign from the club. Within hours, a sign saying 'Don't Go, Steve' was fixed to the lamppost overlooking the manager's parking space outside the Madejski Stadium. Others pleading with him not to resign followed the next day, and the day after that hundreds of Reading supporters massed in and around that parking space in a show of support for the manager who had just relegated their football team.

I don't think that would have happened at any other club, or at any other time. That was how special Steve Coppell was – and still is – to Reading supporters.

Steve Coppell, Manager Reading Football Club, 9th Oct 2003 to 12th May 2009.

Photograph © Reading FC

Lightning Source UK Ltd.
Milton Keynes UK
UKOW01n0735310316

271195UK00001B/1/P